Alfred Gwynne Vanderbilt

The Unlikely Hero of the *Lusitania*

Steven H. Gittelman and Emily Gittelman

HAMILTON BOOKS

A member of

ROWMAN & LITTLEFIELD PUBLISHERS, INC.

Lanham • Boulder • New York • Toronto • Plymouth, UK

Hamilton Books
4501 Forbes Boulevard
Suite 200
Lanham, Maryland 20706
Hamilton Books Acquisitions Department (301) 459-3366

10 Thornbury Road
Plymouth PL6 7PP
United Kingdom

Printed in the United States of America
British Library Cataloging in Publication Information Available

Library of Congress Control Number: 2012945969
ISBN: 978-0-7618-5506-4 (clothbound : alk. paper)
eISBN: 978-0-7618-5507-1

∞™ The paper used in this publication meets the minimum requirements of American National Standard for Information Sciences—Permanence of Paper for Printed Library Materials, ANSI Z39.48-1992

Contents

Acknowledgments

Our interest in the Vanderbilts dates back to 1989 when two events of significance occurred; Emily was born and I became a trustee of the Suffolk County Vanderbilt Museum. By the time I was president of the Board of Trustees and Emily was eight, we began a program of living history at the museum. Emily was a precocious, eager volunteer who quickly filled the role of "Margaret," the seaplane pilot's niece. Thus began a father-daughter journey that has been one of the greatest joys of parenthood that anyone can put into words.

Imagine loading up our family Ford Model A, emblazoned with the moniker "John the Gardener, established 1931." As John, my fictitious character, and Margaret, we piled in for another Sunday of telling tales about Willie K. and other Vanderbilts.

Apparently our journey is not over: John has aged and so has Emily, who is now twenty-one. For the last seven years, Emily played the role of Willie K's obnoxious teenage step-daughter Rosemary, contending with a cantankerous and aging John. Soon we branched into stories about other Vanderbilts, never satisfied to repeat anything that others might have gleaned from the standard tomes. When we finally found ourselves on the threshold of some of the lesser known characters, our fun really began.

Alfred Vanderbilt was one of those little known members of the illustrious family, but given that he went down on the *Lusitania,* complete with inklings of an historic act of heroism, we had to question why he was so poorly known. One would think the Vanderbilt family would openly celebrate "The Hero of the Lusitania." We became obsessed with investigating why Alfred was lost to the pages of history.

We have to thank all those who chose to write about the Vanderbilts and skipped over Alfred. Check out your favorite Vanderbilt text and you are likely to see his tale omitted.

No father and daughter team could ask for more. Imagine waiting at the Hall of Old Records, New York City, for the anointed moment when one hundred years of dust could be blown off a yellowing file and Alfred's sordid divorce testimony was revealed to our gaping eyes. We were entranced as the file was veritably ripped open and the photos and text revealed their entombed secrets.

Michael Dooling and Carole Lindsay provided incredibly invaluable research assistance. Carol Hart, director of the Vanderbilt Museum, was an early reader and a constantly encouraging force. We have found her to be the greatest intellectual stimulus that anyone has provided us.

Elaine Trimarchi and Gretchen Oldrin Monas served as early readers. Jennifer Gittelman provided much needed support and encouragement. We are thankful to Sara Lehn who as an early reader, gifted us with her grammatical wisdom. Charlotte Evans served as a most capable editor.

Many of our images came from the Library of Congress, an unbeatable resource.

Norman Brown, a true coaching aficionado, made his wisdom and image collection available to us.

There were many at my place of employment who provided endless patience, particularly Danielle Leacock who has served as an incredibly able assistant.

Elaine Trimarchi, my partner provided support and patience for my telling and re-telling of chapter after chapter.

Chapter One

Eighteen Minutes

The story of the sinking of the *Lusitania*, a tale of staggering loss, when the British Cunard liner was struck by a single torpedo that shattered the ship and the lives of many, has been told many a time. On May 7, 1915, the 43,000 ton and 785 foot long liner was sunk, killing 1,198 people on board.[1]

Usually a dashing figure that stood out in a crowd, Alfred Gwynne Vanderbilt in a single-breasted charcoal-gray suit and a lively polka-dot foulard bowtie, was tall, athletic, and always handsomely dressed, normally with an assured posture that was reminiscent of disdain. But now he was lost in a sea of other bodies floating in the cold water.

As he waited for the *Lusitania*'s departure, Alfred stood with Charles Frohman, the producer of a number of successful Broadway productions including *Peter Pan*, and Captain William Thomas Turner, Cunard's choice to command the ship. Undoubtedly Alfred was the most dapper of the trio, sporting a stylish tweed cap and pink carnation in his lapel. By contrast, Frohman was a squat, frog-like man clad in dark clothing and aided by a cane. Turner, stocky in frame, appeared thoroughly competent as a British captain attired in the appropriate naval uniform with a gold-braided cap and four thick gold stripes on his sleeves. The press lavished attention upon the three men prior to the ship's departure from New York harbor.

On the day of sailing Alfred had received a cryptic telegram that said, "The Lusitania is Doomed. Do Not Sail On Her." It was anonymously signed, "Morte."[2]

When asked by the press what he thought, he quipped that it was only "somebody trying to have a little fun at my expense." Pressing on, the reporters were particularly interested in Alfred's opinion of the German U-boat threat. "Why should we be afraid of German submarines?" Alfred scoffed. "We can outdistance any submarine afloat."[3]

He wrapped his arms around his second wife, Margaret, and then pointed to a copy of a New York newspaper emblazoned with a recently issued submarine warning from the German Embassy. "Notice," read the quarter-page ad signed by the Imperial German Embassy, Washington, D.C.

> Travelers intending to embark on the Atlantic voyage are reminded that a state of war exists between Germany and her allies and Great Britain and her allies; that the zone of war includes the waters adjacent to the British Isles; that, in accordance with formal notice given by the Imperial German Government, vessels flying the flag of Great Britain, or of any of her allies, are liable to destruction in those waters and that travelers sailing in the war zone on ships of Great Britain or her allies do so at their own risk.[4]

"Well, how ridiculous this thing is," Alfred insisted. He was later quoted saying boldly in the May 16th issue of *The New York Times*, "The Germans would not dare to make any attempt to sink this ship."

Placing his hand on Vanderbilt's shoulder, Captain Turner salted the eventual wound. "Do you think," he asked confidently, "all these people would be booking passage on board the *Lusitania* if they thought she could be caught by a German submarine? Why, it's the best joke I've heard in many days, this talk of torpedoing!" Turner and Vanderbilt turned to each other and guffawed, a joke that turned into irony as the voyage went on.[5]

Later, as he conversed in his comfortable *Lusitania* cabin with a fellow New Yorker, the unflappable Vanderbilt reaffirmed his dim views of German behavior. "They have disgraced themselves," he spat, "and never in our time will they be looked upon by any human being valuing his honor, save with feelings of contempt. How can Germany, after what she has done, ever think of being classed as a country of sportsmen and of honor on a par with America, England, and France?"[6]

Tales of valor and bravery are lexicon to the *Lusitania* legend, and have been well documented by her 761 survivors. Perhaps it was the gentility of her passengers, where a true gentleman or gentlewoman is trained never to panic. Most tragically, it was the likely mistaken belief that there was no need for panic, since a ship of such size and girth would naturally take some time to slip into the endless deep ocean waters. Instead, the *Lusitania* surprised all. She took a mere eighteen minutes to sink. No matter how the history books depicted the event, or how subsequent politicians spun it, there was nothing graceful about the end of the *Lusitania* or the way her passengers desperately fought for survival.

The *Lusitania* was moving so fast before she was struck that the bubble trail of the torpedo appeared to approach at an angle and she continued moving so fast after impact that lifeboats were torn from their davits. The listing was so abrupt that starboard lifeboats quickly leaned against her plate sides and had their frail bottoms torn out by protruding rivets. Port lifeboats hung precariously away from the ship, creating a gap insurmountable for all but the most athletic. She moved so fast that when her bow submerged, it ploughed into the sea bottom before the stern had a chance to right itself. With no place to go but up, the stern rose and then fell in groaning agony, echoing the gasps of those who erroneously thought they had so much time to spare.

Charles Frohman awaited the rising waters with his consort, the actress Miss Marguerite "Rita" Lucile Jolivet. Rita was terrified of drowning, despite the life jacket she had secured around her body. In an attempt to make the going quicker, she pocketed a revolver to use at precisely the right time. Knowing the end was near, Frohman suggesting that she lean on the rail to conserve her energy. Quoting his favorite play *Peter Pan* by James Barrie, he asked calmly, "Why fear death?" "It is the most beautiful adventure that life gives us."[7]

As soon as he had recited these words to Miss Rita, a vicious wall of green water swept her away, sucking the boots off her feet even as it stole the breath from her lungs, robbing her of her chance to use the revolver.

On the night before the torpedo struck, Alfred attended a benefit concert for the Seaman's Charities with Charles Frohman and his entourage. On the way in, a Canadian woman named Phoebe Amory was selling programs for ten cents. Alfred insisted on paying five dollars for the program, saying to Charlotte, "There, that's for your lovely smile."

Oliver Bernard, a class-sensitive gentleman who disliked Vanderbilt with a passion, witnessed the exchange between Alfred and Phoebe. Bernard had been dislodged from a *Lusitania* dining table in favor of a wealthier patron, and he had observed the separation of the wealthy into "dismal twos and threes . . . not on speaking terms with anybody." Bernard surmised, darkly, "a submarine would have at least socialized the audience."[8]

Frustrated, Bernard took a brief walk on deck to clear his head and stopped to gaze out at the sea. The clarity he sought was soon interrupted when an American woman standing next to him observed something in the water.

Bernard was struck by recognition too sickening to allow for a response. Horrified, he watched helplessly as "a frothy track was snaking up to them like an express; an experiment, a signal, his mind tried to register, to persuade him anything but that it was a torpedo!"[9]

Through his nausea he experienced a reverberating shock through the hull, a towering white column of water and a shower of debris. It was everything he might have expected of a direct hit, and nothing like what he might have imagined. Through a surging sea of humanity, Bernard made his way to the Promenade Deck, where an attempt was being made to lower boats. At the entrance to the first-class saloon he had a near collision with Alfred Vanderbilt, who remarked casually with an unforgettable grin, "Well, they got us this time, all right."[10]

It was Alfred's trademark smile, appropriate for every event. The rest of the passengers were frenzied and screaming but Bernard thought Alfred looked almost excited, as if "he was waiting for the next race at Ascot."[11]

A steward noticed one particular woman that Vanderbilt was attempting to save. Alice Middleton, like many others, kept falling down on the deck as the ship shook and the bow plunged forward. Noticing that she did not have a lifebelt and not finding one available, Alfred Gwynne gave her his own, before crashing waves separated them.

The die was cast; the choice was made. The millionaire could not swim, and the unforgiving sea showed no mercy. Undeterred by his handicap, Alfred continued his heroic efforts until the end. The ship's barber witnessed him placing children in their life jackets. He instructed valet Ronald Denyer to "Find all the kiddies you can, boy."

Vanderbilt loaded armfuls of children onto the lowering boats. Survivors witnessed him as being as calm as a man waiting for a train. His last effort, ever so pitifully desperate and so painfully heroic, was to lash babies in their wrappings to life jackets so that they might float away from the ship unharmed. So much of his effort was futile as many of the babies perished within a few minutes of casting out to sea yet he did not pause for a moment.

Owen Kenan was one of the last to see Alfred Gwynne. Kenan jumped with Vanderbilt's valet, Denyer, at the very end as the Atlantic Ocean threatened to swallow up the Lusitania. Turner had already given the order to abandon ship and all crew hands had jumped, saving their own skins. Vanderbilt, by all accounts, did not follow and Denyer did not survive. The sea came in a giant wave and he was washed away. Alfred Vanderbilt's body was never found.

The dichotomy proved striking and Alfred's actions striking. What had driven this man to blithely sacrifice his own life to save those of women and children even in the very last moments when all hope was seemingly lost? Alfred G. Vanderbilt, a man known for his appetite for life and notorious adulterous affairs, had redeemed his thirty-eight years of existence in the last eighteen minutes of his life.

NOTES

1. Butler, Daniel Allen. 2000. *The Lusitania The Life, Loss, and Legacy of an Ocean Legend.* Stackpole Books. Mechanicsburg, PA. Pg. 263.

2. Preston, Diana. 2002. *Lusitania: An Epic Tragedy.* Penguin Group Inc. Pg.100.

3. *Hoehling, A.A. and Mary Hoehling. 1956. Popular Library Edition.* New York, N.Y. Pg. 25.
4. Ramsay, David. 2001. *Lusitania Saga and Myth.* W.W. Norton Co., N.Y., N.Y. Pg. 53.
5. *New York Times*. May 16, 1915. Pg. 1
6. *New York Times*. May 16, 1915. Pg. 5
7. Preston, Diana. 2002. *Lusitania: An Epic Tragedy.* Penguin Group Inc. Pg. 253.
8. Oliver, Bernard P. 1936. *Cock Sparrow: A True Chronicle*. Jonathan Cape Ltd. London. Pg. 154.
9. Ibid.
10. Preston, Diana. 2002. *Lusitania: An Epic Tragedy.* Penguin Group Inc. Pg. 209.
11. Oliver, Bernard P. 1936. *Cock Sparrow: A True Chronicle*. Jonathan Cape Ltd. London. Pg. 156.

Chapter Two

The Unlikely Heir

It was an interesting turn of events to say the least. Alfred Gwynne Vanderbilt, just twenty-two years of age, sat quietly in his father's home in one of the library's stiff Queen Anne chairs. He was remarkably composed considering the news he had received a few hours prior. His uncle William Kissam Vanderbilt I, brother to his father Cornelius II, had summoned him from Japan to attend the reading of his father's will, rushing him back via steamboat,[1] special train, and tugboat.[2] The return trip had been a global spectacle of no small repute. But it had given him ample time for reflection.

Tall, handsome, and athletic with a striking countenance and light blue eyes, Alfred did not need family money to command the attention of his playmates where he enjoyed the spoils of society's limelight. He was known for his social prowess more than for any workman's talent, given his fun-loving, light-hearted,[3] and capricious manner. The young Vanderbilt was the quintessential playboy, ready for adventure at a moment's notice.

Despite his father's ill health, Alfred had embarked on a global jaunt with fellow graduates from Yale. Given the family physician had speculated the likelihood of his father's demise while Alfred was gone, some might have questioned the wisdom of leaving on such a long journey. However, there was a tendency for Vanderbilt men to marry young, and his mother supported the venture, hoping to buy time and avoid that critical error.

In fact, some had said that Cornelius had resolved his fate and awaited his end with spiritual serenity.[4] There was no sense in keeping Alfred home, when staying could not change his father's condition. To some extent, his father's death had been expected. The surprise lay in the will that Cornelius II had left behind; for it was here that the fortunes and lives of all the other members of the Vanderbilt clan would be determined.

The long shadows of the afternoon sun cast dark silhouettes on the smooth cold marble floors of the library. Alice, Alfred's mother, paced up and down in mournful black, her head bowed, her hands clasped with resilient determination, and her face visibly pinched with pain.[5] Her Cornelius was dead and the future of all she had known in her long married life would be revealed in the will he had decreed. Despite her pain, there was much at stake, and the fates of so many lives lay in the balance. At the turn of the century, the legacy of Cornelius Vanderbilt's empire—who received what, where, and how—would finally be brought to light.

Alice's petite frame belied her strength of will. She was the quiet force that kept the 137-room mansion immaculate and magnificent. She had urged her husband to build this four-story chateau of marble, brick, and stone with its opulent halls, Baccarat chandeliers, and red draperies. Every piece of furniture, each painting and architectural flourish, had to undergo her scrutiny and it was her impetus that had completed construction of the *Breakers* mansion in Newport, Rhode Island, in just two years at a time when all construction was done by hand.[6] She was no ordinary force to be reckoned with.

Also seated in the library were the other members of the direct family: Alfred's older brother Cornelius III ("Neily"), his younger brother Reginald, and his two sisters, Gertrude and Gladys. Behind them, tall glass bookcases held thousands of fine and rare illustrated books,[7] all personally selected by Cornelius II himself. Near the archway of the library, there was a bronze bust of William Henry Vanderbilt II, the first-born son who had died of typhoid in 1892. A large painting of the Cornelius II in the classical style hung opposite the bust, immortalizing the appearance of a man whose presence shook the world far beyond his lifetime.[8]

Known for his commitment to work, Cornelius II was diligent, thrifty, hardworking, and apparently quite mild-mannered.[9] His appearance was by most standards, quite ordinary, with rounded shoulders and wire-rimmed spectacles, graying dark brown hair, and a Roman nose. Cornelius resembled any one of the accountants in his own office, wielding a conservative approach to his vast fortune. His was not the method of bold conquest or domination but rather that of careful counting and slow growth.

Cornelius loved his work and took pride in knowing the precise worth of every aspect of his railroad business. Alfred revered his father's dedication to the Grand Central Railroad, the central of all Vanderbilt Railroads, as well as the legacy left by his great grandfather, the Commodore. While the public viewed Cornelius II as an upstanding citizen who contributed to charities and hospitals, Alfred knew how much his father's dedication to his work cost him. Cornelius II was a workaholic; a man who did not take vacations or who stopped to take breaks. Alfred, like all the other members of his side of the family, had grown accustomed to his father's long working hours and abhorred the shackles of the railroad business.

How did this steward and bastion of society, this upstanding citizen pass away? Cornelius II was fifty-six years old when his physician pronounced him deceased. His death was a shock to many outside the family for he had always been a healthy and robust man, albeit with a slight tendency towards portliness. Yet he had never been one to indulge in heavy liquors, spirits, wines, or Bacchalian revelries; Cornelius's life was in many ways a model of Puritan moderation apart from the periodic festivities that he maintained according to Vanderbilt tradition.

It was common knowledge that on July 17, 1896, Cornelius had suffered a debilitating stroke that had left him temporarily incapacitated and unable to speak. It would take several months before he fully recovered from that event. His wife[10] Alice waited upon him, acting as a nursemaid, silencing all noise outside their palatial residence, where even the neighboring streets of New York magically became quiet as a tomb. Later, the couple returned to their summer resort, the *Breakers*, where Cornelius could enjoy a more leisurely pace of living and convalescence. He slowly made progress, but age prevented his body from making the rapid recovery his mind so naturally attained.

By April 1898, almost two years later, after a short sojourn to a health spa in Europe, to his wife's delight, Cornelius began to show a remarkable improvement in his overall physique, assuming many of his former activities.

It was the afternoon of September 11, 1899,[11] a crisp fall day, when Cornelius left the *Breakers* with Alice at his side, and traveled aboard his own private railroad car to New York to attend a private meeting of railroad directors. Cornelius and Alice traveled in car No. 493 with its four large staterooms and associated pantry, kitchen, library, dining compartment, and saloon replete with musical instruments and offering rich English oak interiors with exquisite blue velvet furniture.[12]

Acting like his normal self, Cornelius commanded the full attention of his board of directors upon his arrival in New York City. Alice was content, as her husband had at last returned to his former level of social engagement and business activity. Thus it came as a terrifying shock to her the following morning in their New York mansion on West 57th Street[13] when at six o'clock she heard her husband scream out her name in desperation, "Alice! Alice!" Rushing forward, she reached him just in time to see Cornelius's head drop backwards as she cradled him to her bosom. Within minutes of yelling, "I think I am dying!" to his wife, Cornelius fell unconscious in her arms, his face turned blue, while his brain bled from a cerebral hemorrhage.[14]

Senator Chauncey Depew, the principal lawyer for two generations of Vanderbilts, was the first of the close-knit assemblage of friends to arrive at the residence to console a weeping Alice and thirteen-year-old Gladys. While the physician, Dr. Frances Delafield,[15] who had been hurriedly summoned soon after Cornelius had collapsed, attended to the overwhelmed spouse, Depew mourned the loss of his most intimate friend.[16] He was soon joined by all of Cornelius's living brothers. Uncle Willie, Cornelius's partner, best friend, and brother, was immediately put in charge of sending telegrams to the immediate family. Depew had the task of seeing to funeral arrangements.

The first person Uncle Willie called was the eldest living son, Neily, who upon hearing of his father's death, immediately departed to join the family; his grief was visible.[17] Gertrude and Reginald, two of Alfred's younger siblings, arrived from Newport later in the afternoon of the same day.[18]

Alfred, however, was hard to locate because of his travels abroad. Uncle Willie sent telegrams to every residence and port of call where the young Vanderbilt had been sighted, including places in Hong Kong and Yokohama,[19] Japan. Eventually, word came back that A.G. had been spotted in China, and a cable was dispatched[20] to summon the young man home.

Depew took care of the press. When asked for his opinion about the death of his dear friend, Depew spoke at length and with obvious emotion, declaring that, "Mr. Vanderbilt and I were the most intimate friends . . . I was closer to him and he was closer to me than any other man."[21] Depew expanded upon Cornelius's role in society as a bright, intelligent, and socially responsible citizen whom he considered among "the most charitable of men."[22]

Young Alfred Vanderbilt. Undated. Culver Pictures.

At ten o'clock the next morning, the funeral was held privately at St. Bartholomew's Church, a place of worship that Cornelius II had been known to frequent. All of his living children (except for Alfred, who was rushing home) friends, and family were present. After the service, the body was borne in a casket filled with fragrant American Beauty roses, Catalyea orchids, and lilies of the valley[23] to the end of 42nd Street and carried by boat to Staten Island to be buried in the Vanderbilt family vault.

Thousands lined the street, eager to get a glimpse of the casket of a man not only known as a railroad leader but also well respected in the community for both his contributions to charities and his religious convictions. People were there to pay their respects to a beloved public figure, whose demise filled them with a mixture of both fear and hope; fear of changes in the railroad that Cornelius had managed with such intensity and upon which they depended heavily for daily transportation to work and their families, mingled with hope that the new heir would offer them a new and optimistic future.[24]

In just over two weeks since the funeral, the reading of the will was scheduled in order to accommodate the young Vanderbilt who had cut short his

The Breakers, *the Newport address of the Cornelius Vanderbilt branch of the Vanderbilt family, ca. 1904. The stone mansion with its waterfront location was purchased from the Lorillard family by Cornelius Vanderbilt II, Alfred's father. A wooden house soon burned and was replaced by this impregnable fortress. Library of Congress. Bain Collection.*

Vanderbilt Hall Yale ca. 1901. Brothers William Henry, Cornelius III and Alfred Gwynne all attended and completed their educations at Yale. It was at this dormitory building donated by their father in honor of William Henry who died while in attendance from typhoid that brothers Cornelius and Alfred shared two years in residence. Young Alfred shifted his attentions to the ladies when the more serious Cornelius (Neily) finished two years before him. Library of Congress. Bain Collection.

trip. The family was impatient, eager to know the outcome of how the inheritance would be divided among the siblings. This event, so important to the fortunes of every one of Cornelius' children was to be decided at the reading held in the library of the *Breakers* mansion.

Drawing inspiration from both classical French and Italian Renaissance architecture, the library with its Circassian walnut wood paneling, gold leaf motifs, and Spanish leather, offered an inviting contrast to the colossal and imposing marble floors and halls of the *Breakers* mansion. At one end, there was a sixteenth century stone fireplace from a Burgundy chateau with carefree French words etched on the marble mantelpiece that read: "De gran bien ma rie, et poinct ne default; Il n'est qu'adresse, quant tout prevault."[25]

"Little do I care for riches, and do not miss them, since only wisdom prevails in the end."[26]

The only sounds in the room were the hushed murmurs of the young people gathered there, each of them deeply invested in the outcome of the reading of the will. Mrs. Cornelius Vanderbilt sat down, her petite body disappearing in the expanse of a large red velvet refectory chair.[27] Every single one of them eagerly anticipated the result and Neily the eldest, was by far most concerned, having the most to lose.

Neily seated. Harpers Weekly.

William Henry's unexpected death from typhoid in 1893 at age twenty-one had left Neily the next in line to inherit the vast Vanderbilt fortune by the rules of progenitor. Unlike William Henry, who was a sailor, athlete, social playboy, scholar, and golden boy of the family[28], Neily was a quiet young man of studious bent who loved to tinker with mechanical toys and inventions, occasionally suffering from bouts of rheumatism. Possessing a brilliant mind and a penchant for work, Neily had worked with dedication at his father's New York Central Railroad office.

Despite the dramatic difference in personality, the brothers had shared one enormous interest that would drastically alter their lives: Grace Wilson. Known for both her classical beauty and sophisticated charms, Grace opened doors wherever she went. She was an intelligent woman with many suitors. Neily, like his older brother, fell head over heels in love with her.

Both Cornelius II and Alice were greatly dismayed by Neily's fixation with Grace and tried their best to divert his attention by exposing Grace and her family for their social-climbing ways, which the Vanderbilt family found disgraceful. They were appalled by Grace's unseemly willingness to quickly become the consort of yet another member of the Vanderbilt clan so soon after W. H.'s demise. However, when Neily showed no signs of quitting his courtship, Cornelius II threatened Neily with cutting off his inheritance. The press exacerbated the situation by heralding Neily as a romantic who was willing to give up his inheritance for love while his parents were cast as insufferable tyrants. As the tension built up between father and son, the silence between them grew so that even though they shared the same living quarters and worked in the same building, they never spoke a word to each other.

Whispering servants revealed in painstaking detail how conflict broke out between father and son one hot humid afternoon in June 1896 at the Vanderbilt mansion on Fifth Avenue. Trying his best to prevent the union between his son and the notorious Grace Wilson, Cornelius II ordered his son to go to the *Breakers*. Enraged and forced into a corner, Neily, viewing this as yet another controlling measure from his autocratic father to prevent him from being with the woman he loved, exploded with the force of a volcano,[29] striking his father and stormed out. Cornelius II suffered a stroke that paralyzed his right side and forced him to bed rest for another three months. The vigorous man, who was known for his twelve-hour workdays, was diminished to a feeble[30] and frail skeleton of his former self, leaving the management of his formidable railroad company to his brother, William K. while Cornelius II retreated to the protection of the massive *Breakers* estate. Father and son did not speak again and the enormous mansion could not put enough distance between them. Neily moved out and in less than a month, married his sweetheart. While Grace Wilson enjoyed being the center of attention with the press, Cornelius II raged at the *Breakers*, furious at his son's flagrant disobedience.

Stubbornness, the family trait that both riveted public attention and created an empire, was also the characteristic that would break the family apart. Neither Cornelius II nor Neily could forgive each other. No warm words ever passed between them again and despite Neily's remarkable successes as an engineer and inventor of a locomotive firebox, his frequent letters, and even after the birth of his first child[31] whom he secretly brought home to meet his mother, no word of encouragement, forgiveness, or acknowledgement issued forth out of the stony walls of the *Breakers*.

Under the Vanderbilt roof with its gilded memorial plaque in honor of their late brother, Neily and Alfred had shared living quarters at Yale, where Neily had excelled at school and Alfred in society. Despite sharing the same blood, Alfred and Neily could not be further apart in temperament and inclinations. Neily had graduated with a degree in engineering, eager to take on the responsibilities of heir to the vast Vanderbilt Empire. Alfred, on the other hand, would have none of this, deploring the heaviness and routine of daily life at the New York Central Railroad. Departing instead with his friends Ernest Iselin, William F. Burden, and Douglas Cochran in a lavish private car boudoir

No. 493 of the *Venturer* upon graduation, the young Alfred Gwynne Vanderbilt set out to explore the world, declaring simply, "We are going to see the entire world, or as much of it as we can, and we expect to have a good time."[32]

Uncle Willie stood by the narrow alcove adjoining the library, staring at the mid-eighteenth century Dutch clock with its elegant long gold arms and delicate wood inlay. A long richly tapered red Kurdish rug lay on the cold marble floor. It was only a few hours since he had quietly met with Alfred in the Grand Central Depot to inform the young man of his father's death and the changes in the will. The young man had rushed to keep his appointment at the former offices of his deceased father where the meeting was held in strict confidentiality behind locked and padded doors.

A.G.'s return home[33] was described at great length by all the major newspapers. Warmly greeted by his brother Reginald and his brother-in-law Harry Payne Whitney, the three young men traveled in a hurry to Newport[34] to reach the *Breakers* on October 15, 1899. While the press remarked upon the meeting between the young Vanderbilt and his Uncle Willie and why Neily who "would have been the head of that family"[35] and fueled rumors about the will being contested, in actuality, the contents of the will were kept a "profound secret."[36]

William Kissam had further expanded a family fortune and the railroad dynasty of power and privilege. The will to be discussed contained the details of how Cornelius intended to divide his $100 million estate. Uncle Willie had insisted that the family wait until Alfred returned before the will could be read. The Vanderbilt fortune was the most royal inheritance in America, one of the largest in the world. Every newspaper carried daily accounts of Alfred's journey and his progress homeward. Time moved slowly while the world and family waited anxiously for the arrival of the young man to commence the reading of the will.

A heavy silence permeated the library as all anxious eyes fixated upon the senior lawyer who was vested with the responsibility of reading the will. Reginald, who at a mere nineteen years of age was the apple of his mother's eye, had been pacing back and forth and now froze in his steps as one of the lawyers stood up and began to shuffle his papers from his heavy leather portfolio. The glow of the bright fire in the expansive fireplace illuminated his face from below, giving it an unnatural cast. The man was none other than Chauncey Depew, a family friend and Chairman of the board of directors of the New York Central Railroad Company, known for both his sound advice and his gift as an orator. The only sounds in the room were those of an occasional crackling from a log in the fire or the background murmur of ocean waves beating against the cliffs, above which the mansion loomed majestically.

Unlike his siblings, Alfred's demeanor of quiet self-assurance spoke of hidden knowledge. Attired in Bond Street black-and-white linen finished with a diamond stickpin,[37] Alfred was a fashionable, poised youth. He presented a striking contrast to his brother Neily, whose clothing and demeanor revealed the stress of a busy working man.[38]

The Cornelius branch of the Vanderbilt clan waited with bated breath. All except Alfred and Uncle Willie were unaware of what would unfold. Would obedience to Cornelius' desire be reflected generously in the will? Or would a more prudent business choice prevail? Reginald, though adored by his mother Alice, was too young to inherit the mantle of authority and Alfred was too much of a social butterfly. Neily was definitely more equipped to handle the challenges of running a railroad business than his siblings. Yet, no one else in the family had incurred the wrath of Cornelius as much as Neily by his choice of bride.

Out of the shadowy cluster of legal counsel, Depew emerged to begin the reading of the will, holding aloft a sheaf of papers extracted from a leather portfolio. Like the dark clouds that gather in the sky before a thunderstorm, the air in the library was charged and ponderous with the weight of these conflicting desires and thwarted ambitions.

Depew read in a carrying voice, "I give and devise to my beloved wife Alice G. Vanderbilt, for and during the term of her natural life, my dwelling house on Fifth Avenue and Fifty-Seventh Street," continuing to describe how Alice, Cornelius's dear wife inherited all of the property, artwork, horses, stables, and furniture of their opulent homes. Depew enumerated every home and possession in detail, including the *Breakers* where they were gathered. The will further postulated that upon Alice's death, each possession would be given to the children in the following order of Alfred, Reginald, Gertrude, and Gladys.

Again and again, Depew read the same decree for each and every residence, save the Oakland Farms estate in South Portsmouth, Rhode Island, which went to Alfred alone. To Alfred also passed the gold medal of 1864[39] that was handed down like a rite of passage from each Vanderbilt head of household to the next scion.

Conspicuously absent from every bequest, however, was Neily's name. As the reading of the will slowly progressed, Neily's anguish intensified. The verdict was the same in all cases: five children, of which four received fortuitous inheritance, while one had been painstakingly ignored.

Depew spoke loudly and clearly. There was no mistake in what he read and with every syllable that escaped his lips, the more final pronouncement of judgment. A few items of art were saved for Alfred: "I expect from this bequest the portrait and bust of my grandfather and the portrait of my father, and the two portraits bequeathed to me in the will of my grandfather, all of which I give my son Alfred."

Depew's voice rang out clearly and decisively with the precision of a knife cutting through the pin-drop silence. Alice received the *Breakers* and a $7 million trust fund while Alfred, Reginald, Gertrude, and Gladys each received $5 million apiece. Neily was granted nothing.

While he seethed internally with rage, his mind tormented by the decisions of his father that sealed his fortune, Neily, gripping his fists so tightly that the whites of his knuckles were exposed, did not lose his laser-like focus for one moment. Was even his child, an innocent wee babe and Cornelius's grandson ignored and left out of the will?

As Neily was well aware, Depew was not finished. The fate of the bulk of the estate had yet to be told. For Neily, $500,000 was bequeathed along with the income from a $1 million trust fund of which he could only reap the interest during his lifetime. The principal of the $1 million fund would remain inaccessible and reserved for his children. This amount, while sizeable for the time, was a mere pittance in comparison to the Vanderbilt inheritance, a drop in the vast ocean of that formidable empire.

What then of the remaining $42,500,000 million estate? Neily wondered, quickly calculating, his heart sinking.

Depew clearing his throat announced that Alfred was to receive the entire residuary estate of exactly $42,575,000.[40]

Alfred, the playboy of Yale society, voted in 1899 the "social light" of his class, was now the heir to one of the greatest fortunes in the world! The final blow was struck.

Neily leaned back in his chair in shock. With a devastating finality, Depew read the last words of the will, "I have to this in my last Will and Testament, set my hand and seal of the city of New York, this 1st day of June in 1896."[41] The father's final decision was to divide a fortune based upon emotion rather than rationality. Obedience had won out over any business considerations in the old man's heart.

Neily sat stricken upon hearing these fateful last words; "The 1st day of June in 1896" for that day was no less than the date Neily had set to marry Grace Wilson. The date immediately brought back a fresh reminder of a stinging hurt from that ominous day when he had quarreled with his father.

He could hardly believe it. His father had changed his will the very day that Neily had defiantly announced his betrothal to Grace and here, no less than three years later, Neily's fortune or lack thereof, had been so preemptively dictated. The rift between Cornelius and his eldest living son was of such epic proportions that the rules of progenitor were abandoned and the legacy of an unforgiving father unleashed in a torrent of resentment. How could his father described as a generous man of "sensitive conscientiousness"[42] who "promoted the wealth of humanity"[43] known for his "benevolent enterprises"[44] and "courage"[45] sustain such an intense hatred of his own son?

No words could soothe Neily, as the library grew suffocating and oppressive to him. While his father had extended his vengeful spirit beyond the grave to effectively strangle any claims Neily made to his wealth, Neily experienced a deep hollow rejection in the present when none of his family members comforted the unhappy son but instead rallied to the unexpected and most unlikely of heirs, Alfred.

NOTES

1. *Los Angeles Times*. "Peking in Port." Oct 10, 1899. Pg. 1.
2. *The Atlanta Constitution*. "Rushes from Ocean to Ocean." Oct. 10, 1899. Pg. 1.
3. *The Atlanta Constitution*. "In the Public Eye." Sept 20, 1899. Pg 6.
4. *The Chicago Daily*. "Sudden Death of Vanderbilt." Sept 13, 1899. Pg. 1.
5. *The Chicago Daily*. "Vanderbilt Will Read." Sept 16, 1899. Pg. 7.
6. Vanderbilt II, Arthur T. Fortune's Children: The Fall of the House of Vanderbilt. New York, NY: William Morrow and Company. 1989. Pg 187.
7. The Washington Post. "Death of Vanderbilt: Head of the Family Stricken Down at New York." Sept 13, 1899. Pg. 1.
8. Tschirch, John. "The Breakers." NPS Report. The Preservation Society of Newport County. Feb 22, 1994. Pg. 6.
9. Vanderbilt II, Arthur T. *Fortune's Children: The Fall of the House of Vanderbilt*. New York, NY: William Morrow and Company. 1989. Pg. 180.
10. Ibid. Pg. 220.
11. Ibid. Pg. 221.
12. Ibid. Pg. 221.
13. *The New York Times*. "Mr. Cornelius Vanderbilt Dead." Sept 13, 1899. Page 1.
14. Ibid. Pg. 223.
15. *The Chicago Daily*. "Sudden Death of Vanderbilt." Sept 13, 1899. Pg. 1.
16. *The New York Times*. "Mr. Cornelius Vanderbilt Dead." Sept 13, 1899. Page 1.
17. Ibid.
18. *The Chicago Daily*. "Sudden Death of Vanderbilt." Sept 13, 1899. Pg. 1.
19. *The New York Times*. "Will of Mr. Vanderbilt." Sept 28, 1899. Pg. 5.
20. *The Chicago Daily*. "Sudden Death of Vanderbilt." Sept 13, 1899. Pg. 1.
21. Ibid.
22. Ibid.
23. *The New York Times*. "Mr. Vanderbilt's Memory: Honored by the Foremost Railroad Men and Financiers." Sept 15, 1899. Pg. 12.
24. *The Washington Post*. "At Vanderbilt's Bier: Prominent Clergy and Laity To Gather Around Tomb." Sept 14, 1899. Page 3.

25. Vanderbilt II, Arthur T. *Fortune's Children: The Fall of the House of Vanderbilt.* New York, NY: William Morrow and Company. 1989. Pg. 222.
26. Perschler, Martin. "Historic Landscapes Project: The Breakers." Newport, RI: The Preservation Society of Newport County, 1993.
27. Vanderbilt Jr., Cornelius V. *Queen of the Golden Age: The Fabulous Story of Grace Wilson Vanderbilt.* New York, NY: McGraw-Hill Book Company. 1956. Pg. 127.
28. Vanderbilt II, Arthur T. *Fortune's Children: The Fall of the House of Vanderbilt.* New York, NY: William Morrow and Company. 1989. Pg. 202.
29. Vanderbilt Jr., Cornelius V. *Queen of the Golden Age: The Fabulous Story of Grace Wilson Vanderbilt.* New York, NY: McGraw-Hill Book Company. 1956. Pg. 54.
30. Ibid. Pg. 103.
31. Ibid. Pg. 108.
32. *The New York Times.* "Vanderbilt Party Off: Young Millionaires Started Last Night from This City on Their Trip Around the World." July 27, 1899. Pg. 7.
33. *The New York Times.* "A.G. Vanderbilt Coming Here." Oct 16, 1899. Pg. 1.
34. *The New York Times.* "A.G. Vanderbilt At Home." Oct 15, 1899. Pg. 1.
35. *The New York Times.* "A.G. Vanderbilt In the City." Oct 17, 1899. Pg. 1.
36. Ibid.
37. Vanderbilt Jr., Cornelius V. *Queen of the Golden Age: The Fabulous Story of Grace Wilson Vanderbilt.* New York, NY: McGraw-Hill Book Company. 1956. Pg. 137.
38. Ibid. Pg. 136.
39. Vanderbilt II, Arthur T. *Fortune's Children: The Fall of the House of Vanderbilt.* New York, NY: William Morrow and Company. 1989. Pg. 223.
40. Ibid. Pg. 221.
41. Ibid. Pg. 223.
42. *The New York Times..* "Mr. Vanderbilt's Memory: Honored by the Foremost Railroad Men and Financiers." Sespt 15, 1899. Pg. 12.
43. Ibid.
44. Ibid.
45. Ibid.

Chapter Three

The Gift

Despite the massive attention that he drew, the dapper young Alfred carried himself with remarkable grace under this familial onslaught. A.G. was well aware that he was ill equipped to bear the heavy mantle of responsibility that his father had bestowed upon him. Perhaps acknowledging his own poor decision, Cornelius II had pleaded with his brother William Kissam to act as trustee of his estate, ensuring that the wheels of the Vanderbilt railroad empire would still operate smoothly. As guardian of his brother's estate, William Kissam now wielded more power than ever before in his lifetime along with his own considerable inheritance.

The young Vanderbilt known for his expensive tastes and extravagant lifestyle could easily squander away the family fortune and it was up to Uncle Willie to prevent that. At best, the railroad would remain as it was, since there was no leader left to challenge, take calculated risks, and build new profits and enterprises. It would be up to Uncle Willie and his own son, the energetic and willful sportsman Willie K., who was no more inclined to work than Alfred, to master the reins of the powerful Vanderbilt railroad legacy and empire.

Uncle Willie was uneasy with the weighty burden of responsibility that he now bore. His brother Cornelius II had pleaded with him to carry on as leader of the railroad. It was with great reluctance that William Kissam assumed these duties. He was torn between conflicting interests: his own personal desire to avoid familial responsibility and loyalty to a dying brother who had begged for his support on his deathbed. William Kissam viewed money to be a handicap to happiness[1] but he knew of the tremendous financial benefit of a possible global transportation monopoly.

The family dispersed after Depew's last words. The will had been read and Cornelius' iron will had wrought its final judgment upon all of his

Alfred with top hat ca. 1907. Alfred was clearly a man to be dealt with when it came to fashion. Here in this three quarter formal portrait he is a man about town. When he drove his coaches he deferred on the fancier dress leaning more towards lighter colored clothes or the fabrics of a working taxi man. Library of Congress. Bain Collection.

descendants. Despite the public hunger for information on just what had been revealed, none of the executors[2] would disclose its contents. With everyone gone, Alfred spent Sunday with his mother at the *Breakers*.[3]

The next morning, A.G. traveled to New York and met with his brother, Neily, at the Waldorf-Astoria hotel, along with lawyers for a "genuine brotherly meeting." The two brothers agreed to wait to offer the will for probate until Uncle Willie returned from his cruise[4] on the *Valiant*, at which time the will would become public knowledge. It was on Oct 26, 1899, exactly 11 days after the reading of the will at the family home, that the will became public knowledge.

The actual distribution of the fortune after $2,000,000 was gifted to Mrs. Cornelius Vanderbilt[5], was approximated as shown in Table 3.1.[6]

The late Cornelius cemented Alfred's position as principal heir to the Vanderbilt fortune in the seventeenth clause:

> Seventeenth, all the rest, residue and remainder of the estate including all lapsed legacies and the principal of annuities, is given to the executors in trust to hold and invest and re-invest and collect rents, income, and profits for the use of his son Alfred.[7]

Alfred's new holdings included and were not limited to the New York Central Railroad, the Lake Shore and Michigan Southern Railroad, the Michi-

Table 3.1. Distribution of the Cornelius Vanderbilt II estate

Alfred G. Vanderbilt	36,375,000
Mrs. Gertrude Vanderbilt Whitney	8,375,000
Reginald C. Vanderbilt	7,375,000
Gladys Moore Vanderbilt	7,375,000
Cornelius (Neily) Vanderbilt	1,375,000
Relatives, friends, and servants	656,000
Churches and institutions	1,020,000

gan Central Railroad, the Pittsburg and Lake Erie Railroad, the Beech Creek Railroad, and the Pullman Company.

Cornelius also appointed six executors of the will in the nineteenth clause: Alice his widow, A.G. his second son, Willie Kissam his brother, Chauncey Depew his trusted railroad chairman, Edward W. Rossiter his legal counsel, and Reginald his youngest son when he was of suitable age.[8] The will also clearly specified that A.G. would receive only 'equal share of specific bequests'[9] until he was thirty years of age, at which point he would receive half of the residuary legacy. Upon attaining the age of thirty-five years, the young Vanderbilt heir would then come into 'full possession of his fortune.'[10] His younger brother Reginald received the position of heir in the case of Alfred's unexpected death with the same stipulations.

Alfred gave his brother Neily $6 million from the residuary legacy[11] in a gesture that Chauncey Depew insisted was "voluntary"[12] and conducted in a "most beautiful brotherly way,"[13] thereby making Neily's fortune the same as that of his brother Reginald and sister Gladys.

The front page of every national newspaper speculated about a family so obviously divided in a will and the charitable act of A.G., who was now "head of the Vanderbilt family,"[14] towards his brother Neily, whose marriage to Miss Wilson, was bitterly opposed by Cornelius[15], sparking deep displeasure from his father.[16] Neily was disinherited for marrying Grace Wilson. Declaring Neily the "luckless one,"[17] rumors circulated that A.G.'s present was to prevent the will from being contested.[18]

Neily's love affair with Grace Wilson aboard the steamship White Ladye of Ogden Goelet in the summer of 1895 was discussed at great length. His "devoted attentions to her"[19] in the Mediterranean fueled a dark resentment from both friends and family of the Vanderbilts who opposed the courtship of the young woman. The public revisited all the old hurts: Neily's subsequent stubborn insistence upon continuing the relationship after threatening statements from his father; his suffering from the reappearance of his childhood rheumatic bouts;[20] his ensuing conflict with his father resulting in blows; his father's stroke and their lack of communication for three years. He was the prodigal son, admired for his love of Grace but reviled for hitting his father. Neily would have none of this, his pride hurt by every insult the press hurled at him. When asked at his residence at 608 Fifth Avenue,[21] "Have you anything to say concerning your brother Alfred's act in presenting to you $6 million from his portion of the estate left by your father?,"[22] he balked at their language, hesitating in particular over the words "presenting" and "from his portion of the estate" before replying to their questions and insisting that his only comment was, "A family settlement was reached and Carter & Ledyard acted as my attorneys. That is all I have to say."[23]

Depew tried to defuse the heat, immediately rushing to the defense of the Vanderbilt family, saying that the arrangement was reached with perfectly good feelings on both sides,[24] denying that Neily had attempted or would attempt to contest the will. He declared that "Alfred's act was not the result of a threat to contest the will on the part of Neily. There will be no contest. This settlement suits all parties, and it has been achieved without friction."[25]

The public eye turned to the new heir with interest. Who was Alfred, the new head of the Vanderbilt house? His study at Yale, his trip abroad, and above all, his personality were discussed at great length as speculations about his spending habits and nature rose to the surface. The press described him as being "unostentatious"[26] and not even "conscious of his father's millions."[27] He was also said to be a "democratic and frank"[28] young man with a "genuine sense of humor"[29] whose popularity was evident in his selection to the exclusive Skull and Bones Society of Yale.

A long discourse by a correspondent of *The New York Sun*, reprinted in the *Los Angeles Times*, titled *You're All Right, Alfred,*[30] took an intimate look at Alfred's decision to "act contrary to his father's wish and will by making a free-will gift to his brother of $6 million of the money his father wished to keep from him."[31] A.G. had to choose between two opposing conflicts, "the duty imposed by filial piety, the obligations of a young son to his father" and that of "the duty or impulse of fraternal affection."[32] Which of these would A.G. choose and "which should be more binding on the conscience, the obedience to your father and the execution of his will, or fraternal affection which compels a contrary course?"[33]

As the principal heir, the young Vanderbilt had every right to do what he deemed fit with his inheritance, and by his act of gifting $6 million to his elder brother, he showed that he was "distinctly of the right sort—a good fellow and a good brother."[34]

While opinion of Alfred rose favorably in the public limelight, Neily rebelled, filled with the anger of one who has been unjustly condemned and judged. He called forth the press to make a statement to denounce that his brother had given him a gift, saying vehemently that "It is no gift, but the result of a compact entered into before my father's demise. By this compact, I was to receive no less than $20 million."[35] When pressed about whether there would be an amicable settlement of the residuary estate, Neily refrained from commenting and ended the press conference, declaring, "I will not discuss the matter further. I just wish to be set right before the public. All my interests are in my lawyer's hands."[36]

The Wilsons, Grace's family, were horrified. Her sister Belle wrote Grace a letter saying that she was "trembling and quivering with the wickedness and injustice of it all." Belle continued to say that it was "the greatest wickedness of the 19th century — when a son has been as good and upright and pure and honorable as Neily to brand him in the eyes of the world as an evil-doer."

The two brothers would barely speak after the will was settled. There was hardly any indication that Alfred spent time working at the New York Central Railroad but on the very day that Alfred was brought to his desk at the treasurer's office, Neily quit his job and never went back again.

NOTES

1. Vanderbilt Jr., Cornelius V. *Queen of the Golden Age: The Fabulous Story of Grace Wilson Vanderbilt.* New York, NY: McGraw-Hill Book Company. 1956. Pg. 65.
2. *The New York Times.* "Vanderbilt Will Conference." Oct 17, 1899. Pg. 10.
3. *Chicago Daily.* "Vanderbilt Will Not Filed For Probate." Oct 17, 1899. Pg. 4.
4. Ibid.
5. *The New York Times.* "Vanderbilt Will Changed By Heir." Oct 27, 1899. Pg. 1.
6. *The New York Times.* "Vanderbilt Will Changed By Heir." Oct. 27, 1899. Pg. 1.
7. *The Washington Post.* "The Vanderbilt Will." Oct. 27, 1899. Pg. 1.
8. *Los Angeles Times.* "Vanderbilt's Will." Oct 27, 1899. Pg 4.
9. *The New York Times.* "Vanderbilt Will Changed By Heir." Oct. 27, 1899. Pg. 1.
10. Ibid.
11. *The New York Times.* "Vanderbilt Will Changed By Heir." Oct. 27, 1899. Pg. 1.
12. *Los Angeles Times.* "Vanderbilt's Will." Oct 27, 1899. Pg 4.
13. Ibid.
14. *The Washington Post.* "The Vanderbilt Will." Oct. 27, 1899. Pg. 1.
15. *The Chicago Tribune.* "Son Is Cut Off By Vanderbilt." Oct. 27, 1899. Pg. 1.
16. *The Washington Post.* "The Vanderbilt Will." Oct. 27, 1899. Pg. 1.
17. *The Chicago Tribune.* "Son Is Cut Off By Vanderbilt." Oct. 27, 1899. Pg. 1.
18. Ibid.
19. *The Chicago Tribune.* "Vanderbilt Will: Only $1,500,000 Left to the son Cornelius." Oct 27, 1899. Pg.1.
20. Ibid.

21. *The New York Times*. "Vanderbilt Will Changed By Heir." Oct 27, 1899. Pg. 1.
22. *The Chicago Tribune.* "Son Is Cut Off By Vanderbilt." Oct. 27, 1899. Pg. 1.
23. Ibid.
24. *The New York Times*. "Vanderbilt Will Changed By Heir." Oct 27, 1899. Pg. 1.
25. *The New York Times*. "Vanderbilt Will Changed By Heir." Oct 27, 1899. Pg. 1.
26. *The Chicago Tribune.* "Son Is Cut Off By Vanderbilt." Oct. 27, 1899. Pg. 1.
27. Ibid.
28. Ibid.
29. Ibid.
30. *Los Angeles Times*. "You're All Right." Nov. 4, 1899. Pg. 8.
31. Ibid.
32. Ibid.
33. Ibid.
34. Ibid.
35. *Boston.* "It is no gift." Oct 28, 1899. Pg. 3.
36. Ibid.

Chapter Four

An Equal Match

Within two days of the public reading of the will, Alfred's social engagements went from being the pastimes of a young man of leisure to those of the youngest, most eligible bachelor in America.

Alfred met with his childhood playmate and friend, Miss Elsie French, in New York. Tall with auburn hair and hazel eyes,[1] the young Miss French, at eighteen years of age, was beautiful and wealthy in her own right, being the daughter of the deceased F.O. French, the president of the Manhattan Trust Company.

Meeting Elsie again brought vivid memories back to the young Vanderbilt of his most recent travels abroad and the joyful and lighthearted energy at the farewell party prior to his departure. He could remember the sparkle in her eyes and the boisterous energy of his friends, ready to set sail on the adventure of a lifetime. They were carefree, without the ties or shackles of a heavy responsibility.

His mother had insisted upon a large dinner party to which all of their friends and family were invited.[2] After that sizeable social gathering, Alfred and an intimate circle of young friends, Elsie included, all gathered together for a picnic Saturday afternoon at Oakland Farms in Portsmouth, R.I. It was a marvelous time, ending with swimming and a barbecue at *Bailey's Beach.*

The entire week itself had been one day after the other of surprises and events, concluding with the paper chase at Jamestown on July 24, 1899. With a head start of ten minutes, George P. Messervey played the fox, disappearing rapidly from the ferry landing where they had just arrived. Quick to mount, their fast young group of eight, Miss Evelyn Burden, Miss Gerry, Miss French, Miss Fish, Alfred Gwynne Vanderbilt, Robert L. Gerry, Harry Payne Whitney, and Milton S. Barber[3] took up the pursuit rapidly.

Hot on the chase, the eight hunters did not stop for even a moment to pause, ruthlessly invading meadows, ditches, fences, and ditches to chase the fox. Faster and faster they chased but George kept eluding them. Giddy and laughing, the eight, despite the most valiant of efforts, could not prevent George the fox from returning to the ferry in the nick of time. Miss Elsie French and Harry Payne Whitney led the pursuit and were also the first to arrive back at the ferry, horsetails flying and bodies glistening.

The young Vanderbilt retained that level of excitement when he arrived in New York two days later with his friends. He was to depart for his yearlong tour of the world. Overwhelmed by the vast array of options now available to him and the heavy responsibilities that lay ahead of him, A.G. returned to what was familiar and enjoyable: the companionship of his friends. Described as "four handsome, sturdy, good natured youngsters," the traveling entourage consisted of Alfred, William P. Burden, Ernest Iselin, and Douglass Cochran.

Since the party consisted of "young men who are possessed of independent fortunes,"[4] Depew, who had arrived to see the young men depart from Grand Central Station and to do the finishing touches for their departure, said, "it seems reasonable to predict that they will have a good time and not pinch themselves in the matter of comfort.'[5] Dressed in a gray Scotch suit[6] with turned up trousers and a straw hat at a jaunty tilt, Alfred was light, carefree, and ready to learn about the world and what lay beyond the familiar. He was ready to continue the travels that had been interrupted by his father's death.

As planned, Alfred sailed on the *Teutonic to* Liverpool and made his way to London, joining his three traveling companions. They intended, if possible, to visit Siam and lower China, Hindustan, Afghanistan, India, Persia, Egypt, and the Nile. They planned to be away until late in July or possibly September, their "return depending entirely upon the whim of the moment."[7]

The easy banter, joie de vivre, and raucous enthusiasm of his friends during the day offered Alfred pleasant distractions, allowing him to escape his new worries. He had inherited the mantle of glory descending from the commodore, and the heavy responsibility that came with it, which he was poorly equipped to handle. On top of his new undertakings, restlessness kept bringing Alfred's mind to Elsie.

He had hardly put down his bags before he announced his intention to meet up with her for a few days. The threesome were surprised, especially Ernest.[8] Ernest tried to convince Alfred to accompany him to St. Moritz to see his sister[9] who had won a series of skiing and tobogganing events, becoming a local heroine in recent months.

A.G. refused to budge. Alfred surprised even himself by his desire, although it was in his nature to embrace such a spontaneous decision. In affairs of the heart, Alfred had never revealed the kind of susceptibility his mother feared.

Elsie French, Alfred's socially acceptable bride.

The very next morning he left, sailing the English Channel to get to Paris. The journey had been a long one, but upon arriving in Paris, he did not pause to rest. Eager to see Elsie, he hurried to her residence, only to find that she was out for the evening with her mother and her uncle, Amos Tuck. Tuck was a wealthy and refined businessman who had made no qualms about expressing his desire to see Elsie marry royalty. In fact, he had been introducing Elsie to as many suitable bachelors as possible, including French Prince Henri d'Orleans.[10]

Money was not the most appealing factor to Amos Tuck; instead, he valued refinement, education, and love of arts and culture. These values had been deeply entrenched in him for as long as he had been living in France. Alfred was not new to such inclinations: his uncle Willie had expressed similar sentiments and was also educated in Europe. Nonetheless, Alfred was aware of his competition and eager to act upon his interest.

When Alfred arrived at Elsie's door the next morning, the butler announced that she was out for her morning walk in the gardens and took him to her, quietly departing without a word. The early morning light was soft and gentle, silhouetting her frame with an ethereal quality.

Alfred could scarcely believe his eyes as he reached Elsie. Looking at her in this Parisian environment, Alfred appreciated how his childhood friend had grown into an exquisite woman. She was tall and slender, with gorgeous tamed brown tresses, a soft mouth, and gentle eyes. The sweet womanly face beneath her elegant Parisian ensemble delighted him beyond measure. Alfred knew Elsie well enough to recognize their mutual love of freedom. Her time in Paris had further developed her fine sensibilities. She had become a very charming young woman.[11]

Their childhood banter was now replaced by a serious courtship, one that accelerated in a short period of time. As Alfred struggled internally with the family drama surrounding his father's death, he felt deeply relieved to be in the company of someone like Elsie, whom he loved and respected and who shared a similar upbringing and background as he. It was easy for Alfred to confide in Elsie because she was his friend of many years. Yet the fervent feelings he was now experiencing for her was not easily explained.

All ideas of further travel to the exotic lands of Persia and the pyramids of Egypt were dispelled. In fact, Alfred never got past Paris and the Riviera.[12] Every morning, Alfred would get ready, longing to see Elsie. He spent every day with her and every night he would retire to his lodgings impatient for the next day.

With Elsie, Alfred was unhindered, free of judgment and restraint in a way that he never been afforded before, while paradoxically being challenged enough to whet his curiosity and stimulate his interest. He relaxed into his new daily routine, being careful to not invoke the ire of her uncle while at the same time, adroitly positioning himself in the good graces of her mother. He had grown accustomed to putting on his public face, even sometimes to his friends, denying his emotions and choosing to be socially pleasant and agreeable, while also suffering from acute bouts of loneliness and confusion. Always debonair and ready for a good laugh, Alfred was described in the society papers as the quintessential ladies' man and playboy.[13] Yet with Elsie, Alfred had no social masks. He could be himself entirely. Some of his natural reticence and almost proletarian inclinations began to surface in her companionship.

Elsie read frequently and Alfred enjoyed debating and conversing with her. Her charm disarmed him and he found himself willing to discuss topics that hitherto had been taboo. He felt courageous and at ease with himself in her company, accepted for his own thoughts, even if they radically departed from those of his deceased father or his elder brother Neily. In the public's eye, Alfred was perceived to be a kind and generous soul, despite his irresponsibility and devilish lifestyle. Encouraged by Elsie's philanthropic leanings,[14] A.G. felt more comfortable embracing a simpler lifestyle.

As his Uncle Willie and his mother urged him to return to New York to resume his responsibilities as the heir to the Vanderbilt fortune and legacy,

Alfred rebelled internally. He admired his father's hardworking nature and loyalty, but viewed the railroad company and associated responsibilities as dull, tiring, boring, and overwhelming. To him, the railroad lifestyle was devoid of joy and he loathed becoming shackled to the family business. Alfred longed to stay in Europe, but at the behest of his mother, finally returned to New York, promising Elsie that he would return.[15]

The newspapers and tabloids ate up the story of Alfred's consuming passion for Elsie, but Alfred spent his time divided among his responsibilities at the New York Central Railroad, his family, looking at various properties near Newport, Rhode Island,[16] the Vanderbilt farm known as Oakland Farm bequeathed by his late father,[17] and acquiring the quaint Rocky Hall, a cottage on Bellevue Avenue, as his new summer home in Newport.

It was not long before he traveled again to Europe, splitting his time between the two continents before he joined Elsie in London in March of that year. Elsie's natural diplomacy helped ease some tension in Alfred's familial relationships as she skillfully maneuvered them out of harm's way. By late April, as the papers circulated with rumors and contrasting tales of possible union and separation, Elsie and Alfred prepared to address the press. The young couple formally announced their engagement on April 23 to the London *Times*.

The papers went wild. *The Boston Globe* had several features running in tandem daily, titled: "Youthful Head of Famous House Has Millions of His Own,"[18] to "Bride-Elect an Heiress to a Vast Fortune,"[19] and "Golden Match."[20] The public fell in love with the image of the young couple, childhood companions that had been born into homes of remarkable wealth, prestige, and power. *The New York Times*[21] described the engagement as "a little romance in itself. They have been sweethearts since childhood."

Graduated from Yale at the age of twenty-two, Alfred was described as being a "good horseman, an excellent whip" who excelled at all outdoor sports and was very "fond of the theater" being "well-built" and possessing the "characteristic, clear cut features of the Vanderbilts."[22] Elsie too attracted considerable attention. Elsie's father Francis O. French, owner of the Manhattan Trust Company, had built a sizeable fortune. The French family had powerful connections, wealth, and a reputation to defend. Educated and groomed in Europe under the protective eye of her uncle, Elsie was not just a talented and beautiful young woman, but also quite wealthy in her own right, coming in to $15 million from her father.[23] Alfred had inherited a staggering $42.5 million. The Vanderbilt family was the American equivalent of royalty, and this proposed union between the Vanderbilt and French families was a marriage of equals in many ways.

One of the remarkable differences from other recent Vanderbilt unions that had been filled with intrigue, conflict, and family drama, the engagement of

Elsie French to Alfred Vanderbilt was received by the press as a "foregone conclusion" with the approval of the late Cornelius Vanderbilt as well as Mrs. Vanderbilt, who apparently was quite fond of young Elsie.[24] Elsie too enjoyed the approval of Mrs. Harry Payne Whitney, a sister of Alfred. Marriage too, it seemed, was another sore point between Neily and Alfred.

Soon after the engagement announcement, Alfred left Elsie in Europe and returned to New York with his mother, Reginald, Gladys, and Gladys' two children.[25] Back and forth Alfred went from Europe to America, until finally Elsie and her mother decided to return home. Arriving off the steamship *St. Louis* together in New York on July 22, with Elsie "armed with collection of trunks that might contain the fripperies of a Princess of the blood royal,"[26] the young couple departed for Wickford Junction in Newport[27] three days later in Alfred's private car. Elsie and her mother took up temporary residence at a local boarding house for five days while their villa *Harbor View* was being prepared for their occupancy. Five days later, they moved in to their new villa.

The young couple announced a tentative marriage date of September at Trinity Church and a reception at *Harbor View*. As the months passed, without any further announcements, this proposed wedding date came under increasing scrutiny and public pressure.[28]

Any young man in love with a newfound passion would have his head in the clouds. Alfred was likely no exception. He was very outgoing during his courtship with Elsie, attending parties and social events throughout the year.[29]

Elsie was his perfect playmate, someone who could enjoy jaunts in the country and fast coach rides and yet due to her grace and wit, she could hold her own among high society's elite. Soon after her return from Europe, Elsie joined him in his coaching adventures, frequently accompanying him on short trips. His engagement to Elsie and his love of coaching filled his days with color and vivacity. By all accounts, they were the perfect pair.

A few months before, when looking at properties with his friend Potter, Alfred had explored Oakland Farm. Alfred's pursuit of coaching grew into a lifestyle that he adopted with vigor, passion, and notoriety. Being athletic and winsome, he possessed the knack of getting friends, family, and even onlookers enthusiastic about his interests.[30] Alfred took up coaching with great passion. Cultivating his sport and gaining a reputation as an expert whip, the young Vanderbilt attempted to establish a coaching record time[31] on August 25, 1900 for the distance from Newport to Boston and back with a four-horse brake. Relays of four horses each were set up along the way in Fall River, Taunton, and Stoughton. It was a Saturday morning and quite early when Alfred headed out with four friends[32] and two footmen, planning to get to Boston in record-time. Alfred wanted to break the previous record made by O. H. P. Belmont four years prior to traverse the 70-mile stretch from Newport to Boston.[33] However, members of the traveling party vehemently denied this desire when they arrived in Boston later that night, claiming instead that they were only having a "simple pleasure trip."[34]

The heat beat relentlessly and the horses struggled up the hill in Tiverton, where one of them collapsed and had to be left with a nearby farmer for resuscitation. Alfred still pushed on with just three horses to the coach in a spike team,[35] but the heat did not let up.[36] Despite his best efforts, they were still late so that by the time they reached Taunton at 2 p.m. forty-five minutes behind schedule, they decided to call off the record-breaking part of the trip. Continuing along to Boston, they got there by sundown and exhausted by the conditions, retired there for the night. After a day's rest, the party set out again at 8 am in excellent spirits to return to Newport from Boston, picking up Elsie along the way at Tiverton. Alfred did not appear to be deterred by his previous setback. With Elsie seated beside him in the box seat, Alfred holding the ribbons, made record time and successfully drove the entourage, stopping first at Stoughton to change four more horses to the coach, and then two more stops at Taunton and Fall River, before arriving back to Newport.[37]

Arriving at Rocky Hall at 7:25 p.m., Alfred was 15 minutes faster than his trip out to Boston and a whole 30 minutes before the scheduled time of arrival.[38] The party was elated but declined to say much to the awaiting press although Alfred hinted of possible new record-breaking attempts in the future.

Sharing a great love of the outdoors and competitive sports, the young couple engaged frequently in hunting events. Counted among the most skillful and adventurous of Newport's cross-country riders, Elsie and Alfred participated with friends in long meets, often by Quaker Hill near the kennels of Hillside Farm by Newport. Even when A.G.'s horses were indisposed or being treated at the veterinarian's, the young man ever wanted to miss out on horse racing and hunting events. Intense competition among friends was likely and during one such fox hunt in September about two weeks after their Newport-Boston incident, both the young Ms. French and Mr. Vanderbilt actively pursued the chase, where Mrs. Adolph Ladenburg,[39] a friend of the family, outran all her competitors, landing all the jumps, making the kill, and setting a new record, while her competitors fell behind, some even sustaining serious wounds. So hot was the pursuit that the young pair had to move constantly to keep pace with the action, running from one vantage point to another to view the hot-blooded chase. Never to give up, A.G. went out with the same hunting crowd a few days later[40] when his horse was recovered, with Elsie cheering him on and garnering fourth place for the last hunt of the season.

Their shared passion lent itself to a remarkable closeness that never went unnoticed. While the press barraged them with questions about their approaching marriage[41], the dynamic duo was able to remain cool and collected. Their social graces were always evident. The day after the last Newport hunt, the young Vanderbilt surprised the public with a declaration to return to work after an informal dinner with Elsie, her mother, and some close friends. The young man said, "I'm going to go back to my father's desk and try to take up the work where he left off. I want you to wish me good luck,[42]" while Elsie looked on with approval.[43]

Just as Alfred embarked on yet another change in his life, strongly supported by his fiancé, the papers lavished attention on the subject. *The Atlanta Constitution* described A.G.'s commitment to work as "Alfred Gwynne Vanderbilt, the head of the house, has abandoned his polo outfit and will go to work. He will be his own paymaster."[44] The *Chicago Daily Tribune* compared him favorably to his cousin William K. Vanderbilt Jr., saying that the young Vanderbilt "had wisely chosen to learn the business in which so much of his wealth is invested instead of devoting himself to polo, automobiles, and golf."[45]

The papers loved him. He appeared to have become some kind of hero overnight, inspiring other wealthy young men to earn their own living "by honest toil."[46] Every day, the young heir went into work as an accountant like other gentlemen who worked for the company. However, a big difference lay in how much he received every week. Alfred's paycheck, close to $60,000,[47] was a sharp contrast to the young workers who took home $25 a week. Despite being born with a silver spoon in his mouth, Alfred showed a willingness to pull up his sleeves and do the "dirty work" which endeared him to the public and the press.

The young Vanderbilt continued along his new chosen path of work and pleasure. In fact, thoughts of social pleasure and being with Elsie were never far from his mind. Within less than a month, Alfred rented the majestic and charming property of *Chastellux*[48] in Newport as a summer rental for the next year, an acquisition that garnered immediate attention because of its attractive appearance and desirability for entertaining. With a sweeping view of the harbor, *Chastellux,* the summer residence of Lorillard Spencer, was made of gray stone and was considered one of the most stunning villas in the area.

In November, just as rumors began to fly once again with questions about this "marriage of love between childhood sweethearts," the pair's forthcoming wedding was announced publicly[49] for January 18th 1901 and then amended to January 14th at the behest of Elsie's mother a few days later. Congratulations were in order for the young couple and a public outpouring of support mixed with curiosity was evident in all the major newspapers, with speculations about elaborate wedding preparations including special trains for guests and lavish decorations. Soon after their announcement, Alfred's mother Alice returned from a long sojourn in Europe with her daughter Gladys and was met by the young couple. Mrs. F.O. French left Newport to meet with Mrs. Cornelius Vanderbilt to plan the wedding of their children in January.[50] The mothers of the bride and groom started preparing for the wedding.[51]

By December 3rd, the young couple had selected a church for the wedding, the Zabriskie Memorial Church of St. John the Evangelist on Washington Street in Newport.[52] The buzz and excitement about their upcoming wedding gained a momentum in December that did not abate till long after the actual event. Mrs. Cornelius Vanderbilt hired numerous contractors and servants to get their Newport Mansion the *Breakers*, ready for a welcoming reception for all of their guests that would arrive a week before the wedding in January while Mrs. F.O. French arranged for automobiles for all of her guests and sleighs for backup in case of inclement weather. The Vanderbilts brought their horses, 130 in total, to the *Breakers*.

Gifts began to pour in and were sent to the *Aquidneck National Bank* for safekeeping. Decorations including evergreens, holly, trees, and wreaths were shipped in large quantities to Mrs. F.O. French, who was hosting both the wedding breakfast and the wedding reception at her villa. The newspapers chronicled wedding preparation details such as the arrival of the gowns in waterproof containers to the removal of more than 200 storm windows in the large Newport residence.[53] Every little detail was being taken care of with style.

Going out to 250 guests, mostly family and friends, the invitations were simple and read:

> *Mrs. French requests the honor of your presence at the marriage of her daughter Elsie and Alfred Gwynne Vanderbilt, on Monday, the 14th of January, at 12 o'clock, at St. John's Church, Newport R.I.*

The newspapers too began to focus more on Elsie, writing whole feature articles about the future wife of Alfred G. Vanderbilt. Described as being tall, blonde and stronger than most women, Elsie was a "veritable young Brunhilde", one who "out of doors there is no sport in which she does not excel."[54] Her love of clothing and disdain for heavy jewelry was analyzed and described in great detail, as well as the flowers she enjoyed wearing. Her audience was both entranced and mystified by her simplicity: "Violets she frankly prefers to jewels, for it is one of the refreshing charms of this young lady to adopt perfectly unconventional tastes without any affectation or assumption of a pose."[55] The mother of the groom made arrangements for the weddings guests such as special trains with carriages waiting for them at the station to take them to the church with a special organ recital by the choirmaster William H. Boone just for the guests.

The newspapers kept public curiosity and excitement fed by describing the arrival of guests and wedding items with much attention to detail. Long articles about wedding cakes, gowns, flowers, and the improvements being made to the *Breakers* and the *Harbor View* residence abounded.

But not all news was trivial. Two days before their wedding, Alfred and Elsie procured their wedding license amidst glaring ice, the frightening remnants of a dangerous hailstorm and survived a slippery ride when their carriage careened down a hill.

Despite the alarming experience, Alfred and Elsie remained in buoyant spirits, as they got to see the wedding gifts that were being safeguarded at the vault.[56] Among the many presents there was a $75,000 pearl and diamond necklace, a gift from Alice to the young bride. Elsie's mother, Mrs. F.O. French, said it "was the most beautiful necklace she had ever seen."[57] The same day Alfred gave his future wife the sum of $3.7 million in gold-edged bonds in a silver case.[58]

Elsie's request for simplicity[59] was mentioned only briefly in the papers as the press preferred to carry ornate descriptions of elaborate dinners and preparations such as "Wedding at Newport Marked by Gorgeous Display of Gowns, Elaborate Decorations, and Millions Represented" and comparisons between Elsie and Alfred, listing their respective advantages.[60]

Some had contrasting and conflicting descriptions such as the "grandeur of arrangements" and "social standing of the participants" with lengthy descriptions of the wedding details, along with a statement of how neither the bride nor the bridegroom cared for "any display of wealth."[61] Spending with reckless abandon was fast becoming socially inappropriate. Elsie preferred a simple and elegant style, reflecting her own refined sensibilities.

After much anticipation, the big day arrived. Decorated "with gorgeous lavishness" the wedding ceremony was lovely in every aspect, with the church being "exquisitely decorated[62] and "everything in good taste."[63] Two clergymen entered to the tune of the *Lohengrin* march, followed by the bridegroom and his younger brother, Reginald, who acted as best man. The bridal procession started with the ushers leading, followed by the four bridesmaids. All friends of Alfred's, the eight ushers were attired in frock coats with lavender ties and pearl pins. Carrying bouquets of fresh American beauty roses, the four bridesmaids wore pearl gray crepe de chine[64] with liberty gauze and delicate gray hats adorned with a gold knot in front. The maid of honor, Miss Gladys Vanderbilt, Alfred's sister, was similarly dressed.

Following the last bridesmaid slowly, the future Mrs. Alfred Vanderbilt[65] approached the aisle, leaning on Amos Tuck French's arm. Elsie was dressed in a remarkably simple yet striking gown made of rich white satin in ivory, with a train extending as far as three yards, a lace high collar corsage, long, fitted sleeves trimmed with soft lace, and a skirt with delicate sprays of orange blossoms and tulle, to create a dazzlingly effect of loveliness. Over her head, Elsie wore a long bridal veil that extended down to the train of her gown.[66] Carrying a simple bouquet of white lilies and orchids, Elsie did not wear any jewelry and yet was resplendent in her beauty.

Meeting Alfred at the altar and smiling, the pair turned towards the Reverend Morgan who read the betrothal part of the service, after which they moved towards the chancel and were pronounced husband and wife by the Reverend Beattie. Despite an elaborate buildup, the ceremony was brief.

All the guests and the newly married couple headed over to *Harbor View* for the wedding breakfast and reception. At Mrs. French's request, none of the guests incurred any expenses, as she provided all the automobiles for transportation and dining. Served at round tables, the wedding breakfast lasted about two hours, after which the guests convened in the large drawing room that had been converted into a floral bower. Alfred and Elsie received their friends and family as a newly married couple, accepting congratulations and enjoying their company.

The guests were ready to celebrate and there was much feasting and clinking of glasses. The couple entertained their guests graciously for several hours before leaving for Boston. They took a special train and arrived at the Back Bay Station where the radiance of their smiles "could not but have impressed some people of the happiness they felt."[67]

The papers were sure to be ablaze. The most eligible bachelor was now wed! A new period in Alfred's life had begun with Elsie, now together as one.

On their honeymoon, the pair was inseparable, frequently sighted in public, attending art events and theater performances.[68] The newly married couple, blissful in their union, stayed several days in Boston and the Berkshires before taking a private car to New York, where they boarded the *Oceanic*[69] for a honeymoon tour of Europe. They were supposed to be in Europe for a few weeks but returned to America sooner than expected to search for a new residence in New York and spend time with their families. By February, they had taken up residence back in Newport again, where their winter adventures and sleigh riding[70] were discussed with great admiration.

Despite Alfred and Elsie being two months married, the newspapers continued to describe their wedding with much gusto, elaborating upon the display of the wedding cakes, flowers, gowns, and gifts all the way into March. Mrs. Francis O. French could bear it no longer and issued a statement to the press from her home in London to "correct impressions"[71] conveyed through the English press obtained from "various irresponsible newspapers" about her daughter's marriage. She denied the large expenditures attached to the cost of flowers, wedding cakes, and bridal wear. Mrs. F.O. French said she had read the local papers "with considerable distress" and was requesting that these papers correct their information to represent the facts.

Elsie's traveling apparel was the biggest draw in the arts and culture section of the newspapers as they all described, in minute detail, every item in her traveling trousseau such as the broad wale called South Sea blue for her jacket trimmed with skeleton plaid veloutine.[72] For Elsie, having the press chronicle the mundane details of her travel wardrobe and her day-to-day life as a newlywed was exhausting, if not intrusive. Elsie quickly became fully cognizant that as the wife of Alfred Gwynne Vanderbilt, her life would never be the same.

NOTES

1. *Boston.* "Young and Beautiful" Oct 28, 1899. Pg. 3.
2. *The New York Times.* "The News of Newport." Jul 14, 1899. Pg. 7.
3. *Boston Daily Globe.* 'Society's Paper Chase." Jul 25, 1899. Pg. 12.
4. *Boston Daily Globe.* "Tour of World." Jul. 27. 1899. Pg. 2.
5. Ibid.
6. Ibid.
7. *The Chicago Daily Tribune.* "Plans of Travel for Young Vanderbilt." January 31, 1900. Pg. 4.
8. Ernest Iselin, son of Mr. and Mrs. Adrian Iselin.
9. *The New York Times.* June 13, 2001. "What Is Doing In Society." Pg. 7.
10. *The Chicago Daily Tribune.* "May Lose His Sweetheart: Uncle of Elsie French Opposed to Alfred Gwynne Vanderbilt as Suitor for Her Hand." March 12, 1900. Pg. 2.
11. *Los Angeles Times.* "New York Society: The Vanderbilt-French Wedding, the Astor Ball, and Other Social Functions at the Great Metropolis." Jan 27, 1901. Pg. B2.
12. *The New York Times.* April 29, 1900. "Vanderbilt Engagement: Miss Elsie French to become Alfred Gwynne Vanderbilt's Wife." Pg. 7.
13. *The Atlanta Constitution.* April 29, 1900. Pg. 2.
14. *The New York Times.* "The News of Newport." April 22, 1900. Pg 6.
15. *The New York Times.* "What is Doing in Society." May 2, 1900. Pg. 9
16. *The Washington Post.* Jan 28, 1900. Pg. 2.
17. *The New York Times.* "A. G. Vanderbilt in Newport: The Visit Causes Revival of Report of His Coming Marriage."
18. *The Boston Daily Globe.* "Golden Match." April 29, 2001. Pg. 1.
19. Ibid.
20. Ibid.
21. *The New York Times.* "Vanderbilt Engagement: Miss Elsie French to become Alfred Gwynne Vanderbilt's Wife." April 29, 2001. Pg. 7.
22. *The New York Times.* April 29, 1900. "Vanderbilt Engagement: Miss Elsie French to become Alfred Gwynne Vanderbilt's Wife." Pg. 7.

23. *The Washington Post.* "Vanderbilt to Wed Millions." April 29, 2001. Pg.1.
24. *The New York Times.* April 29, 1900. "Vanderbilt Engagement: Miss Elsie French to become Alfred Gwynne Vanderbilt's Wife."
25. *The New York Times.* "Vanderbilt Engagement: Miss Elsie French to become Alfred Gwynne Vanderbilt's Wife." April 29, 2001. Pg. 7.
26. *The Chicago Tribune.* July 22, 1900. "General News." Pg. 6.
27. Boston Daily Globe, July 26, 1900. "Miss French Arrives." Pg. 8.
28. *The New York Times.* "Vanderbilt-French Wedding." August 1, 1900. Pg.7.
29. Chicago Tribune. July 29, 1900. Pg. 42.
30. *The New York Times.* August 13, 1900. "The News of Newport." Pg. 7.
31. *The New York Times.* August 25, 1900. "A.G. Vanderbilt's Coach Run: To Drive from Newport to Boston Today in Record-Breaking Time." Pg. 1.
32. *The New York Times.* August 28, 1900. "Vanderbilt Coaching Trip: Party Returns After Boston to Newport After Successful Run." Pg. 1.
33. *The New York Times.* August 27, 1900. "Will Try for Record Today." Pg 1.
34. *The New York Times.* August 27, 1900. "Hurt by Heat."
35. Ibid.
36. *The New York Times.* August 25, 1900. "A. Vanderbilt's Coaching Trip: Heat Balks His Effort to Establish a Record from Newport to Boston." Pg. 1.
37. *The New York Times.* August 28, 1900. "Vanderbilt Coaching Trip: Party Returns After Boston to Newport After Successful Run." Pg. 1.
38. *Boston Daily Globe.* August 28, 1900. "To Newport in His Coach." Pg. 6.
39. *The New York Times.* Sept 18, 1900. "Fox Hunters at Newport: Mrs. Ladenburg in at the Death After a Hard Ride." Pg. 9.
40. *The New York Times*. September 30, 1900. "Newport's Last Hunt." Pg. 8.
41. *Los Angeles Times*. Jan 27, 1901. "New York Society: The Vanderbilt-French Wedding, the Astor Ball, and Other Social Functions at the Great Metropolis." Pg. B2.
42. *Boston Daily Globe*. October 1, 1900. "Richest Young Man Going To Work: Alfred G. Vanderbilt Surprises His Friends by Announcing that He will Try to Learn the Railroad Business." Pg. 7.
43. *Boston Daily Globe.* October 1, 1900. "Richest Young Man Going To Work: Alfred G. Vanderbilt Surprises His Friends by Announcing that He will Try to Learn the Railroad Business." Pg. 7.
44. *The Atlanta Constitution.* October 3, 1900.
45. *The Chicago Daily Tribune.* "Opening the Dramatic Season." October 3, 1900. Pg. 6.
46. *Boston Daily Globe.* "Fashion's New Fad." Oct 9, 1900. Pg. 6.
47. Ibid.
48. *The New York Times*. "What Is Doing In Society." Oct 16, 1900. Pg. 7.
49. *The New York Times*. Nov 6, 1900. "Vanderbilt-French Wedding: Date is Now Definitely Settled for Jan.18 Next." Pg. 3.
50. *The New York Times.* Nov 13, 1900. "The News of Newport." Pg. 7.
51. *The New York Times.* "Coming Vanderbilt Wedding." Dec 22, 1900. Pg. 1.
52. *Boston Daily Globe.* "Plans for Vanderbilt-French Wedding."

53. Ibid.
54. Ibid.
55. *The Atlanta Constitution.* Jan 6, 1901 "Mr. Vanderbilt's Bride." Pg. C5.
56. *The New York Times.* "Mr. Vanderbilt at Newport: Spends the Day with Miss French Completing Wedding Arrangements." Jan 2, 1901. Pg. 9.
57. *The Chicago Daily Tribune.* "Vanderbilt Gives $3,700,000 to Fiancée." Jan 12, 1901. Pg.4.
58. *The Atlanta Constitution.* "With His Wealth Vanderbilt Endows Miss Elsie French." Jan 15, 1901. Pg. 1.
59. *Los Angeles Times.* "Vanderbilt Wedding." Jan 14, 1901. Pg. 4.
60. Boston. "Vanderbilts Here." Jan 15, 1901. Pg.1.
61. *The Chicago Daily Tribune.* Jan 15, 1901. "Splendor at a Wedding." Pg.7.
62. *The New York Times.* Jan 15, 1901. "Alfred G. Vanderbilt Marries Miss French." Pg.1.
63. *The New York Times.* Jan 15, 1901. "Everything in Good Taste." Pg. 2.
64. *The Hartford Courant.* "Vanderbilt-French: Preparations for Today's Wedding at Newport." Jan 14, 1901. Pg. 2
65. *The Washington Post.* "Vow Said At Newport." Jan 15, 1901. Pg. 2.
66. WhiteHern Museum Archive, Jan. 15, 1901. Rev. Calvin McQuesten.
67. *Boston.* "Vanderbilts Here." Jan 15, 1901. Pg.1.
68. *The New York Times.* "To Have and To Hold." Feb 19, 1901. Pg. 6.
69. *The Washington Post.* "Social and Personal." Feb 25, 1901. Pg. 7.
70. *The New York Times.* "The News of Newport." Feb 8, 1901. Pg. 9.
71. *The New York Times.* "Mrs. F.O. French Distressed: She Issues a Statement Correcting Reports about the Vanderbilt
72. *The Chicago Daily Tribune.* January 31, 1900. "Plans of Travel for Young Vanderbilt." Pg. 4.

Chapter Five

Working Man: Whips, Skirts, and Coattails

Society was entranced by the exploits of the young heirs to some of the world's largest fortunes. With more than $2,400,000,000 in stock[1] divided among a few, the entire wealth of the nation seemed concentrated in the hands of young men. Most of these were the eldest born sons of wealthy financiers, who faithfully followed the practice of primogeniture. Cornelius Vanderbilt alone was the exception, having named his third-born son his inheritor.

Who would follow in the footsteps of the late Vanderbilt Senior? Andrew Carnegie had said that despite the law of primogeniture, "there was no country where it was so true that a family went from shirt sleeves to shirt sleeves in three generations as in the United States."[2] Who among them would choose leisure and who work? Many a millionaire's son went to work as a clerk in the bottom tier of his father's operation. They strived as businessmen to earn reputations that matched their inheritances. A.G., like the sons of Hill, Mackay, Gould, Green, Whitney, and Rockefeller[3], also prepared himself for railroad management, working as a clerk for $10 a week during his apprenticeship. Yet unlike his peers, Alfred did not stay at the railroad offices for very long, returning as quickly as possible to his rural pastimes.

While expanding his residences at Oakland Farms in Newport, R.I., as well as his extensive camp in the Adirondacks, he kept a smaller apartment in New York to oversee his coaching trips. A.G. spent all of his free time fixing up the stables at Oakland, acquiring new horses for his coaches, participating in numerous horse show events, and altogether, retreating from the working world of his father.

Alfred merely played at business, a luxury he could well afford. He could have purchased yachts like his cousin Willie K., spent most of his time at the track like his brother Reginald, or wandered across Europe like his uncle and friends, but A.G. preferred to spend his time as a whip behind a four-in-hand.

Alfred Vanderbilt holding whip and in coaching attire. In later photos he sports a moustache, but he always seemed adorned with a carnation. Ca. 1905. Culver Pictures Inc.

A family friend, speaking to the *Herald*, revealed his doubts: "Here is one of the greatest properties in earth without a single one of the younger generation of Vanderbilts to look after it in the future. Here is a great house, akin in this country where money is the power to royalty in another land, without a single descendent of the man who planned it, who saved and worked for it, to keep it on its career."

It was not that Alfred Gwynne did not like work *per se*; in fact, he delighted workers when he formally recognized the importance of labor unions "for the laboring man." A.G. enjoyed wearing a workingman's clothes at his rural residences and adopted a lifestyle there far simpler than those of his family and friends. With exquisite taste and a love of fashion, Alfred would mix together expensive objects with a rustic lifestyle. He was a man of contradictions; displaying his pleasure in a rustic lifestyle which shocked some of his peers, as he shirked his financial obligations; and yet, with his exquisite taste and love of style, bringing in expensive elements into these rough and tumble surroundings and encouraging the sport of coaching.

The newspapers ate up stories of regality, splendor, adventure, courtship, and financial dealing. Like a child bored of her dolls and looking for a new toy, society began to lose interest in Alfred Gwynne as his commitment to coaching deepened.

Sitting in a backless cushioned seat, Alfred as the driver, or *whip*, drove a carriage that was reminiscent of the style of a previous era before the advent of automobiles: a three thousand pound road coach with four-foot wheels.[4] It was as though A.G. wished desperately to return to a previous era where once again, four horses would lead a magnificent coach. His coach was well kept, shining and immaculate. The Vanderbilt name carried the colors of maroon,[5] which contrasted nicely with A.G.'s shining black horses. Coaching required elegance, skill, swift maneuvering, and a certain showmanship; it was not a sport for the ordinary individual and it demanded a considerable level of upkeep that only a sizeable fortune could maintain. Understated with dark wood interior paneling finished with gold trim, the carriage that Alfred drove possessed an upper level for passengers that was almost nine feet off the ground,[6] and a small windowed cabin better suited for storing luggage than for seating people, showing his own apparent preference for beauty and movement than mere comfort. Mounting the coach carriage was no ordinary endeavor for women in their long corseted gowns,[7] who struggled to climb aboard. There was a definite pecking order to seating aboard this vehicle, with the most celebrated and valued guest sitting next to the whip, and other passengers placed behind these two frontrunners, in seats of gammon with cushioned metal. While the coachmen wore black top hats, the owners wore grey and people on the streets instantly could recognize who was in charge, simply by their hat.[8]

In Paris, A.G. cultivated his love of coaching under the guidance of Edwin Howlett, a man famous for his adroit handling of horses in carriages and teams. Howlett was a Swiss man based in Paris who had written the book *Driving Lessons* in 1894.[9] Under his tutelage, the young Vanderbilt drove in the Bois du Boulogne with Howlett's son Morris, an outstanding whip in his own right.

A.G.'s relationship with his horses was hard to explain. He was not the quintessential horseman nor was he the sole financier wishing to make huge profits at the track. The young man was athletic and of a good build, enjoying a good competition; a man who took extremely good care of the animals in his stable, and yet could not be fully bothered to agonize over every detail in breeding horse shows. Alfred was a true showman who reveled in being the center of attention as a young dashing coachman with a flower in his lapel. He enjoyed riding atop his four-in-hand coach, drawing widespread attention from crowds of appreciative people. He was not the sole rider but rather the darling of society, who brought color, vivacity, and a certain panache wherever he went, enjoying the exuberant reactions he evoked from strangers and people he met along his travels, as he played to the crowds.

Alfred and Elsie sharing a carriage with Alfred at the ribbons. His passion turned to coaching early on and Elsie was an obliging spouse. The sport had lost its favor among society until Alfred provided renewed interest and funding. Truth was it appeared to become an unhealthy obsession. Library of Congress. Bain Collection.

The young man immersed himself in the stables, spending most of his free time with his horses, practicing and getting ready for events. Maybe it was the pure exhilaration and freedom of unrestricted movement that his prize horses exhibited with their gleaming eyes and flaring nostrils; their manes whipping as their shiny flanks and necks rippled with taut, glistening, and powerful muscles that thrilled the young heir. While he did not bear the brunt of responsibility as head of the Vanderbilt legacy, having left the running of the railroad business in the hands of his uncle William Kissam, Alfred spent his time and efforts in pursuing his newfound love of coaching and thoroughbreds.

Spending a mere $100,000 a year on his coaching, a paltry sum in comparison to his income as well as standard expenses for other members of the Vanderbilt family, Alfred established his practice of driving coaches at Oakland Farms, the gorgeous country estate of his father on the southern end of Aquidneck Island about six miles away from the bustling metropolitan center of Newport.[10] Making Oakland Farms his primary residence with the construction of an elaborate country villa,[11] A.G. plunged headlong into his new lifestyle, donning the clothes of the workmen at his estate; building horse barns and practice areas; taking horses to private shows, sales, and events; and competing with an unrivalled generosity of spirit. As his commitment to the sport and lifestyle intensified, the young Vanderbilt initiated the building of the largest private riding ring in the world, a private hippodrome at Oakland Farms. Under his direction beginning at the end of the summer of 1901,[12] Alfred transformed his estate from an idyllic rural retreat to one of the most famous horse farms of its time.

Alfred spared no expense. Described as a 'mammoth ring' of epic proportions, measuring 265 feet long and 125 feet in width, with a 65 foot high ceiling, the ring was a horseman's paradise, connected to numerous additional rooms that included a swimming pool, roof garden, trophy room, library, squash and tennis courts, and a balcony for 200 people.[13] Adjoining this colossal horse ring was a magnificent stable for no less than 90 horses that rivaled that of the finest horse stables in the world, an accompanying carriage house, and a covered walkway to bring horses and carriages directly into the ring without exposing them to inclement weather.

For a little while, A.G. tried out automobile racing, indulging his love of speed and competition, as he attempted again to set a record, driving a 16

As part of the spoils of inheritance Alfred received Oakland Farm outside of Newport. It was not the house pictured here that astonished admirers as much as did the barns. Shingle style often sported gambrel roofs that were a perfect complement to barn architecture. This shingle style lacked in the glamour that was apparent at nearby Newport. Town and Country, April 20, 1907.

Four views of the barn at Vanderbilt's Oakland farm outside of Newport. Barns come in all sizes and shapes but few could match the fanciful castle like structure that Alfred built. Few would boast a trophy room and a swimming pool. Even fewer witnessed the wild parties that occurred in this one. Town and Country, *April 20, 1907.*

horsepower car[14] from Newport to Lenox, R.I. His brother Reginald competed against him, but withdrew less than half-way through the trip after one of his tires gave out. Alfred was frustrated since his automobile did not even make it out of his residence. He refused to move forward despite over almost a week of work by machinists in preparation for the race.[15] A certain tenacity revealed itself in the young Vanderbilt when only thirteen days later, he attempted to once again set an automobile record, from Newport to Boston and back, on his own, averaging seventy miles per hour.[16] He confidently announced that he could beat the express train with ease if he tried it again.

Alfred did not stay long behind the wheel. After receiving a series of traffic tickets, A.G. turned his back on automobile racing and took up coaching as a means of travel for short trips. In contrast to the reputation of his reckless, speed-loving cousin Willie K., young Alfred surprised the press by not only giving up racing but also adopting local habits and predilections, decrying speeding and advocating traffic law enforcement. When the chauffeur of the wealthy diamond merchant, St. John Wood, carelessly sped past A.G.'s *Pioneer* coach on its way from the Holland House to Ardsley Casino,[17] crippling one of his horses, Alfred Gwynne took up the case in court. He passionately called for punishment of the driver and punitive damages of $1,000 for the horse.

While A.G. was stirring up debate in the courts, his sister-in-law Grace pulled off the social success of the year by capturing Prince Henry, who sat as her guest in her box at the Metropolitan Opera. She was now deemed "*the* Mrs. Vanderbilt."[18] Alice, Alfred's mother, fretted and called upon Elsie and Alfred Gwynne to entertain. They obliged her, acting as gracious young hosts, entertaining guests for Reginald's engagement[19] and upcoming wedding, and hosting large luncheon parties for over a hundred guests[20] at their estate.[21] Anointed "citizen of Newport,"[22] A.G. and his wife attended fashionable events such as the much touted arrival of Alice Roosevelt, daughter to the president Theodore Roosevelt and erstwhile playful companion of James H. Hyde, to Rhode Island society.[23] Polo was still the rage and Alfred's competitive game in the Westchester team[24] drew forth some notice in societal columns. Still, the focus remained upon Reginald, the latest Vanderbilt to wed and for whom A.G. would be best man.[25]

Reginald supported his brother's love of coaching. He began to show his own horses at local events by the end of the summer and the following year.[26] Alfred's playmate, James Hazen Hyde, also started coaching. Both Hyde and Reginald accompanied A.G. on his frequent trips. Elsie came along less frequently as the year progressed,[27] preferring to spend time with her own companions and fostered, instead, her love of sailboats.

As his interest in coaching deepened, A.G. traveled far and wide to witness and participate with friends, including his brother-in-law Harry Payne Whitney,[28] in polo tournaments in Saratoga Springs, long a bastion of the Vanderbilt clan,[29] New York, and across the ocean to London, where he participated in numerous International Horse Show events. Famous for its illustrious residents and rejuvenating spas, Saratoga Springs was a fashionable resort area, renowned for its sumptuous living, health spas, and smooth horse tracks. Unlike other American social watering holes such as Newport[30] that excluded any discussion even of mistresses, it comfortably wore a disreputable air of illicit affairs between gorgeous belles resplendent in their organza, chiffon, taffeta, and silk gowns, and rough, tobacco-spitting men.[31]

In a time when human beings traveled with ease by rail, it was hard to imagine that for hundreds of centuries human beings had to rely upon their feet or animal power to travel by land. As Prince Phillip wrote in *The History of the Coaching Club*'s foreword, "The Road Coach and Park Drag, drawn usually by four horses and driven by a Coachman, were the very last - and most technically advanced - of the long line of animal-powered transport vehicles."[32] These exquisitely designed and stately vehicles would have completely vanished if not for the efforts of amateur drivers who had created the Coaching Club in New York in 1871, attracting more followers in the next decade such as A.G. who would revive the sport of driving a four-in-hand and bring attention again to this lifestyle.

The popularity of coach riding accelerated during the end of the nineteenth century, becoming a "required accomplishment of a man of fashion"[33] in New York and London and other European cities. New York's Coaching Club hosted two annual meets during the "London season" where coaches would start out in Hyde Park in the late afternoon and arrive in the evening at last for dinner at a hotel.

It was not long before Alfred's appetite for competition compelled him to challenge an existing record. A day before his departure, newspapers picked up the story of the prosperous youth[34] who was about to create a new coaching record from New York to Philadelphia and back within a stretch of sixteen and a half hours, a race against time to set a precedent of what coachmen could potentially achieve.

With this goal in mind, Alfred Gwynne and his friend James H. Hyde, the twenty-four year old eligible bachelor and heir to the Equitable trust fortune, who had planned the trip one year in advance and paid for all the expenses, running a tab of at least $2,000, left New York's *Holland House* on October 9, 1901 at 6 a.m. for Philadelphia, planning to return the same day back to New York at 1:32 a.m. Most notable among the seven other passengers that accompanied them was Maurice E. Howitt, the legendary French "whip" who won James' prize for four-in-hand coaching at the horse show the previous year.

Heir apparent to hundreds of millions of dollars, sitting atop the reserves of the investment fund of the Equitable Life Assurance Society[35], James shared many things in common with Alfred. Both of them were handsome young men whose fathers had oddly died the same year in 1899, leaving both of them the inheritors of enormous fortunes; and both thoroughly relished the elegant sport of coaching. As James grew in stature in the coaching world, his visibility concerned the board of the Equitable Insurance Company who read about his exploits and questioned where he was spending his time and money.[36]

With sixteen teams of four horses ready along with several six-horse teams for the more treacherously sandy areas of the trip, Hyde and A.G. had spared no expense for the trip, with special trains, ferryboats, and employees waiting on hand to switch horses. Initially, Alfred had expressed a desire to be part of the team effort, but then he appeared to lose interest. Hyde then sent him a torrent of telegrams[37] and finally, just four days prior to the scheduled race, the young Vanderbilt responded at last with an apology, "My part of the transaction has been a perfect fizzle just from forgetfulness and inexcusable poor judgment. I see it now only too well and regret it with all my heart."[38] A.G. agreed to participate, joining Hyde and reiterating his enthusiasm and willingness to match James in his "commitment of horses, tack, and men to the endeavor."[39]

Leaving the Holland House in New York early in the morning on Oct 9, 1901 in the coach *Tantivy*, Alfred drove the coach, racing out of the city at full speed and alternated with Hyde at every horse exchange. Akin to a vaudeville act, fatigued horses were pulled off and replaced by fresh colts, ready to run in two minutes and fifteen seconds. At every stop where horses were exchanged, crowds had gathered in anticipation, with nearly 2,000 waiting in New Brunswick alone.[40] Despite poor roads, loose sands, broken cobblestone, and intense heat, the pair kept to their schedule, fighting against time. Howlett described this later: "Even between villages there were massed hundreds of eager faces urging us on to victory: it was thrilling!"[41] The horses pushed forward at full speed, their manes swishing, bodies gleaming with perspiration; as their sculpted muscles engaged. A.G. held the reins firmly, cracking the whip from time to time, yelling enthusiastically. Back and forth, the two young men swapped reins, alternating between relays.

It was past midnight when they reached the outskirts of Newark, led by the light of a headlamp of a young Western Union messenger on a bicycle who guided them through the streets,[42] as they entered Newark promptly at 12:25 p.m., the Hyde party took another forty-two minutes to finally approach the Pennsylvania ferry in Jersey City.

Tearing forward to Exchange Place at breakneck speed, the carriage rushed into the ferry house without even slowing to draw rein. Under Alfred's direction, the coach did not slow down, making a "last dash for the finish";[43] cracking up the gangway plank, as the horses panted and snorted for breath, flying forward till the wheels of the carriage hit the deck. Held from 10:30 p.m. the previous night, the boat that had awaited them, a special ferry brought by Hyde for this last leg, quickly cast off at 1:07 a.m., rushing the party across the river, "in motion before the coach wheels had even stopped turning."[44]

Pulling up at last in front of the Holland House in New York at 1:32 a.m., exactly three hours and two minutes behind their scheduled time, the party was met by thousands of eager coaching fans, clubmen, and various automobiles and cabs, all of whom had arrived early and waited patiently for them. Triumphant, the young drivers hopped off the coach, as the photographer clicked away. They had succeeded in creating an entirely new record for coaching travel between the two great cities of New York and Philadelphia, clocking in at nineteen hours and thirty-two minutes in total. A reading from an odometer attached to Hyde's coach revealed that a distance of 224 miles in total had been traversed along this roundtrip, at an effective speed of 14 miles per hour.[45]

While reports of the race filled newspapers, with flattering descriptions of both James and Alfred, the young Vanderbilt gained more attention in the favor of society's press, perhaps because "Vanderbilt was an irresistible name."[46]

Alfred's attention so long devoted to his handsome stallions was diverted the next month, distracted by an event that entirely affected his perspective: the birth of his first child, William Henry Vanderbilt, named after his great-grandfather, on November 24, 1901.[47]

At ten o'clock in the evening, William H., a healthy eight-pound baby boy[48] was born at home at the Vanderbilt residence on 727 Fifth Avenue.[49] Now A.G. had an heir, a child who would inherit his vast empire. Yet, the young father had no legacy to impart to his first-born. What would he share with his child? Would it be the feats of his own youth? Never having displayed any enduring interest in his father's company, Alfred Gwynne embarked upon a significantly different kind of investment two days later: the purchase of new real estate.

Quite unlike his own father who had, in some respects, small real estate holdings, A.G. set about to acquire property for speculative purposes, buying 127 lots in Washington Heights.[50] He announced that this would be the beginning of many more similar transactions in the future. The next day, the young father put a bid on the illustrious iridescent Hope diamond owned by the New York millionaire Simon Frankel, for three hundred and fifty thousand dollars[51] as an early Christmas present for his wife.

While Elsie stayed busy with preparations for the christening of the baby, congratulations on the birth of the newborn issued forth from all parts of the family. His brother Neily was the only notable exception; he drove up to the gates to read the posting but did not enter.

Six months later, A.G. was back again in the coaching seat, this time with a different agenda. In the spring of 1902, James Hazen, along with A.G., came up with a plan to charge guests for coaching trips. They converted his coach into a public conveyance with $12 a ticket for guests, $15 for the box seat next to him, and $100 for the entire vehicle, which held between twelve and fourteen passengers. It was a trifle in comparison to the actual cost of running the whole operation, estimated at roughly $40,000 per vehicle for the whole season.[52] Coaches were retrofitted, painted in the colors of each house (scarlet and black for Hyde and maroon for Vanderbilt), with accompanying coachmen and livery. Hyde sent out a detailed flyer with a timetable of coach arrivals and departures, leaving New York promptly at eight-thirty in the morning three times a week.[53] Hyde invited numerous guests, including financiers and debutantes, and kept up the practice until the end of the 1903 summer season, at which point he sold his horses and left for Paris.[54] A.G., however, did not stop.

For the entire season, Alfred tooled about as the whip of the coach *Pioneer* in New York almost every day in the summer, taking up residence in his apartment there in a six-bedroom flat for $6,000 a year[55] and picking up socialites and strangers along the way. Proper etiquette for coaching dictated that the whip be dressed and treated simply; yet with A.G. at the helm, few guests aboard his coach abided by this. Instead, they spent most of their time trying to win his approval, drawn to his impeccable manners, graciousness, and the Vanderbilt name. His guests included many women who were strangers to New York and did not know what clothes to wear, often dressing in colorful hats and flimsy, light clothing[56] that accentuated their curves and elegant silhouettes, as was the fashion that season. Entirely unprepared for high winds, rain (Alfred never paused for the weather) and jumpy rides, these women, who had zealously waited to get a ride, shivered when they were aboard the coach, looking deeply relieved when they got to their final stop.

Alfred soon acquired a reputation for being a considerate coachman. On one occasion, Alfred, seeing an elderly black man walking wearily on the road, unexpectedly yanked his carriage to a screeching halt and gave the surprised man a lift to his destination. Another time, he pulled up his coach to carry a hatter by the name of Charles Hallen,[57] who had fought violently with a friend in the street and lay battered on the ground. A.G. was on his way from New York to Morristown and instead, diverted the coach to Milburn to have Hallen's wounds mended at a local doctor's office.

The family also made an attempt to mend its wounds, as reconciliation efforts between Neily's family and the rest of the Vanderbilt clan bore fruit. Reginald's wedding and the birth of the two first-born sons for both the eldest Vanderbilt men encouraged peaceful relations. Neily and Grace made a formal call upon Mr. and Mrs. Alfred G. Vanderbilt at Oakland, reaching by the end of that summer in 1903 a "satisfactory understanding."[58]

Rumors circulated that the healing was the efforts of Reginald and Alfred since the wedding and that friends such as Martha Johnston and De Lancey Kountze were sending messages of good will and harmony.[59] An entirely new generation of Vanderbilts had begun with three children: Neily's son, A.G.'s toddler, and Reginald's newborn arriving in September.[60] Perhaps peace was borne out of love for them and for their sakes.

Neily also no longer had to compete with his younger siblings for success. As a celebrated inventor, he was doing exceedingly well, with no less than thirty-one patents to his name. He was building a formidable reputation in his own right for his creative genius, and the press, who had so quickly denounced him a few years earlier, began to court his approval once more. Surrounded by eager reporters at the Atlantic City Horse Show, A.G. initially refused to comment to the press upon the reconciliation.[61] However, when the press reappeared outside his Windsor hotel residence later and questioned him directly again, the young Vanderbilt replied, "Besides, you understand, this is a family reunion. No half measures will be adopted in this case. We have extended the olive branch. He accepts it in the spirit in which it is offered and everything is adjusted."[62]

When reporters impudently persisted in asking whether Neily's decision to marry Grace was a factor in causing his father's death, A.G. withdrew immediately, his smile fading, frostily replying, "That is a subject I prefer to say nothing about, Sir. I think I have given you all the information you require."[63]

Willie K., Alfred's cousin, now took up the business of running the railroad, acting as financier at Grand Central Terminal. Reputed to be a "keen business person of whom great things may be expected,[64]" Willie K. contrasted severely with A.G. who was "seldom at his desk."[65]

Uncle William Kissam and Cousin Willie K. were immediately faced with the problem of having to rebuild Grand Central Terminal after an accident occurred in Danbury, Connecticut on January 2, 1902. Smoke had filled the tunnel, obscuring the vision of the train conductor. In the head-on collision that ensued, fifteen people were killed and hundreds injured. The public was infuriated. The railroads were given until July 1, 1908 to completely stop using steam locomotives, within city limits, and switch to electricity. Wilgus, the chief engineer for the project, offered a plan that was vast in both scope and expense. He conceived the proposal by 1903 and began construction but had to build the new terminal while the old terminal functioned unabated.

By far the largest and most complicated construction project ever undertaken in an American city, the project was originally estimated at forty million dollars but actual expenses skyrocketed to seventy-two million dollars, presenting daunting challenges, met with grace, leadership, and tact by the senior Willie Kissam Vanderbilt, Alfred's uncle. Going from a structure that the New York Times called "unpleasant,"[66] "wretched,"[67] and an "inconvenient" behemoth in 1899, the Grand Central Terminal was transformed radically into a. symbolic masterpiece of both excellent planning and harmony. As the city rail lines switched to electric, stretching further and further outward, commuter traffic began to spill out towards the Bronx, Rockland, and Westchester counties. In less than five years, New York City became the largest suburban city in the world; a city unlike any other in America through the stroke of creative genius of two key men: Wilgus, who developed the plan, and William Kissam Sr., who had the boldness to implement it. This fervor of excitement filled the younger Willie K.

Unlike his cousin and uncle, Alfred did not involve himself in the workings of the business. Instead, he was more likely found engaged in the more social aspects of business, such as handing out $5 gold pieces[68] as holiday gifts to all of the conductors and motormen of the railroad near *Oakland Farm.*

The Commissioner of Public Works, Joseph M. Patterson, upon tendering his resignation to the Mayor, passionately spoke about the need for reform and called into question A.G.'s work ethic or lack thereof,[69] using him as an example of what was wrong with society:

> He doesn't turn a wheel, he doesn't move a locomotive, he doesn't do a thing for the railroad. He simply owns it. He doesn't contribute towards making the road safe. Those men earn so much money from him. Suppose he should give to them what they earn, instead of taking it himself?[70]

Alfred busied himself with his coaching routines, entering horse shows, his family life, and attending social extravaganzas such as Hyde's ball. Alfred Gwynne's social counterpart, James Hazen Hyde, had established a lavish tradition of entertaining guests at his four hundred acre estate, *The Oaks* in Bay Shore, Long Island where he had laid miles of coaching road, and entertained famous guests that included the crown prince of Siam and the mistress of King Edward VII.[71] At a time where wealth and extravagance had become resented within populist America, the wealthy styled themselves after Continental aristocrats. However, the nature of popularity in society tends toward sudden shifts, and as James gained more power in the Equitable Life Society he had inherited, criticism of his extracurricular activities grew as well.

Balls were paradoxical: they were exclusive and yet also public entertainment. At the time that Hyde threw his magnificent ball, society recognized the importance of the ball as being *the* foremost social event of the year. From gilded bird cages and swans roaming the grounds to expansive profusions of flowers to themed decorations ranging from the Wild West to ancient Egypt, these parties of the Gilded Age showcased wealth, pomp, and splendor; being the meeting place where social and sexual alliances were forged. Guests in exquisitely tailored costumes, glittering with jewels and Southern heirlooms, resembled royalty.

On January 31, 1905, James Hazen Hyde threw his ball at the Sherry Hotel. While his guests reveled in their elaborate costumes, James appeared as himself[72] dressed in a bottle green coat,[73] a stiff white shirt, red vest, black stockings, and shiny black dancing shoes; the traditional attire of a coachman. The theme of the party was eighteenth century Europe with an alternative of coaching attire and Hyde and his coat tails fit in seamlessly with the skirts and ball gowns of that era. After weeks of preparation involving the planning of the seating for six hundred guests, Hyde successfully hosted a magnificent party with some of society's most famous and powerful luminaries such as the Equitable board of directors including Astor, Depew, Gould, Belmont, Alfred Vanderbilt, Roger Winthrop, and E. Harriman.

James Hazen Hyde appeared to have led a parallel life to Alfred. Also a coachman he would spend a fortune on his passion to the intense disfavor of Equitable Life Assurance LC the company his father had built and whose assets he squandered. His reputation was shattered when he spent equitable money on a vast costume party. He was soon ousted by the board of the Equitable and reappeared in Alfred's life when the two men escaped to London. Library of Congress. Bain Collection.

However, reports began to trickle in speculating that the ball had actually cost no less than $200,000![74] Hardly a week after the ball, in a flurry of secret meetings[75] that culminated in the signing of a petition circulated among shareholders an attempt was mounted to force Hyde into relinquishing his power at Equitable. An infuriated Hyde refused to cave in and assembled his own rebuttal team.

The *World* did a count and there were twenty-four directors supporting the opposition initiative with, surprisingly, Chauncey Depew among them; and twenty directors that supported Hyde, including friend Alfred G. Vanderbilt,[76] Brad Johnson, and H.R. Winthrop,[77] three of Hyde's close coaching companions.

A scandal broke in the *New York Times* when the cost of the ball was bandied about.[78] Equitable Life Society was imploding as further rumors of Hyde's personal expenses and Francophile lifestyle intensified.

Hyde could not hold out for much longer. The country got caught up in the scandal. Within less than two months of throwing the most extravagant and exquisite ball in New York City, Hyde had not only lost his position at

Equitable, as the company had entirely restructured itself, but also fallen from grace, losing his reputation as well.

While A.G. enjoyed being society's golden boy, rumors began to circulate about him quietly, first as whispered tales in conjunction with his former coaching companion. Alfred had been on the board of Equitable but resigned after the Hyde Equitable scandal reached its peak.

At the private Equitable meetings[79] that ultimately sealed the fate of the young man, Hyde's private expenses were discussed at great length. These expenditures included coaching trips where Alfred G. Vanderbilt accompanied James Hyde from the *Holland House* to the Arsdale Casino in New York during the previous summer.[80]

These rumors began to spill out into the public arena. The credibility of coaching as a business was a laughable proposition and therefore any expenditures made in that vein were considered improper. It was inconceivable that Hyde could ever regain more than one-tenth of the money he had put towards his coaching entourage, even with a full coach of passengers paying $10 a head, when the cost of maintaining his coach alone was estimated at $50,000.[81] Hyde not only sealed his own fate but eradicated any possible claim that Alfred might have mounted to justify coaching as a reasonable business occupation of his own. Coaching was forever relegated to being a rich man's sport, never to be considered real work.

Hyde, however, was a skeleton of his former self, and eventually retreated to a lifestyle far simpler than ever before as the final curtain on the Equitable implosion dropped.

NOTES

1. *The Chicago Daily Tribune.* "Wealth in Hands of Fifty." Jul. 26, 1903. Pg. 19.
2. Ibid.
3. *The Chicago Daily Tribune.* "Rich Men's Sons are Hard Workers." Aug. 2, 1903. Pg. 19.
4. Ibid. Pg. 78.
5. Ibid.
6. Ibid.
7. Ibid.
8. Ibid.
9. Ibid.
10. Garman, James. E. *A History of the Gentleman's Farm of Portsmouth.* City: 2003. Pg. 66.
11. Ibid. Pg. 74.
12. Ibid. Pg. 73.
13. Ibid. Pg. 74.

14. *Boston Daily Globe.* "To Smash Record." Jul 5, 1902. Pg. 3.
15. *Boston Daily Globe.* "Gave Up Run To Lenox." Jul 6, 1902. Pg. 6.
16. *The Washington Post.* "Vanderbilt's Auto Exploit." Jul. 20, 1903. Pg. 1.
17. *The New York Times.* "A.G. Vanderbilt Sues Owner of Automobile." April 25, 1903. Pg.1.
18. Vanderbilt II, Arthur T. Fortune's Children: The Fall of the House of Vanderbilt. New York, NY: William Morrow and Company. 1989. Pg. 299-300.
19. *The Washington Post.* "Miss Neilson His Choice." August 4, 1902. Pg. 7.
20. *Boston Daily Globe.* "Ready for Guests." April 13, 1903. Pg. 1.
21. *The New York Times.* "Newport Society Surprised by Collier-Van Alen Wedding." Jul 27, 1902. Pg. 26.
22. *Boston Daily Globe.* "Citizen of Rhode Island." Aug. 23, 1903. Pg. 26.
23. *Chicago Daily Tribune.* "Miss Roosevelt at Newport." Aug. 3, 1902. Pg.6.
24. *The New York Times.* "Lively Polo at Newport." Aug. 2, 1903. Pg. 14.
25. *Boston Daily Globe.* "Reginald C. Vanderbilt Announces Ushers for his Wedding." April 3, 1903. Pg. 6.
26. *The New York Times.* "Clubs and Clubmen." April 26, 1903. Pg. SM6.
27. *The New York Times.* "What Is Doing In Society." April 28, 1903. Pg. 9.
28. *The New York Times.* "Society Marks The Decline of Summer." Aug. 25, 1901. Pg. 7.
29. Ibid. Pg. 148.
30. Ibid. Pg. 150
31. Ibid. Pg. 149.
32. Ryder, Tom. *The History of the Coaching Club: 1871-2000.* London: J.A. Allen, 1999.
33. Ibid.
34. *The Chicago Daily Tribune.* Oct. 9, 1901. Pg. 1.
35. Ibid. Pg. 124.
36. Ibid. Pg. 121.
37. Ibid. Pg.118-9.
38. Ibid.
39. Ibid.
40. Beard, Patricia. *After the Ball.* New York: Harper Collins, 2003. Pg. 119.
41. Beard, Patricia. *After the Ball* New York: Harper Collins, 2003. Pg. 120.
42. Beard, Patricia. *After the Ball.* New York: Harper Collins, 2003. Pg. 120.
43. Chicago Daily. "New Coaching Record Is Made." Oct. 10, 1901. Pg. 1.
44. Beard, Patricia. *After the Ball.* New York: Harper Collins, 2003. Pg. 120.
45. *The New York Times.* "Mr. Hyde's Coaching Trip." Oct. 13, 1901. Pg. 24.
46. Ibid. Pg. 121.
47. *The Los Angeles Times.* "Flashes From the Wires." Nov. 25, 1901. Pg. 2.
48. *The New York Times.* "Alfred Vanderbilt a Father." Nov. 25, 1901. Pg.1.
49. *Chicago Daily Tribune.* "Heir is born to Head of the Vanderbilt Family." Nov. 25, 1901. Pg. 2.
50. *Chicago Daily Tribune.* "Alfred G. Vanderbilt Tries New Investment." Nov. 27, 1901. Pg. 5.

51. *Los Angeles Times*. "Half A Million for Hope Diamond." Nov. 28, 1901. Pg. 3.
52. Beard, Patricia. *After the Ball*. New York: Harper Collins, 2003. Pg. 126.
53. Ibid.
54. Ibid.
55. *Chicago Daily Tribune*. "Vanderbilt In Flat." Nov. 16, 1903. Pg. 1.
56. *The New York Times*. "Told In Her Boudoir." May 3, 1903. Pg. SM13.
57. *Los Angeles Times*. "Coachers Were His Samaritans." May 20, 1903. Pg. 6.
58. *The Chicago Daily Tribune*. Sept. 11, 1903. Pg. 2.
59. *The Chicago Daily Tribune*. "Bride to Be May Settle Vanderbilt Feud." Oct. 4, 1903. Pg.6.
60. *Boston Daily Globe*. "Stork Coming." Sept 16, 1903. Pg. 7.
61. *The New York Times*. "Alfred G. Vanderbilt Silent." Jul. 17, 1903. Pg. 1.
62. *Boston Daily Globe*. "Confirms Story." Jul. 17, 1903. Pg. 7.
63. Ibid.
64. *The New York Times*. "W.K. Vanderbilt. Jr., Clerk." Dec. 4, 1903. Pg. 1.
65. Ibid.
66. *The New York Times*. Oct 3, 1899. Pg. 14.
67. *The New York Times*. Oct 3, 1899. Pg. 14.
68. *The New York Times*. "The News of Newport." Dec. 27, 1903. Pg. 7.
69. *The New York Times*. "Convert to Socialism Quits Dunne's Cabinet." Mar 3, 1906. Pg. 4.
70. Ibid.
71. Beard, Patricia. *After the Ball*. New York: Harper Collins, 2003. Pg. 60.
72. Ibid. Pg. 151.
73. Ibid. Pg. 171.
74. *The New York Times*. "Attack by Knowles on Tarbell's Methods." May 2, 1905. Pg. 2.
75. Beard, Patricia. *After the Ball*. New York: Harper Collins, 2003. Pg. 183.
76. *Wall Street Journal*. "Equitable Life." Feb, 17, 1905. Pg. 4.
77. Beard, Patricia. *After the Ball*. New York: Harper Collins, 2003. Pg. 190.
78. *The New York Times*. "Hyde's Complaint Against Alexander: Full Text of Petition." May 14, 1905. Pg. 10.
79. *The Wall Street Journal*. "Equitable Life." Feb. 17, 1905. Pg. 4.
80. *The Chicago Daily Tribune*. "Hyde Must Quit or be Exposed." Apr. 1, 1905. Pg. 1.
81. *The Washington Post*. "Young Hyde's Unique Method of Expenditure." Jul 23, 1905 Pg. FP6.

Chapter Six

A Serpentine Curve: A Failure to Stop

As they approached the dreaded curve, A.G. held on to his seat for dear life as his reckless Italian chauffeur Paul Sartori, veered the ninety horsepower Fiat[1] at full throttle round the Mineola section of the course.[2] Harder and harder Sartori pushed, trying to reach the outer rim of the course to gain ascension, racking up the speed on the hard turns at a swift ninety miles per hour.[3] It was a trial run but the duo did not hold back and Sartori, instead of letting up, slammed down on the gas pedal, until the very last thirty yards before the Serpentine curve at Albertson Station,[4] when he suddenly slapped the brakes down.

As the crowd gasped in horror, the Fiat's wheels screeched and skidded across the gutter, as the car spun out of control, launching into the gutter, and by less than a fraction of an inch, Paul and Alfred were thrown out of the car a good fifteen feet,[5] landing on a bed of soft earth. The automobile, barely missing three tall telephone poles that lay directly ahead, sped along a little further and then turned over, wheels spinning.

In stunned silence, the large crowd that had gathered to watch the spectacle, waited. When the two young men stood up, wiping the dust off their jackets, and righted the machine, a huge cheer broke out. A.G. and Sartori got back into the vehicle and finished the course.

It was only a year since William K. Vanderbilt II had established the Vanderbilt cup on Long Island,[6] now considered "the greatest sporting event" for automobiles in America.[7] Alfred Gwynne had enthusiastically signed up, purchasing a fancy new Italian vehicle and procured a skilled and daring driver to boot.

A.G.'s love affair with cars was brief, tumultuous, and thrilling, full of unexpected twists, expensive vehicles, foreign competitions, and thrilling accidents where the "drivers narrowly escaped injury or death."[8] An accident occurred when Elsie, Alfred's wife, narrowly escaped from a head on collision with a speeding motorcyclist while driving the coach from their estate to pick up Alfred at the Wickford boat ramp.[9] Her driver had adroitly reined in the horses, turning them into the curbstone, narrowly missing a direct collision, but overthrowing one of the horses as Mrs. Alfred G. Vanderbilt leapt out of the carriage. Badly shaken, Elsie got back into the carriage and continued on to the boat dock to meet her husband.

Maybe it was that event or her own love of the open seas, but Elsie began to pay more attention to sailing and acquiring her own boat the thirty-foot *Caprice*. She was able to hold her own against the other Vanderbilt men as a skillful sailor.[10] A.G. had also dabbled a bit in yachting, purchasing the steam yacht *Vixen* the previous year, later renamed *Adroit,*[11] which Elsie now maneuvered skillfully on the water. While his wife did not accompany him to purchase new horses, she did go with Alfred to inquire about new yachts for sale.[12] The Vanderbilt family alone possessed more yachts than any other family in the country and almost the entire world, with twelve boats costing approximately $2,000,000.

Despite winning a string of regional events[13] and beating existing records,[14] his chauffeur Paul Sartori had developed a bad reputation for speeding along the local roads[15] as he tested out new vehicles, racking up large speeding fines[16] footed by the young Vanderbilt.[17]

With numerous failed attempts caused by mechanical failures such as overheating of the engine in his sleek Mercedes,[18] Alfred Gwynne did not exhibit the same winning streak that he had in coaching with his new hobby of car racing. He spent an exorbitant amount on his foreign and specially crafted cars that often fell apart on the course or failed to live up to expectations.

In December, hoping to extend his success in the coaching realm towards his car racing efforts, Alfred entered the highly competitive Daytona Beach race[19] for the swiftest of the world's automobiles[20] with his new sixty horsepower vehicle driven by Sartori.

After another daredevil automobile incident where Sartori swerved into a fence, stripping away boards and iron piping,[21] and accidentally injuring a sixteen-year old boy who was peering through the rails to watch a local race, A.G. threw in his hat with some frustration but did not give up entirely. He decided to enter one last competition and let the outcome decide the fate of his racing hobby.

The young man recognized that these races aroused American manufacturers to compete with Europeans who dominated all the racing events. Picking up the gauntlet, A.G. built his own 250 horsepower goliath[22] for the next Ormond event in early 1906. Choosing a location on West Thirty-Ninth Street, Alfred built his own machine shop[23] and spent no less than $15,000 on

Cousin Willy K. Vanderbilt was setting speed records at Ormond Beach Florida causing Alfred to join in the battle for speed. He built this goliath 250 horse power automobile at extraordinary expense with Sartori. Here in 1906 is Sartori behind the wheel of Alfred's race car. The vehicle was over the weight limit and became bogged down in the sand having to be towed back to the shops. The two men ended up in a lawsuit about fees with the builder winning. Alfred soon condemned anyone who went too fast. Library of Congress. Bain Collection.

building his own vehicle with light aluminum. Sartori was behind the wheel again. With an estimated speed of 152 miles per hour, Alfred's powerful new engine could achieve a mile in 23 and 2/3 seconds, beating the world record of 32 4/5 seconds and was believed to be the "most powerful racing machine in the world."[24]

Stories of the remarkable speed of this automobile spread like wildfire and when the car was towed to the beach, a crowd of no less than one thousand people waited eagerly to watch the demonstration of its virile strength. Yet not only did the car fail to move fast, it hardly moved at all. Sartori was forced to drag the vehicle back into the shop[25] for feverish repairs. The bill racked up and the press commented heavily upon these expenditures, questioning how any man could willingly "sink $30,000 in a 250 horsepower car"[26] as the young Vanderbilt offered. The vehicle was deemed to be too heavy for the event, weighing an extra 200 pounds, and vibrated so much that the wheels would sink into the sand.[27] Running out of time, A.G. was forced to pull the car out of the race.

When his sixty horsepower Mercedes was ruined in a devastating fire, the young man gave up entirely. After nearly a two-year stint, A.G.'s interest in automobile racing began to wane and he retired his fancy vehicles, relegating them to domestic use, while putting all of his energy in full force towards his coaching.

He enjoyed being a top competitor in coaching events both at home and at the London Horse Show.[28] Eager young women thronged the entrance of the *Holland House* during the two-month coaching spree where the young man offered $2 rides through town. In fact, the pleasure of riding with Alfred Gwynne, affectionately called "Alfie", in Newport and New York social circles, far surpassed a need for transportation for these passengers. Considered a man of "amiable disposition[29]" with an "unimpeachable record,"[30] the young Vanderbilt began the 1905 coaching season with a special $10 ride for his fourteen fellow passengers, where he took them from the *Holland House* to the *Ardsley Club* and back, an entire distance of nineteen miles that included changing the horses three times. Three times a week, A.G. took his guests to the *Ardsley Club*, enjoying a pleasurable champagne luncheon at the casino.

A.G. acquired the famous champion four-in-hand coaching team comprised of *Rustling Silk, Full Dress, Sweet Marie,* and *Polly Prim* from J. Hobart Moore explicitly for horse show events.[31] Atlantic City's busy season picked by June as both Alfred and his brother Reginald, who continued to enjoy a friendly spar, arrived to feature their horses. With entries in every event, Alfred Gwynne went on to win blue ribbons for his handsome team of grays at Atlantic City, perfectly handling his four-in-hand team and winning large applause from the audience as judges pinned ribbons to his team.[32] The young scion was among the very best in the amateur arena and was a force to reckon with in the four-in-hand event with his fine team of horses, considered the best in the country. With his victories, A.G. also enjoyed popular support in the press as stories of his frugal expenditure in comparison to other illustrious members of the Vanderbilt clan emerged. With his fine stable and obvious inclination towards coaching culture, Alfred Gwynne spent his money only on his horse endeavors and his home at *Oakland Farms* which, although pleasant, was "not at all the sort of place you would expect one of such wealth to live in."[33]

Colonel William D'Alton Mann, who published the societal gossip paper *Town Topics,* approached A.G. with an idea of how to buy good press through the creation of a publication that would promote its subscribers to the public and establish good reputations that could not be tainted by even the wrongdoings of its elite members. The young man embraced the idea, allowing Mann to promptly fleece him and two other Vanderbilts, his uncle

Willie and his brother Reginald, for the subscription amount of $1500 as the Colonel published *Fads and Fancies*.[34] Through this paper, the three Vanderbilt men hoped to be untouchable while also promoting their individual causes: William K. Vanderbilt desired to be labeled as a railroad executive of considerable prowess; Reginald as similar to the Commodore with a "sunny disposition;" and finally A.G. pictured in his handsome four-in-hand coach, traveling to his estate in the Adirondacks.[35] The actual paper spoke little and on first glance, did not reveal much. Why would Alfred Gwynne spend $1500 for a subscription that contained little information of any value? Maybe A.G. learned the value of guarding a reputation after watching his coaching companion Hyde suffer in the public limelight after the Equitable scandal.

As the cold winter lingered in New York, Elsie embarked upon a voyage[36] to Europe where she met and befriended Prince Albert of Schleswig-Holstein, the grandson of Queen Victoria and the first cousin of the German Empress,[37] at a party given by her sister, now Lady Chylesmore, at her lovely villa in Cannes. The young prince agreed to visit Elsie and Alfred at Newport when he arrived in America that spring.[38] Alfred too made efforts to court royalty in conjunction with the London Horse Show.

That summer, Alfred entered his first show in London,[39] an event that he worked hard to both promote and participate in. James Hazen Hyde acted as secretary for the National Horse Show for the American counterpart. Hyde's efforts bore fruit with the acceptance of powerful Englishmen to these events, thereby promoting a global competition. First hosted at the Olympia building in London, the show as an annual event would next move to Paris and would include on its list of prestigious members, both the Prince of Wales and King Edward.

Alfred continued to rake in the prizes, as he masterfully drove his coach *Venture* with magnificent grays to win several blue ribbons,[40] winning three 1st place prizes and two 3rd places[41] at the Challenge Cup.[42] He was again in top form with crowds of adoring and cheering fans. Yet, a different wind of far colder gales blew upon him at the Bay Shore Show when A.G. won the Hyde Cup by a narrow margin, as spectators booed, hissed, and complained, showing their obvious disapproval for his victory. Competing against only one other coachman, J. Campbell Thompson, who led a team of four big bays, Alfred Gwynne won the event as Thompson's team ran into the fence. Thompson's team however was in better physical form and the judges' decision was greeted by loud hisses from the crowd and a "mincing manner"[43] from Thompson.

He was, however, a skeleton of his former self, and eventually retreated to a lifestyle far simpler than ever before as the final curtain on the Equitable implosion dropped.

Younger brother Reginald followed in Alfred's footsteps. In life he would spend money like water and drink alcohol similarly but on that day in June of 1908 he would take first place at the Plainfield horse show with his prize horse Phoebe Watton. Library of Congress. Bain Collection.

With Alfred's indoor horseman's paradise at *Oakland Farms* as the setting, the couple planned a party[44] for June 15th, sending out invitations to friends and farm neighbors in Newport and Portsmouth. A.G. drew up plans for a private horse show with Reginald akin to the Nationals at Madison Square Garden where each class would be called out by a bugler for every event, including a circus event for the children with professional performers.[45] However, just one week before the affair, on July 8, 1906, Alfred Gwynne called the entire event off, postponing the opening indefinitely.[46] It seemed Mr. and Mrs. A.G. Vanderbilt were no longer in the mood to entertain together.

Discussions about the new Olympia building in London that would host the first International Horse Show were also underway.[47] Both A.G. and his brother Reginald signed up as exhibitors for the next year. Competitors constantly changed in the local shows but Alfred Gwynne and Reggie kept up their friendly rivalry, with their own sibling scorecard, each time one of them won against the other, enjoying a good laugh. When either one walked away with the first blue ribbon as Reginald did with *Dr. Selwonk* at the Philadephia Horse Show at St. Martin, Alfred followed with second place with his spanking gray, *Polly Prim.*[48]

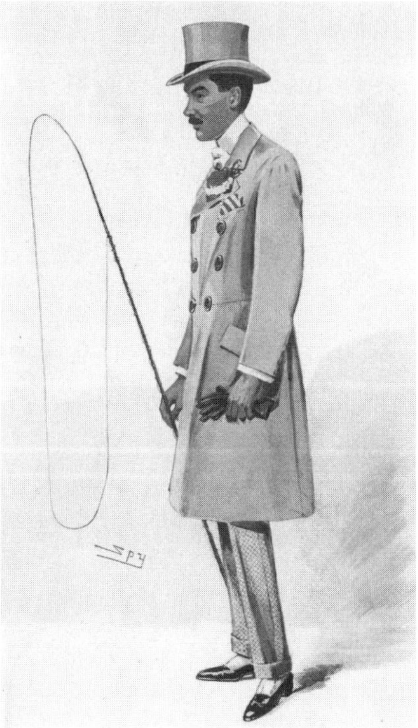

In this 1907 cartoon penned by "Spy" and appearing in Vanity Fair Alfred appears as the whip. It was past time for the young man to move on and become a productive part of society. He never did.

Alfred at the ribbons of Polly Prim in Bay Shore Long Island, ca. 1906. George Grantham Bain, 32 Union Square East, N.Y.

Since Alfred G. was spending so much time leading his coach in New York City, Elsie oversaw the renovation, expansion, and tasteful decoration of a new luxurious apartment for them on the corner of 46th Street and Greenwood.[49] She accompanied A.G. to the large and expensive sale of forty-four *Pioneer* coach horses of the Durland Academy in Central Park ten days later, where many interested buyers and spectators had gathered to watch and purchase the fine animals in perfect form and of good size, measuring each fifteen to sixteen hands in height, and in the spring of youth still at five or six years of age.[50] She also hosted with her husband the fourth annual picnic at Southwick's Grove[51] for the children of the Sunday school of the Thames Street Methodist Episcopal Church, beginning with a trolley ride, followed by an evening of entertainment with a full orchestra and minstrel troupe.[52]

As the next Atlantic City event approached, A.G. experienced a slight conflict of interest since the horse show was scheduled for the same day as the circus. He also encountered a few obstacles, namely in regards to his traveling from the hotel directly to the horse show grounds at Inlet Park by his coach. As the word got out about his plans, local busmen created a fuss to show their disapproval with the mayor, protesting favoritism. Conflict had already been brewing between the busmen and the local police over how, why, and when certain regulations were enforced by town hall.[53] Consequently, the mayor was forced into the position of demanding that Alfred Gwynne follow the same passenger vehicle laws that pertained to all other such vehicles within the city limits by acquiring his own busman's license.

While the young scion agreed to get the license, he sent his coaching hand and superintendent Charles Wilson to the mayor's office to submit the paperwork and reply to the press inquiries. When asked, Wilson replied laconically, "Anything to keep the peace."[54] Charlie Wilson was a good thirty years older than Alfie. He was a somewhat heavyset man known for his considerable coaching experience, but decidedly different from other employees. His appearance was somewhat deceptive; he seemed to be a mild-mannered and unobtrusive character. Yet upon closer interaction, Wilson's fiery temperament was revealed as well as his predilections for the fairer sex. Waiting until the last minute, Wilson appeared at the office a half hour before noon on the eighteenth of July, ready to be initiated. Reading the provisions of the license, Wilson smiled visibly at the clause that required licensees to "keep the Sabbath day in orderly fashion."[55] Signing his name, paying the fee of $12, and acquiring the necessary license, tag, and badge number 24, Wilson drove the coach. Alfred would arrive much later. On July 18, 1906, A.G. became the first Vanderbilt to acquire the status of an officially licensed bus driver, carrying the nickel badge in his breast pocket while he tooled around in the *Venture*.

Increasingly, Alfred adopted more somber and subdued colors in his coaching apparel that resembled the clothing of local busmen, such as his "black serge sack suit"[56] with a "seedy slate hued top hat."[57] His new outfits gave him the appearance of a "second man" near his coach, the *Venture*, resembling more of a busman than his Vanderbilt siblings. On the second day of the Atlantic City horse show, as A.G. waited outside the Windsor Hotel for his passengers, a rotund and florid man precariously walked down the boardwalk. Making up his mind, he looked at the ornate coach and came up to the young man, offering him a nickel and a dime for a ride, the typical bus fare from the Boardwalk to Atlantic Avenue.[58]

> 'Jush gimme tha' mush worth o' ride,' said the fat one with the leftover to the owner of the coach.
>
> 'Fare is $2,' pleasantly replied Mr. Vanderbilt, not offering to accept the 15 cents.
>
> 'Thasso?' said the bunned adipose one; with an expression of surprise....and after a considerable sorting over of twenties and fifties, he finally found a two dollar bill and offered it to Mr. Vanderbilt, who of course, made no move to accept it.
>
> 'Coach is full,' said Mr. Vanderbilt, most affably.[59]

Alfred G. was accompanied on most of his coaching trips by his Dalmatian "Rogue", who had become the mascot of his four-in-hand coaches, following "the fortunes of *Venture* on foot every day and adds a touch of picturesqueness [sic] as he trots beside the horses all the way to Belmont Park and back."[60] Rogue was the only exception that would cause A.G. to wait a minute before leaving. The faithful dog was nimble and confident, as he "picks his way with the ease of a mounted policeman among the cabs and carriages of Fifth Avenue."[61] Rogue would stay by the coach while Willie was watching the event.

A few weeks later however, the Dalmatian wandered off into the lower part of the grand stands between the boxes and reserved seats, followed by a large bulldog that attacked him. Rogue did not run away but "fought back for all he was worth"[62] as women screamed, hurriedly fleeing their seats, upsetting chairs and causing mayhem in general, until stablemen arrived to separate the animals. As Alfred G. walked away with the "lion's share of prizes"[63] that afternoon, the conversation in the stands had little to do with the horse competition and instead revolved around the "fighting abilities of the two dogs."[64] Later interpretations of the clash declared that Rogue's "performance was not a tribute to the animal's training as a working Dalmatian."[65]

Atlantic City, unlike previous years, did not bring the usual Chicago contingent and hardly any competition worthy of recognition for A.G. In fact, tooling around as a whip was losing credibility. Maybe it was the behavior of Hyde that had brought shame and ridicule to his activities, now deemed irresponsible, flamboyant, extravagant, and frivolous. Or maybe it was the incident with Rogue that changed the way society viewed Alfred Gwynne. Regardless, Alfie, who had enjoyed being at the top of his form and the darling of society for the last year, also began to lose favor with the public.

The world of horse culture was distinctly different from anything else and the stable life was a dividing line between two vastly separate lifestyles, between the owner of the mansion who sat in the carriage and the driver who handled the reins. Yet for Alfred, this demarcation was no longer distinct and while his wife Elsie and his family lay in the former category, he moved freely between both worlds.

NOTES

1. *The Wall Street Journal*. "A.G. Vanderbilt Narrow Escape." Oct. 14, 1905. Pg. 7.
2. *The Atlanta Constitution*. "Alfred Vanderbilt Thrown." Oct. 14, 1905. Pg. 14.
3. *The Washington Post*. "Vanderbilt in Spill." Oct. 14, 1901. Pg. 1.
4. *The Wall Street Journal*. "A.G. Vanderbilt Narrow Escape." Oct. 14, 1905. Pg. 7.
5. *The Atlanta Constitution*. "Alfred Vanderbilt Thrown." Oct. 14, 1905. Pg. 14.
6. *Boston Daily Globe*. "Advance Guard." Jul. 19, 1904. Pg. 3.
7. *The New York Sun*. "From Touring to Racing." Aug. 1904. Pg. 20.
8. *The Chicago Daily Tribune*. "Covers Mile in 59 1-5 seconds." Jun. 12, 1904. Pg. 9.
9. *The New York Times*. "Narrow Escape in Newport Accidents." Jul. 10,1904. Pg. 7.
10. *The Boston Daily Globe*. "Learning to Sail Yacht." Sept. 22, 1905. Pg. 16.
11. *The New York Sun*. "Vanderbilts' Yachts." Aug. 1904. Pg. 20.
12. *The New York Times*. Mar 8, 1906. Pg. 6.
13. *The Chicago Daily Tribune*. "Covers Mile in 59 1-5 seconds." Jun. 12, 1904. Pg. 9.
14. *The New York Times*. "Vanderbilt's Auto Wrecked in a Race." Jul. 19. 1904. Pg. 5.
15. *The New York Times*. "Motor Wouldn't Go Slow." Jan. 2, 1905. Pg. 1.
16. *The Boston Daily Globe*. "Vanderbilt Surprised." April 2, 1904. Pg. 17.
17. *The New York Times*. "Alfred G. Vanderbilt Arrested for Speeding." Apr. 1, 1905. Pg. 1.
18. *The New York Times*. "Vanderbilt's Auto Wrecked in a Race." Jul. 19. 1904. Pg. 5.
19. *The Atlanta Constitution*. "Swiftest Autos in the World to Compete in Daytona Beach." Dec. 11, 1904. Pg. B4.

20. *The New York Times*. "Fast Auto Drivers to Meet at Ormond." Dec. 25, 1904. Pg. 8.
21. *The New York Times*. "Jul 4, 1905." Pg. 1.
22. *The Washington Post*. "A Wonderful Auto." Jan. 13, 1906. Pg. 6.
23. *The Washington Post*. "It Happened in New York." Jan 18, 1906. Pg. C1.
24. *The Chicago Daily Tribune*. "Will Go a Mile in :23 2-3." Pg. G15.
25. *The Boston Daily Globe*. "Off on its First Trial." Jan 22, 1906. Pg. 5.
26. *The Chicago Daily Tribune*. "The Referree." Jan 21, 1906. Pg. A1.
27. *The Chicago Daily Tribune*. Jan 23, 1906. Pg. 8.
28. *The New York Times*. "America's Best Horses to be Shown in London." Jul. 29, 1906. Pg. 6.
29. *The Los Angeles Times*. "First Coaching Party." Apr. 25, 1905. Pg. 15.
30. Ibid.
31. *The New York Times*. "A.G. Vanderbilt's New Team." Dec. 21, 1904. Pg. 10.
32. *The New York Times*. "Vanderbilt Horses First." Jul. 19, 1905. Pg. 4.
33. *The Washington Post*. "Alfred Vanderbilt is Inclined to Economy." Jul 23, 195. Pg. FP6.
34. *The New York Times*. "Fads and Fancies: A Rich Man's Book." Dec. 10, 1905.
35. Ibid.
36. *Boston Daily Globe*. Nov. 18, 1905.
37. *The Washington Post*. "Newport to Entertain Prince Albert." Mar. 11, 1906 Pg. E5.
38. Ibid.
39. *The New York Times*. "America's Best Horses to be Shown in London." Jul. 29, 1906. Pg. 6.
40. *The New York Times*. "A.G. Vanderbilt Wins in Durland Horse Show." April 18, 1906. Pg. 9.
41. *The New York Times*. "Mrs. Gerken Withdraws from Bay Shore Show." Aug. 4, 1905. Pg.8
42. *The New York Times*. "Vanderbilt's Coach First at Hollywood." Jul 29, 1905. Pg. 5.
43. *The New York Times*. "Judges' Award Hissed at Bay Shore Show." Aug. 6, 1905. Pg. BS16.
44. *Boston Daily Globe*. "Newport Plans." Feb 25, 1906. Pg. 47.
45. *The Washington Post*. "Mr. and Mrs. A.G. Vanderbilt Plan Novel Function." Jun 17, 1906. Pg. 15.
46. *The New York Times*. "News of Newport." Jul 8, 1906. Pg. 9.
47. *The New York Times*. "World's First Horse Show to be held in London." May 27, 1906.
48. *Boston Daily Globe*. "Reginald Wins Over Alfred G." May 29, 1906. Pg. 5.
49. *The Chicago Daily Tribune*. "New Apartments for the Rich." Jun 3, 1906. Pg. 2.
50. *The New York Times*. "Pioneer Horses Sold." Jun 13, 1906. Pg. 6.
51. *The New York Times*. "The News of Newport." Aug. 6, 1906. Pg. 7.
52. *Boston Daily Globe*. "Vanderbilt Picnic for Children." Jul 13, 1096. Pg. 3.

53. *The New York Times*. "Atlantic City Horse Show." Jul. 18, 1906. Pg. 4.
54. Ibid.
55. *The Washington Post*. "Vanderbilt A Bus Driver." Jul. 19, 1906. Pg. 7.
56. *The Washington Post*. "Man and Vanderbilt's Coach Both Too Full." Pg. E8.
57. Ibid.
58. Ibid.
59. Ibid.
60. *The Washington Post*. "Rogue, the Brightest Coach Dog." Jun 17, 1906. Pg. E54.
61. Ibid.
62. *The New York Times*. "Dog Fight Witnessed by Horse Show Crowd." Aug. 5, 1906. Pg. 5.
63. Ibid.
64. Ibid.
65. *The Washington Post*. Aug. 26, 1906. Pg. 9.

Chapter Seven

Extramarital Horsing Around

Though Elsie and Alfred seemed to initially share a joy for coaching, it soon became Alfred's passion alone. Elsie stopped going with him to horse shows, leaving her without her husband for weeks at a time. She seemed to be content, however, and satisfied herself with her own hobbies. She visited Europe for an extended vacation in Cannes and embarked upon several sailing adventures[1] near their residence. Alfred Gwynne remained forever at his stables and traveled from one horse show to the other. Their separation, though apparent to friends close to the family, was not yet obvious to the public, which focused on Elsie's winsome appearance as a feminine wife and mother, idealized as "delicate,"[2] "girlish,"[3] and "beautiful."[4]

By 1906, Alfred had been coaching for more than five years and was at the top of his form. It was the one part of his life that he excelled in. Increasingly, he began to adopt the complete lifestyle of the whip: wearing the clothes that smelled of toil, horses, and the working man and willing to ride rain or shine regardless of the weather or the discomfort of his passengers. He spent the majority of his time with his coaching comrades such as his stable manager Charles Wilson. There was no clear line for A.G. that separated him from his stable crew. Their joys and their sorrows were his own. As they made their living professionally working at his professed vocation of coaching, he embraced them as family, sharing with them an intimacy he had never experienced with his siblings or spouse.

When traveling between horse shows, Alfred stayed in his luxury private railroad car, the *Wayfarer*. Similar to the private railroad car 493 of his parents,[5] the *Wayfarer* was expansive. It contained spacious mahogany staterooms, a large dining room paneled in walnut, along with an associated kitchen and pantry, bedrooms with full bathtubs, a library, saloon, and servant quarters for the steward and chef. Painted a dark "Pullman green"[6] with gold

Charles Wilson. Cigar puffing stable manager to Alfred proved to be a sordid connection for the Vanderbilt. It was not that Vanderbilt couldn't find his own women but Wilson served as pimp, adulterer, and bigamist. Where there was smoke there was fire. The Bystander. April 29, 1908.

lettering, A.G.'s personal private railroad car also had a spacious observation lounge with an "open platform for taking in the rolling vistas."[7]

Over time, the *Wayfarer* became more than just a luxury car. It was Alfred's home while he was on the road; the home in which he spent much of his time. He would use it to travel to his board meetings at the New York Central, as well as for his own personal pleasure. However, the *Wayfarer* became more than just a means of travel; it was the site for much of Alfred's lechery, as well as that of his fellow whips.

On October 10, 1906, Alfred Vanderbilt traveled from Jersey City to Richmond in order to attend the *Richmond Horse Show,* tagging his private car the *Wayfarer* on to a special express train that he had previously selected for the event to haul both his horses and wagons. Harry Kempster, Mr. Vanderbilt's personal servant, reported that Mr. Vanderbilt was alone on the trip down to Richmond.[8] However, by October 13th, when A.G. left Richmond, there was an addition to his party.

Vanderbilt patiently waited in *The Wayfarer* while it stood in the Richmond Depot. Acting as the centerpiece for the dining table was the Maryland Cup,[9] which he had won that day. Dinner was prepared, but Mr. Vanderbilt would not eat until his guest joined him. She was the lovely Agnes Ruiz, the wife of the Cuban diplomat.

Lacking financial credentials and impressive lineage, Agnes was of a completely different social class, her origins were simple. The daughter of a farmer in Missouri, Agnes possessed an alluring and stunning beauty that far surpassed all the sophisticated graces of high society women. She exuded a regal poise and a simple elegance that spoke more volumes than the elaborate trappings of wealthy women. It was a beauty that could not possibly have been invisible to A.G.; her graceful demeanor and pleasing appearance. Her thin waist tapered up to her supple breasts, culminating in delicate shoulders that flowed into pleasant arms and charmingly proportioned hands. Alabaster skin covered her sweetly proportioned body and swan neck, fitting of her delicately featured face. Her eyes conveyed a winsome softness which looked out from her gentle cheeks. Agnes Ruiz was far more beautiful than Elsie French or any other woman in Alfred's life; yet the cruel irony lay in that she loved a man who could not love or accept her as his equal.

Harry Kempster later described the living arrangements while aboard *The Wayfarer*. In Stateroom A, where Vanderbilt slept, there was an ordinary sized bedstead. Next to that room was a bathroom and next to the bathroom was room B, which also had a bedstead. The bathroom connected rooms A and B.[10] It's not hard to guess who occupied room B, nor what Alfred and Agnes were doing in rooms that were connected to each other via a bathroom. On October 17th, Alfie, accompanied by Agnes, left to go to the horseshow at Norfolk, Virginia.

Around this time, the public was beginning to become aware of the distance between Alfred and Elsie. They had absolutely no knowledge of Agnes, but Elsie's prolonged absence from A.G.'s side was hard to ignore. Elsie's excuse for not being at the Norfolk show with Alfred was that she was ill. The press noted that "if Mrs. Vanderbilt recovers from her recent indisposition in time, the patrons of the Norfolk show will have the pleasure of seeing both of these celebrated exhibitors in the arena."[11] Despite her apparent indisposition, Elsie seemed fit enough to travel with her mother Mrs. F.O. French up to Sagamore Lodge in the Adirondacks in the first week of October.[12]

While they stayed at Norfolk, Alfred and Agnes had a similar sleeping arrangement to what they had on *The Wayfarer*. During their three-day stay in Norfolk, they slept in the Hotel Adelphi.[13] On the fifth floor of the hotel, there was a room that was supposedly occupied by Alfred. However, Kempster reported that the room was barely disturbed and certainly never slept in. Part of Kempster's responsibilities was to place articles of clothing in the room to make it seem like it was in use to anyone who happened to be poking around.[14]

Instead, Alfred slept on the second floor of the hotel where there was a bedroom that was connected to a parlor by a bathroom. The parlor was changed into a bedroom for Agnes to sleep in. Though Alfred said he would be sleeping in the bedroom that was joined to the parlor, Kempster noticed that the bed in the bedroom had not been disturbed.[15] When Kempster would go into the room in the morning to wake up A.G., Alfred would wander into the bedroom from the parlor in "a suit of pajamas."[16] When Kempster saw Agnes, "she had on a nightdress, but I did not pay particular notice to how she was dressed, being a married man myself."[17] Kempster also noticed that the bed in the parlor was "a large sized bed, and I could see two persons had occupied that bed."

Despite how it may seem, Alfred was in Norfolk for more than just a fun-filled vacation. Norfolk housed the largest coaching arena in the country. At four hundred feet in length by one hundred and seventy-five feet in width, the Norfolk Coliseum could accommodate up to ten thousand spectators. For such a small town, this show was colossal in its impact, with prestigious guests including three possible governors, Governor Swanson of Virginia, Governor Glenn of North Carolina, and Governor Warfield of Maryland, along with the full ensemble of the Fourth United States Artillery Band.

Florence Schenck with white ostrich feather hat. The young beauty fell into the charms of the much older Charles Wilson. She was brought aboard the railroad car, the Wayfarer, at a horse show and soon became part of the stable crowd of Vanderbilt. Library of Congress. Bain Collection.

Sometime during the three day event, from October 17th to the 19th, people were catching onto the affair. However, the press would eventually tell the story of Agnes very differently in later sworn testimony. According to the press, on October 19, 1906, Charles Wilson, Alfred's stable manager, provided Alfred with some "entertainment". Wilson allegedly brought Agnes to Alfred to be Vanderbilt's companion. He also brought with him the young Florence Schenck, a radiantly beautiful young woman from Virginia, for his own amusement. When it was discovered that the two young couples had stayed up together until the wee hours of the night, the press assumed that what had taken place was a wild orgy. Many would, therefore, blame Wilson for Alfred's "debauchery" because it was believed he was the one who had introduced Alfred to Agnes.

The very next day, Alfred was interviewed by a reporter from the Chicago Daily Tribune[18] and made the front page in a rather candid defense of the attention given to the sexual propensities of wealthy men like him. The reporter wrote, "Alfred G. Vanderbilt, who is here with a string of horses for the Norfolk horse show this week, took his thoughts away from the tanbark tonight long enough to condemn the publicity given reports of domestic infelicity among some families in New York's wealthy set."[19] For the record, Vanderbilt said:

> Rich men, or most of them love their families as well as poor men. The child of a rich man is as dear to him as his child is to a laborer. He loves his wife, if she be a good woman, the same as you love yours. Of course, they have their differences the same as other people, but unlike the poor man, their quarrel, no matter how trifling, is made to appear dreadful. No attention would be paid to the same conditions if they occurred in some family other than a rich man's.[20]

Although the Norfolk Horse Show was the first time that people noticed the affair, it was nowhere near the beginning of Alfred and Agnes' relationship. William Wilkinson, the superintendent of an apartment building at 596 Lexington Avenue, had sold Agnes an apartment on October 9th, 1905.[21] The apartment was on the second floor of the building, on the west side,[22] and contained only one bedroom.[23] However, it was not until several months later, that he discovered her name.

Wilkinson often had to enter the apartment "to attend to the steam, the radiators, and other things."[24] One time that he was there, a woman who claimed to be a friend of Agnes' showed Wilkinson a letter that had been addressed to Agnes and told him that her real name was Agnes Ruiz.[25] Before this event, he had no idea of her identity.

Agnes was not alone when she had rented the apartment. Accompanied by another woman, they rented the apartment under the name of Flores. Wilkinson later remembered the woman being with Agnes as the one who was named Flores, and so the apartment was rented to her and not Agnes. However, the woman called Flores never spent a single night in the apartment.

It was not long after the apartment was rented that Vanderbilt made his first appearance. He was first seen going into the apartment on October 11th, only two days after she had first rented the apartment. Wilkinson saw Alfred visiting the apartment frequently; an average of three or four times a week.[26] Alfred Gwynne had his own key to her apartment and let himself in as he pleased.[27]

His visits were not of a very casual nature. He would usually arrive around eight o'clock in the evening and go right into the apartment. He would not be seen leaving until eight or nine o'clock the following morning.[28] During the time that he was there, A.G. was not to be disturbed. He gave his close personal servants the number to the apartment so they could telephone him any messages he might have received, but after dinner the calls would cease. They were not to call unless the subject matter was extremely urgent. Any other messages would have to wait until nine o'clock in the morning.[29]

Alfred's residence in New York City was at 161 Madison Avenue. He would reside there with his wife, Elsie, when they were both in the city. However, as soon as Elsie went out of town, Alfred ceased to sleep at the Warrington. Instead, he spent his nights at 596 Lexington Ave with Agnes.[30]

Alfred's personal valet Harry Kempster would carry over fresh linens and a suitcase full of clothing every morning that he spent at Ruiz's residence.[31] On one occasion, much later in the fall of 1907, Kempster saw A.G. emerge from Agnes' bedroom in just his underwear.[32] During the Madison Square Horse Show of 1907, Alfred would spend the night in Agnes' apartment so Kempster would have to come every morning to bring his clothes. He would usually find Alfred's clothes from the previous night discarded on the floor.[33]

Agnes' servants didn't have their own rooms in the apartment, so they would leave at the end of every day, leaving Agnes and Alfred alone.[34] Though there are no witnesses to what occurred during those long evening hours, it's easy to imagine that the pair was involved in a physical relationship together. A.G.'s friend Thomas Benedict Clarke, Jr., Vice President of the Night and Day Bank,[35] dined at the apartment with the couple about half a dozen times.[36] While in the apartment, he witnessed the lovers kissing[37]and showing other perceived marks of affection.[38] Clarke was impressed that "there was no lack of understanding between them."[39] Agnes Ruiz was apparently devoted to Vanderbilt, waiting patiently at the window for him on days she expected him and if he did not come, she would "evince the greatest disappointment."[40]

By the time of the Richmond and Norfolk Horse Shows, the lovers had been in a relationship for at least a year. Most of the servants aboard the *Way-*

farer were aware of the affair, so there was little reason for Alfred to cover his tracks. On the trip back to New York, Vanderbilt's Steward, William Pirie, found "a lady's nightgown on Mr. Vanderbilt's bed."[41] The nightgown was found in Room A, so Pirie gave it to Kempster, who brought it into Agnes' room. At the time, Agnes was the only woman occupying the car, so the nightgown had to belong to her. There was also another incident, on the same trip, when Pirie went to the observation end and saw that "Mr. Vanderbilt was sitting reading a book, and Agnes was lying down on the sofa with her head on his legs."[42] By his legs, Pirie meant Vanderbilt's lap.

Alfred now had a mistress, a gorgeous and seductive woman, Agnes Mary O'Brien Ruiz, who, like him, was also married. His behavior was scandalous yet A.G. did not hide his sexual exploits and while he did exercise some discretion, other behaviors such as requesting his valet to bring his clothes to Agnes' apartment where he had spent the night, could not hide it either. He had drifted so far away from Elsie that not only were they no longer together, he had traveled beyond the limits of their married life where she could not and would not willingly follow. The break was complete.

For a man conducting an affair, A.G. differed from others, mainly perhaps in that the affairs of millionaires could never be kept entirely secret. Once the press caught onto who Alfie's mysterious mistress was, the couple could not be left alone. On one occasion, in order to avoid suspicious reporters, A.G. followed Agnes Ruiz down a dumbwaiter, arriving in the basement as an astonished superintendent Mr. Pickwell greeted them and assisted the young pair in their escape.[43] Pickwell led them out the yard to a fence behind the building and helped A.G. jump over to escape the notice of reporters still waiting out in front of the building. This event occurred no less than one day prior to the Supreme Court signing the decree of divorce that Elsie had petitioned.

Florence Schenck, the woman that Wilson had brought onto *The Wayfarer,* would become an employee in the Vanderbilt stables at the behest of Wilson who could not resist her beauty. Schenck would travel with Wilson and A.G. to all the horse shows, even as they traveled to London where Alfred Gwynne would serve as host at the International Horse Show and as a coachman along the picturesque road from London to Brighton.[44]

Two years later, barely twenty years old, she would announce to the press that she was the wife of Wilson, a declaration that he would not easily agree to.[45] She could not even afford to pay the $31 customs fee, which she had to beg from Wilson, who, reluctantly after three hours, paid the fee for her. Bitterly, she cried and left the pier with a friend.

Later, Schenck again addressed an eager press, telling them how Wilson begged her to marry him. As Charles heard her, he stormed over towards her and asked her to leave. "You know what you promised," he said.

"I guess you mean Mr. Vanderbilt," said Miss Schenck, "but I will talk anyway, and that settles it."

She told the press about how Wilson had taken her soon after their marriage in October to New York, confessing that he was already married but "she would not be here for long." Schenck bitterly admitted that she did not understand the full "gravity of the matter" until Wilson took her to meet the real Mrs. Charles Wilson six months later. Wilson asked the reporters to refrain from printing the story as it could affect his employment at the Vanderbilt stables.

Not only was the story printed, but Wilson also retained his position at the stables. Try as he might, the young Vanderbilt could not distance himself from the scandals of his stable folk because of their knowledge of his own affair. Charlie Wilson had his claws sunk in so deep into Alfred Gwynne that the millionaire was terrified of what the older man might reveal. Wilson was an excellent whip but with such an obvious reputation for adultery and deception, most employers would have gotten rid of him as quickly as possible. Vanderbilt was his meal ticket and Wilson would not easily let that go.

Despite the enormous proclivity of the press to describe in minute detail Alfred's exploits and Elsie's attire at society functions, not a single word escaped about his sexual escapades and the double life he now led with a mistress whom he lavished attention upon, buying her exquisite gems[46] and other gifts. Was society unaware? Or was it choosing to be silent?

NOTES

1. *The New York Times*. "The News of Newport." Jul 30. 1906. Pg. 7.
2. *The Chicago Daily Tribune*. "How to have a Pair of Pretty Shoulders." Aug. 12, 1906. Pg. C10.
3. Ibid.
4. Ibid.
5. Terminal Railroad Association of St. Louis Historical and Technical Society, Inc. Issue 53-54. "Celebrating 111 Years of the Terminal Railroad." Vol. 14. Winter/Spring 2000. Pg. 5-6.
6. Ibid. Pg. 6.
7. Ibid. Pg. 6.
8. Ellen F. Vanderbilt Vs. Alfred G. Vanderbilt. No. 1908-2273. Supreme Court of the State of New York, New York County. 2 April 1908. Pg. 3.
9. Ibid. Pg. 4.
10. Ibid.. Pg. 5.
11. *The Washington Post*. October 1, 1906. Pg. 4.
12. *The New York Times*. Oct. 3, 1906. Pg. 9.

13. Ellen F. Vanderbilt Vs. Alfred G. Vanderbilt. No. 1908-2273. Supreme Court of the State of New York, New York County. 2 April 1908. Pg. 8.
14. Ibid. Pg. 9.
15. Ibid. Pg. 9.
16. Ibid. Pg. 13.
17. Ibid. Pg. 14.
18. *The Chicago Daily Tribune*. "Rich Men Not Bad: Vanderbilt " October 21st, 1906. Pg. 1.
19. Ibid.
20. Ibid.
21. Ellen F. Vanderbilt Vs. Alfred G. Vanderbilt. No. 1908-2273. Supreme Court of the State of New York, New York County. 2 April 1908. Pg. 81.
22. Ibid. Pg. 23.
23. Ibid. Pg. 24.
24. Ibid. Pg. 87.
25. Ibid.
26. Ibid. Pg. 82.
27. *The Washington Post*. "Vanderbilt Escaped." June 16, 1909. Pg. 3.
28. Ellen F. Vanderbilt Vs. Alfred G. Vanderbilt. No. 1908-2273. Supreme Court of the State of New York, New York County. 2 April 1908. Pg. 83.
29. Ibid. Pg. 22.
30. Ibid. Pg. 38.
31. *The Washington Post*. "Vanderbilt Escaped." June 16, 1909. Pg. 3.
32. Ellen F. Vanderbilt Vs. Alfred G. Vanderbilt. No. 1908-2273. Supreme Court of the State of New York, New York County. 2 April 1908. Pg. 31.
33. Ibid. Pg. 32.
34. Ibid. Pg. 37.
35. Ibid. Pg. 55.
36. Ibid. Pg. 51.
37. Ibid. Pg. 57.
38. Ibid.
39. Ibid. Pg. 72.
40. *The Washington Post*. "Vanderbilt Escaped." June 16, 1909. Pg. 3.
41. Ellen F. Vanderbilt Vs. Alfred G. Vanderbilt. No. 1908-2273. Supreme Court of the State of New York, New York County. 2 April 1908. Pg. 73.
42. Ellen F. Vanderbilt Vs. Alfred G. Vanderbilt. No. 1908-2273. Supreme Court of the State of New York, New York County. 2 April 1908.
43. *The Washington Post*. "Vanderbilt Escaped." June 16, 1909. Pg. 3.
44. *The New York Times*. "Alfred Vanderbilt Loses $15,000. July 2, 1908. Pg. 1.
45. Ibid.
46. *The New York Times*. "$350,000 for Ruiz Gems." Dec. 18, 1909. Pg. 1.

Chapter Eight

A Whirling Abyss

London beckoned and Alfred was hot on the pursuit. By November of 1906, along with his legion of supporters, he embarked upon the process of establishing an International Horse Show in London with fanfare and a grand purse of $35,000 to entice the most talented contestants, soliciting entries from Holland, Spain, Germany, Italy, England, France, and Belgium.[1] Soon after A.G. received his blue ribbons for his four-in-hand,[2] his big win was announced at Madison Square Garden at the National Horse Show. All the prominent exhibitors pledged support. The stated purpose of the London Horse Show at the Olympia building was to promote the best of horse breeding.[3] The Olympia was a grandiose structure with a 305 by 76 show ring that offered twice the space of Madison Square Garden. A.G. put his full attention to making his mark abroad.

The *Los Angeles Times* devoted an entire section to the upcoming event, satirizing the young man and English traditions, especially drawing attention to how coaching was impractical.[4] They went as far as to imply that A.G.'s real occupation lay in socializing with pretty English girls:

> And there are the girls laughing, on the coach . . . so he's a jolly good fellow and with 'such a dear American accent.' . . . And now the driver of the coach, be he Alfred Vanderbilt or some common or garden mortal hired by the day, climbs to his lofty perch beside some favored female.[5]

A.G. went from being the "golden boy" of society to having a more daredevil appeal as a young man who did as he pleased, regardless of societal favor. His impeccable good taste garnered Alfred the fastidious reputation for setting the latest fashions for men and his attire was copied assiduously. He was always dapper with his penchant for darker suits of black chevlot with a

Olympia Roof, the site of many an esteemed horse show. Erected in 1885, by Andrew Handyside of Derby, The Olympia, whose roof is shown here, covered an area of 4 acres. The Grand Hall, 450 feet long by 250 feet wide, was said to be the largest building in the United Kingdom covered by one span of iron and glass. By the 1900s, Olympia was regularly hosting the tournament.

single-breasted waistcoat with a V collar, gray suede gloves, black and white shirt, matching pants, and a dark olive green narrow tie.[6] The young Vanderbilt set the vogue for what to wear in society.

As early as mid-January, A.G. set sail for England on the *Cunarder Carmania.*[7] Twenty-six stallions arrived in late February.[8] The young Vanderbilt leased *Red Hill Farm* at Edgeware in close proximity to London, where he intended to stay until at least the Bayshore Show in the spring.[9]

Elsie, however, remained at home, decorating her Newport residence for entertainment and as her primary residence.[10] The split between A.G. and Elsie grew more apparent as their activities together began to dwindle to mere societal functions at best. Their individual tastes stood out in stark contrast to each other as they carved out their own niches.[11] Their interests, once so interwoven, now rarely even ran parallel to each other.

Winter's glimmering ice crystals and breathtaking beauty in the heart of the Adirondacks provided a delightful retreat; Mrs. Alfred G. Vanderbilt decided to embark upon a little adventure to the ice carnival in Montreal via rail. As

International Horse Show Postcards, June 1908–1913.

the family car *Wayfarer* was hitched on to an Adirondack express train, Elsie departed with four friends, Mr. and Mrs. Arthur Iselin and Mr. and Mrs. Arthur Scott Burden from Grand Central Terminal.[12] The driver of the train was William Kirk, known affectionately as the "father of the Adirondack run."

Since 1902, under the auspices of Uncle Willie K. and his engineer Wilgus, the entire railroad terminal and all of its branches were undergoing electrification, which meant that on many nights, construction crews labored all the way from 42nd Street to Central Park. Many lines still remained unfinished and at night, signal sets were difficult to discern for swiftly approaching trains. Unfortunately for Elsie and all the other passengers aboard that Adirondack express that night, a poorly-lit freight train heading north to Mount Murray, switched on to the passenger track just as the express came hurtling down.[13] Later, officials would explain that the engineer of the freight train had failed to stop because of failing brakes and "slippery,"[14] "frosty"[15] tracks. The lights were dim and the trains moved too rapidly. The head-on collision was inevitable. William Kirk had no warning.

Ripping the string of wooden cars to shreds, the express careened off the tracks and rolled over, crushing the skull of Kirk and the fireman next to him instantly. One by one, each passenger car that followed the heavy engine collided with the freight cars, as shards of glass and sharp wood splinters burst out in rapid fire upon impact. Rudely awakened, passengers fell out of passenger cars, startled and bleeding from sharp cuts. Thrust into the cold evening air, they stood in shock amidst the piles of wreckage. By remarkable grace, Elsie and all the other passengers aboard the *Wayfarer* were spared injury since their car was at the tail end of the spiraling train. They were, however, badly shaken by the experience. Through executive privileges the group was taken immediately to Albany to retire for the night.

Abandoning his plans for *Red Hill Farm*, Alfred immediately set sail for home upon receiving the news in London of his wife's accident.[16] Within a week of ascertaining that Elsie was ok, A.G. returned to his coaching activities and soon after, in less than a month, left for London once more. Elsie's near death experience was terrifying in its impact and even though she escaped unscathed, the event had badly shaken her. Did she find comfort in the arms of her young husband? Alfred's heart was big enough to return immediately to be by her side upon hearing the news of her accident. Calamitous events such as these could reconcile many an estranged couple. Yet for A.G. and Elsie, the gulf remained too vast to leap.

Prior to his arrival home, Alfred Gwynne had already ordered his manager Wilson to load his finest string of champion stallions aboard the *Minnetonka*, an Atlantic Transport Liner[17] to London, for the upcoming show. This was in all probability the finest cargo of horseflesh that ever traveled from America to London. Notable among these champions was the award-winning team of grays that had garnered a blue ribbon at every event they competed in: the *Venture* coach team of *Viking*, *Venture, Vanity,* and *Vogue*. A.G.'s pride and joy, the twenty-seven horses aboard the *Minnetonka,* traveled in style, in special spacious stalls on the cattle deck. The stalls were three times the regular size[18] and were known for their improved ventilation and lighting, with special padding and bedding for protection and comfort.[19] For the sea voyage, Alfred had procured the finest hay and special feed for his herd. Charles Wilson had eight grooms at his beck and call that were stationed in close proximity to the equines. A.G. had planned out every detail, from shipping out entire coaches, hansom, broughams, and gigs, to a workout schedule for the horses upon their arrival at Red Hill Farm. This was no small endeavor as the young Vanderbilt had committed vast resources and his own time and effort to ensure the success of his new venture abroad in England, a country known for its appreciation of royalty and finer pursuits, which A.G. strongly identified with.

Despite being an international event, the only two countries to enthusiastically promote their own contestants were England and America. The Vanderbilt grays had an invincible reputation at home. Would they extend their winning streak across the Atlantic Ocean? The Americans brought enthusiasm, young blood, color, vivacity, and money into the age-old sport of equine competition. The young Vanderbilt himself had revived interest in coaching back home with his friend James Hazen Hyde and others of the New York Coaching Club. Would they be able to hold their own against English coachmen? The American spirit of good natured and friendly competition attracted a lot of attention among the Brits, stirring interest as the English began to register their own contestants.[20]

Arriving in New York, A.G. enthused about the new show:

> Everything is progressing splendidly. The Englishmen are giving American exhibitors many concessions and are holding out great inducements for American horse exhibitors to take their fine stock to London. It will be the biggest horse show that ever took place and great interest is being manifested in it all over the continent.[21]

A fellow passenger confided to the Washington Post:

> If it were not for the generosity of Mr. Vanderbilt, two of his American friends, and a wealthy Englishman, the coming international show could not be a success. The general run of English horse fanciers have not the money to go into such an expensive project at the present time.[22]

As A.G.'s attention was diverted to London, inviting more Americans to go abroad and spend their money at horse shows, New York grew quiet. As the spring of 1907 approached, the *Pioneer* coach missed its principal whip. Who else would tool the coach? Now a staple in the coaching tradition for years, the "toot of the horn"[23] as it made its way from the *Holland House* to the *Ardsley Club* impressed upon the locals the arrival of spring and "herald[ed] the advent of summer."[24] With no one to steer its course, the Pioneer was pulled off the road, remaining "out of commission."[25]

In March, Mr. and Mrs. A.G. Vanderbilt called upon Alice, Mrs. Cornelius Vanderbilt, at her mansion in New York, staying with her for four days.[26] Upon hearing about the death of Pinkie, the canine mascot of the local 39th squad of the Engine Company, Alfred immediately offered a beautiful Dalmatian puppy to take its place, writing to the foreman:

> Dear Sir: The account in last Saturday's papers of the sad event, which so suddenly plunged the members of Engine Company No. 39 into mourning attracted my attention.
>
> To take the place of 'Pinkie,' who was so suddenly taken from this world, I would be pleased to present to the members of your company a Dalmatian puppy that first saw the light nearly six months ago. Its parents were both imported. I have given instructions that the strongest and best marked puppy be sent you by express from my Oakland Farm at Newport, R.I., and I trust that you will accept him or her, as the case may be, with my compliments.
>
> Very truly,
> Alfred G. Vanderbilt[27]

Surprised by the offer, the company graciously accepted[28] the puppy as their new mascot, calling him "Oakie." A far cry from the ragged mongrel that had previously accompanied them, Oakie did not last long at his new post. Placed in the hands of four youngsters who took him for a walk in the noisy and bustling heat of Third Avenue, Oakie withdrew, circling about, "putting his tail between his legs" as he speedily ran away. Apparently, the last sighting of Oakie was his swift departure back towards Fifth Avenue, a reaction that drew gleeful laughter from the fireman who remarked that Oakie was "too swell for us. He's gone to the effete west,"[29] adding, "You ought to know what Third Avenue would mean to a dog of Oakie's breeding."[30]

Initially professing to remain abroad for the duration of the London season, Elsie traveled to England, staying at the residence of her sister, Lady Cheylesmore, but remained less than a month.[31] By April, she was entertaining her niece, Miss Pauline L. French, and fiancé S.J. Wagstaff at Oakland without her husband.[32] A.G. remained in Europe. After a week in Paris, the young Vanderbilt scion arrived on April 12, 1906 in London to spend time with his horses at *Red Hill Farm*.[33]

Alfred had left America, eager to escape the public notoriety from the scandals brewing in his stables and establish a new reputation for himself as a coaching whip of repute with his fine appreciation of custom and horse breeding. As rumors began to circulate like wildfire, mainly due to the escapades of his stable manager Charles Wilson, Alfred Gwynne increasingly came under heat. Yet he not only refuted the complaints or innuendos of the press, he denied any knowledge. The Virginia beauty Miss Florence Schenck was chosen to be a whip for some of A.G.'s horses and when questioned, A.G denied a connection: "'The first knowledge I had that Miss Schenck was in my employ I got from the newspapers,' said Mr. Vanderbilt. 'There is absolutely nothing in it.'"[34]

How could Alfred deny that he knew Florence Schenck was in his employment? His relationship with Wilson was far too close for him to not know about her presence there and in fact, the possibility that A.G. had allowed Florence to drive a coach was very likely. Alfred was enmeshed so deeply into the tangled and sordid affair because of his own adultery. He could not separate himself from Wilson who had intimate knowledge of Alfred Gwynne's affair with Agnes Ruiz. Try as he might, the young man could not avoid the vortex of confusion surrounding his stables. Instead, he slipped further and deeper into a whirling abyss of deceit and adultery as one lie after another furiously kept pace with events that were unfolding rapidly out of his control. The best that he could do was to minimize the impact that Wilson's affairs had upon his own lifestyle and societal standing that A.G. was so eager to improve and create anew in London.

With his characteristic enthusiasm, Alfred launched into full-fledged preparation for the event as the weeks approached. He bought $100,000 of stock in the exhibit company[35] that was managing the event and enjoying social events in London.[36] In May, he was back in New York again to participate in the 27th New York Coaching Club parade through Central Park.

As thousands of eager spectators thronged the streets,[37] A.G. drove his maroon coach led by four magnificent grays festooned with red carnations. Beside him on the box seat sat Elsie, fashionably attired in a "turquoise-blue marquisette costume,"[38] with a satin jacket of black silk, pearls, and a black maline hat with black feather trim. Despite blustery weather and a smaller turnout among the coachmen, the event was deemed a success.

With less than two weeks to go, the excitement surrounding the International Horse Show had reached a fever pitch. A.G. left New York, sailing on the *Adriatic* on May 22, 1907 to seek his fame. He excitedly proclaimed that the event "cannot fail to be a complete and unqualified success."[39]

While he had dominated amateur competition at home, Alfred ironically faced serious competition in England from another American millionaire, the fifty-three year old Walter L. Winans.[40] The two men shared many things in common: they were both American millionaires, scions of massive railroad fortunes, and they both had a strong predilection for coaching. Winans was also a man who had the peculiar distinction of being an American brought up in England, who now wished to return to America to settle down and yet was considered an Englishman by most Americans. Why would Winans want to leave England, the "land where millionaires can enjoy life as they please, without being jumped on[41]" to America "where criticism and denunciation of millionaires is sort of [the] national pastime?"[42]

How would Winans fare in a country that valued rags to riches over the playtime pursuits of rich and idle men? America had a love-hate relationship with its wealthy class; heralding its accomplishments while sarcastically lampooning its failures. A strong work ethic pervaded the ethos of the country from its early Puritan beginnings that was impossible to shake.

Nonetheless, the press, who declared him always an American, welcomed Winans:

> Winans is alert and vigorous, sound in wind and limb, eats well and sleeps well, doesn't know what nerves are, and has none of that feverish hurry up and get through with it air characteristic of the man who measures time by dollars. If happiness be 'our being's end and aim,' then Walter L. Winans must be accounted a shining success.[43]

Winans shared his own point of view freely, summing up his philosophy, "I don't see why a man who starts life with all the money he possibly can have any use for should devote the best years of his life to piling up more. Do you?"[44]

With a royal residence at Surrenden Park housing more than one hundred of the finest equines in Europe, valued at half a million dollars, Winans had enough prize-winning stallions to enter 93 out of a possible 124 upcoming events at the London show. With an undefeated record for winning the four-in-hand all over Europe, Winans single-handedly posed the greatest threat to Vanderbilt's quest for equestrian victory. Despite being American by birth and having a professed desire to move to Baltimore, Maryland, Winans was embraced by the British as one of their own and touted as their prize-winning champion.

Elsie was creating her own headlines as she sailed her thirty-foot *Caprice* in Newport harbor. Six days prior to the commencement of the London Horse Show, Mrs. A.G. Vanderbilt was sailing in the harbor past a German cruiser *Bremen* when an American Government launch rammed right into her vessel.[45] Despite initially sinking, the sloop was able to power its way safely back to the inner harbor. Elsie was clearly annoyed but able to keep her equilibrium throughout the scary incident, demanding compensation from the government. Rear Admiral John Merrill appointed a board to inquire into the issue. Elsie evinced little fear about the matter[46] and A.G. remained in London.

Fragrant blossoms welcomed guests and visitors as they arrived at the First International Horse Show. The festive attire and flowery hats against this backdrop of floral abundance lavished "more color to a picture that was brilliant before."[47] With boxes ranging from $50 to $350 for the entire show, most of the guests were either American heirs or heiresses or European royalty. Aristocracy from principally the two nations had assembled to witness the pick of horseflesh in competition. A majority of the high jumper entries came from America, such as Huge Willet's *Heatherbloom*.[48]

For the four-in-hand coach, the favorite among the Americans was undoubtedly Alfred Gwynne while the English offered two strong contestants: J. Ogden Armour[49] and Walter Winans, whose herd of 100 horses were entering virtually every competition.[50]

All eyes were upon Alfred Gwynne. A.G. commanded attention with his glorious team of grays in his coach of maroon and gold, the colors of royalty and aristocracy. The delicately beautiful Duchess of Marlborough, Alfred's cousin, graced his box. The Prince and Princess of Wales attended the event where Mr. Alfred Vanderbilt exhibited his fine stallions in the four-in-hand competition. Despite the public belief that the Americans, while being incredibly charming, had noticeable weaknesses in their horse carriage and performance, the young Vanderbilt scored a victory when his four-in-hand coach prevailed upon the English.[51] Winans won prize after prize but failed to secure this most coveted of blue ribbons.

Three days later, a full cotillion of royalty arrived with King Edward and Queen Alexandria, along with King Frederick and Queen Louise of Denmark.[52] All the victors brought forth their studs and mares for display, parading their equines before the royals. A.G. drew tremendous applause from the British crowds. With over 200,000 guests attending the event, the show was definitely a success "exceeding all expectations."[53]

Immediately, plans were proposed for a repeat of the event the following year again in London. Conversely, R.W. Rives, the interim head of the New York Coaching Club, who had presided over the event, was sharp in his criticism of the American equines. He declared that the American horses did not "compare with the English in many respects."[54] He went even further to say that "we may catch up with the English some day, but not for a long time. Now they show, I think, the greatest horses the world ever knew."[55]

James Hazen Hyde was quick to defend. As manager of the show for the Americans, he swiftly repudiated these remarks:

> We must remember this is an international and not a mere two-nation show. America had no right to expect to win everything. I think our exhibition did very well, and I'm sure they are satisfied, as real sportsmen should be. The show was a great success in every way.[56]

What did A.G. have to say? When asked if he regretted bringing his horses across the ocean to the event, the young man smiled and remarked only, "Of course, I deeply prize my blue ribbons."[57] Despite A.G.'s victory in the four-in-hand coach, the indisputable victor of the event was Walt Winans, who despite being American by birth and raising American horses, secured victory as a Brit, a classification that intensely irritated the American contingent.[58]

At home too, Alfred Gwynne incurred the criticism of societal gossip columnist Marquise de Fontenay who declared that A.G.'s choice of scarlet and gold liveries, the colors of the Vanderbilt house, were inappropriate in the London setting, since those colors were restricted to royalty:

> There is no statute prohibiting anybody else from putting his domestics in the same garb as those of the reigning house. But the unwritten laws dealing with the matter are infinitely more stringent, and their violation much more strongly resented. It was a most impolite thing to do, and it is difficult to understand how Alfred Vanderbilt should have been allowed to make such a break without being warned by some of his friends of the irritation which it would create.[59]

Like any person that acquires fame receives both adulation and praise, Alfred Gwynne was no exception. Yet, this time perhaps and in the months to come, his armor was penetrated, displaying a noticeable irritation with the press as they lingered in their criticism. When A.G. returned home, a swirling mess of confusion awaited him despite his success and the British public's obvious attraction to the Vanderbilt exhibition.

It was not something that Alfred could easily extricate himself from. A woman by the name of Dorothy Skinner, friend of Miss Florence Schenck, had deserted her husband George Bronson Howard on their honeymoon for the companionship of Schenck during the London horse show. After a four-day amorous courtship, twenty-year old Dorothy Skinner had eloped with George B. Howard[60] and married him in secret. Howard had brought his new wife, a popular Virginia beauty, to London for their honeymoon. However, upon seeing her old chum in London in March, Dorothy immediately became attached to Florence once again and soon left Howard to join a fast lifestyle that she found more entertaining, with numerous dining engagements with eligible bachelors and frequent trips across the channel to Paris.[61] Both women were gorgeous and both wanted to have a good time. They were playmates and social rivals in Norfolk, Virginia. Skinner became ensconced in the stable life. A.G. had denied even any knowledge of Schenck's presence in his stables; and yet, he not only harbored a bigamist Charles Wilson among his employees, but also now a renegade wife.

Schenck's own illicit liaison with Charles Wilson had not even settled with the press before she encouraged her friend to leave her husband. George B. Howard poured his agony to the press, clearly implicating Schenck:

> 'Miss Schenck was the sole cause of the trouble,' said Mr. Howard, 'I told my wife she would have to choose between her and me, and she immediately left me. I guess I plucked a lemon this time. It's another case of wed in haste and repent at your leisure.'[62]

His heart ripped open, Howard, a famous twenty-five year old Baltimore author and occasional actor in his own right, was alternately bitter and conciliatory. Despite his wife's transgression, he offered reconciliation but was promptly refused. As scandalous stories spread, Howard threw his hands up in despair and left for America, while vengefully announcing that he found the company of Miss Florence Schenck entirely disagreeable.

Immediately upon hearing of their daughter's employment as a whip, Dr. and Mrs. Powhatan Schenck publicly disowned Florence, without mincing any words, "As far as we are concerned she is absolutely dead to us. We consider her action very improper."[63]

Mrs. Howard retaliated with her own spiteful response, declaring George to be a difficult man who neglected her and possessed an "ungovernable temper."[64] Dorothy declared that her husband would fly into "terrific passions over trivial things and even went so far as to choke me."[65] She was so miserable that "I didn't care if he did."[66] She defended the reputation of her friend Florence and declared that "his story that Miss Schenck alienated her affections is false." Dorothy intended to sue for divorce right away, adding petulantly that the only gift she had received from her husband, a photograph of himself, was placed face downwards in her trunk.[67] By the time she arrived back to New York fully enraged, she publicly announced the successful wedding of Schenck with Wilson.

That public announcement in turn, foisted its own troubles as another woman who lived in Orange, New Jersey, upon hearing the news, demanded that she was the rightful Mrs. Wilson.[68] She had married Charles H. Wilson fourteen years prior and she had a marriage certificate to prove it. The press went wild, taking punches at the stable hand as he became further embroiled in marital tangles:

> Who is really entitled to call herself Mrs. Charles H. Wilson, wife of the whip for Alfred G. Vanderbilt? It appears that there are two claimants to the title.[69]

Mrs. Charles Wilson living in Orange, N.J., had substantial proof as friends and neighbors rallied forth to confirm that Charles Wilson was her husband

and had been a riding manager in a nearby arsenal building. The couple, in fact, was popular among the horse folk of Orange County. Indignant at Schenck's claim to marriage, Mrs. Charles Wilson, after proving the authenticity of her marriage, declared, "I do not care to talk about this matter, as I abhor the notoriety into which my husband has been brought by this London set."[70]

Florence Schenck began to unravel. When she arrived back to New York from the steamship Minnehaha, the change was apparent. Her parents did not welcome her back home as usual and Schenck was visibly distraught and nervous. She was an outcast at home and the man she had forsaken her name and reputation for, had turned out to be a scoundrel. She was hysterical.

To any reporter who would listen, she declared her innocence and how she had wed Wilson in the Richmond Hotel in New York in October of 1906 without knowing of his former marriage. Angrily and desperately, she cried, "He has blighted my life I am now an outcast, without a friend in the world. Even my father and mother have disowned me."[71]

Baring her arm, Florence revealed large welts and black bruises that she said were caused by Wilson in a rage when he beat her and threatened more than a dozen times to kill her, "knocking her senseless"[72] and "treating her brutally all the way across the ocean."[73] She was homeless and penniless, unable to even afford even her own hotel room. The hotel surgeon Dr. Smith diagnosed her to be suffering from nervous prostration and soon after reaching her hotel, she declined any more visitors.

Wilson immediately denied all such rumors and while he reluctantly paid her custom fee, he announced to the press that Florence had approached him to work in the stables and that he had done her a favor.[74] He had provided her with employment, trips, and money, and had never married her, saying instead that he was devoted to his wife. Wilson also stated that Florence was fully aware of his own marriage.

In Richmond, no such marriage license could be found although the pair was definitely present because of the Richmond Horse Show. Where did A.G. stand in all of this hoopla surrounding his stable folk? He was on the verge of being exposed and walked a delicate line. He could not fire Wilson nor Schenck because of their intimate knowledge of his own carnal behavior aboard the Wayfarer in Richmond. Alfred Gwynne must have been relieved however when Schenck separated from Wilson in the hopes that the whirling abyss of rumors and scandals would quietly subside.

The next day after a night of rest, Florence invited the press back to her hotel room. Propped upon a multitude of voluminous pillows, the attractive young woman was decidedly more at ease. She reiterated that Wilson had married her and that she had no previous knowledge of his earlier marriage.

Schenck also sassily declared that she was a Southern woman and that he was a coward who she would not "hesitate to shoot upon sight." Fortunately for Wilson, Florence did not possess a gun.

Mrs. Wilson told a different tale, saying that the pretty Southern belle had lived with them at Newport and that it did not take her long to realize that her "husband's affections had been alienated."[75] This grew more apparent to her when Miss Schenck accompanied her husband, Charles Wilson, to the London horse show.

Florence's troubles did not cease however as she received a telephone call from her father announcing that her family never wished to see her again,[76] which left her prostrate with grief and guilt. The public, at first loud and harshly critical of her, now began to express feelings of pity for a "girl so deceived"[77] and whose story was "exceptionally pathetic."[78]

When asked whether she would file suit against him, initially Schenck replied that she could not, because, "He is the only man I ever cared for, and I could not make up my mind to send him to prison."[79] She said that Charley was a jealous man, frequently given to fits of rage when Florence even spoke to another man. It was fear for his own life and employment at the Vanderbilt stables that prompted him to "hush me up so that no one would know anything about it. He knew that Mr. Vanderbilt did not want a scandal."[80]

Yet Florence would retract that statement; she did file suit against Charles Wilson for $100,000, charging that he "under promise of marriage, lured her away from her home at Norfolk, Va., in October 1906, following which he brought her to this city, where they lived together as husband and wife. Subsequently they went to London-Returning here, Miss Schenck said, she discovered Wilson already was married."

Closer and closer the circle of scandalous rumor reached Alfred till its effect upon his personal life grew obvious. No longer did Elsie or A.G. make efforts to attend even the same social functions that they had participated in the previous year. Mrs. A.G. Vanderbilt hosted the Methodist Church picnic for children alone that summer at Southwick's Grove on July 1st[81] soon after, she left for Sagamore to entertain a massive house party for the 4th of July followed by an ongoing charity bazaar.[82] No longer was the married couple ever within close proximity of each other; they did not even share the same paragraph within the gossip columns.

A chink in Alfred's armor was exposed as he sarcastically responded to the press, revealing his deep cynicism, when a story spread that he had returned to New York to participate in distributing Vanderbilt millions at Newport in August.

> I read a story to that effect in an English newspaper with great interest. It contained things about myself and my family of which I was entirely ignorant. I

> have come to the conclusion that whenever I desire to learn anything about either my family or myself, I must read the newspapers. I constantly find things in the newspapers about myself of which I had not the faintest knowledge. This article telling about a sort of picnic at which the Vanderbilt millions are to be distributed is absolute news to me; but it must be so, because the newspapers say it is.
>
> Take for instance, the detail that the trustees are going to give me I don't know how many millions in August, when I am not entitled to them till much later. I was delighted to learn this. It will be awfully pleasant to return to the United States and receive all that unexpected money, and I am very thankful that the newspapers have so nicely arranged this affair for me.[83]

The scandal never ends. A.G. employed a young Englishman by the name of Harry S. Brenchley,[84] a handsome young man, six foot and two inches tall, of charming disposition who quickly moved up in the ranks of stable folk in Newport and became Alfred's principal coachman within a few months of his arrival to America, accompanying Vanderbilt on all of his coaching trips. Unfortunately for Alfred, another scandal broke out amidst his horse folk when Brenchley ran off to Europe with Mrs. Alfred S. Dietrich, the attractive young wife of a millionaire,[85] who abandoned her husband hastily to depart with Brenchley on his trip to England as A.G.'s coaching sales agent.

Rumors began to fly about a young Madame Adelaide Flores living on Lexington Avenue whom Mr. Alfred Vanderbilt had called upon in the middle of the night. This woman, recognized as Mrs. Agnes Ruiz, had paid for an automobile in cash for $11,000. Brenchley, the stable hand that ran away with a millionaire's wife, in the keep of A.G., and had acquired and delivered the vehicle for her. When questioned, the woman replied:

> I have no defense for myself because I don't need any. And I have no comment to make upon Mr. Vanderbilt or his visit here yesterday or the cause of it. In regard to the automobile which was bought in my name. All I have to say is that it was bought in my name, I got it and paid for it.

How did Alfred respond to these lurid implications? As he always did, A.G. spoke about his horses, entirely avoiding the subject, and focusing upon his upcoming horse show and coaching venture:

> I am anxious to show the English horsemen that the American-bred trotters are the best for coaching purposes, and I am sure I can do so with the horses I have over there.

Even though Alfred had kept Elsie at arm's length and vice-versa, A.G. could not resist being by his son's side during the Christmas holidays and returned to Oakland to buy expensive gifts for his son, and the children of friends, family, and nearby farmers.[86] This seemed to be a pattern he followed his whole life, he loved children.

Everyone in Newport was stunned by the turn of events and even though the couple admittedly had rarely been seen together, neither conflict nor stress had been outwardly evident to the public. Discussions about A.G.'s personal habits and his obsession with horses were brought up, such as Alfred preferring "the stables to the drawing room." Even apparent friends speculated to the press that the couple had not acted as a husband and wife for more than a year and that the young man had not called upon his mother-in-law Mrs. F.O. French in more than two years. When Elsie refused to visit Alfred's mother Alice in New York, rumors were instantly deemed fact and speculations that a new "legal arrangement" would be reached in the "early future" became rampant.

NOTES

1. *The New York Times*. "Great World's Show of Horses in London." Nov. 24, 1906. Pg. 3.
2. *The Washington Post*. "Vanderbilt Leads." Nov. 25, 1906. Pg. 1.
3. *The New York Times*. "Great World's Show of Horses in London." Nov. 24, 1906. Pg. 3.
4. *The Los Angeles Times*. "This Year' Derby King Versus Belmont." Jun 2, 1902. Pg. 17.
5. Ibid.
6. *The New York Times*. "Men's Fashions at the Horse Show." Nov. 25, 1906. Pg. SM3.
7. *The New York Times*. Jan. 19, 1907. Pg. 16.
8. *The New York Times*. "Many American Horses For the English Show." Feb. 3, 1907. Pg. 10.
9. Ibid.
10. *The Washington Post*. "Society in New York." Feb 2, 1907. Pg. 1.
11. Ibid.
12. *The New York Times*. "Vanderbilt Party in N. Y. Central Wreck." Feb. 9. 1907. Pg. 1.
13. Ibid.
14. Ibid.
15. Ibid.
16. *The Washington Post*. "Social Gossip." Feb 12, 1907. Pg. 7
17. *The New York Times*. "Horses Traveling In Padded Stalls." Feb. 24, 1907. Pg. 13.
18. *The Hartford Courant*. "Horses Well Cared For." Feb 25, 1907. Pg. 14.

19. Ibid.
20. *The Chicago Daily Tribune*. Horse Show Stirring Blood of Britons; Yankees Sure. Feb. 24. 1907. Pg. 1.
21. *The New York Times*. "London Horse Show Plans: A.G. Vanderbilt Says Exhibition Will be Biggest Ever Held." Feb. 27, 1907. Pg. 11.
22. *The Washington Post*. "A.G. Vanderbilt Returns: Enthusiastic Over London Horse Show, Which He Planned." Feb. 27, 1907. Pg. 5.
23. *The Washington Post*. "Social Gossip." Feb. 25, 1907. Pg. 7.
24. Ibid.
25. Ibid.
26. *The New York Times*. "Social Notes." March 6, 1907. Pg. 9.
27. *The New York Times*. "Get A Vanderbilt Mascot: Alfred G. Gives Fireman a Dog in Place of One Which Was Killed." March 13, 1907. Pg. 1.
28. Ibid.
29. *The New York Times*. "Vanderbilt Mascot Quits: Couldn't Stand Third Avenue When Presented to a Firehouse." March 24, 1907. Pg. 1.
30. Ibid.
31. *The Washington Post*. Mar. 29. 1907. Pg. 7.
32. *The Washington Post*. "Guests of Mrs. Vanderbilt." Apr. 7, 1907. Pg. 1.
33. *The New York Times*. "A.G. Vanderbilt Back In London." Apr. 13, 1904. Pg. 4.
34. *The New York Times*. "London to Have An Early Season." April 14, 1907. Pg. C2.
35. *The New York Times*. "American Features to Lead." Apr 21, 1907. Pg. C1.
36. *The New York Times*. "Mr. Reid Presides at Dante Meeting." Apr 28, 1907. Pg. C3.
37. *The New York Times*. Society Turns Out for Coach Parade. May 12, 1907. Pg. 1.
38. *The Washington Post*. "Social Gossip." May 13, 1907. Pg. 7.
39. *The New York Times*. "Vanderbilt Seeks Blue Ribbons." May 22, 1907. Pg. 9.
40. *The Chicago Daily Tribune*. "Winans Will Be Real American." May 26, 1907. Pg. B1.
41. Ibid.
42. Ibid.
43. Ibid.
44. Ibid.
45. *The New York Times*. "Mrs. Vanderbilt's Sloop Run Down." Jun 1, 1907. Pg. 1.
46. *The Chicago Daily Tribune*. Jun 1, 1907. Pg. 1.
47. *The New York Times*. "AMERICAN HORSES AT OLYMPIA SHOW." June 8, 1907. Pg. 3.
48. *The New York Times*. "American Features to Lead." Apr 21, 1907. Pg. C1.
49. Ibid.
50. *The Washington Post*. "Will Exhibit Noted Stud." Apr. 21, 1907. Pg. S1.
51. *The New York Times*. "Vanderbilt Four First in London." June 9, 1907. Pg. S1.
52. *The New York Times*. "King Edward Visits the Show." Jun 12, 1907. Pg. 10.

53. *The Washington Post*. "London Horse Show Ends." June 14, 1907. Pg. 9.
54. *The Washington Post*. "English Horses Lead." June 16, 1907. Pg. 10.
55. Ibid.
56. *The Washington Post*. Jun 14, 1907. Pg. 9.
57. Ibid.
58. *The Chicago Daily Tribune*. "Yankee Horses Inferior." June 16, 1907. Pg. B1.
59. *The Chicago Daily Tribune*. "Marquis de Fontenay." Jun. 19,1907. Pg. 8.
60. *The Hartford Courant*. "Author Deserted: Blames Wife's Chum." Jun 15, 1907. Pg. 1.
61. Ibid.
62. *The Washington Post*. "Preferred Girl Chum." Jun 16, 1907. Pg. 16.
63. Ibid.
64. *The New York Times*. "Mrs. Howard Says Husband Is Wrong." Jun 19, 1907. Pg. 5.
65. *The Washington Post*. "Woes of Mrs. Howard." Jun 18, 1907. Pg. 3.
66. Ibid.
67. *The New York Times*. "Mrs. Howard Says Husband Is Wrong." Jun 19, 1907. Pg. 5.
68. *The Washington Post*. "Two Call Him Spouse." Jun 21, 1907. Pg. 3.
69. Ibid.
70. Ibid.
71. *The Washington Post*. "Her Romance Over." Jul 9, 1907. Pg. 1.
72. Ibid.
73. Ibid.
74. *The Washington Post*. "Says She'll Shoot." Jul 10. 1907. Pg. 1.
75. *The New York Times*. Jul 10, 1907. Pg. 4.
76. *The Washington Post*. "Grief Makes Her Ill." Jul 11, 1907. Pg. 3
77. Ibid.
78. Ibid.
79. Ibid.
80. Ibid.
81. *The New York Times*. "Methodist Picnic at Oakland Farm." Jul 2, 1907. Pg. 9.
82. *The New York Times*. "Mrs. Alfred Vanderbilt Returning." Jul 7, 1907. Pg. 7.
83. *The Washington Post*. Jul 7, 1907. Pg. 13.
84. *The Chicago Daily Tribune*. Dec. 22, 1907. Pg. 5.
85. *The Los Angeles Times*. Dec. 22, 1907. Pg. 11.
86. *The New York Times*. "Vanderbilts Santa Claus to Hundreds." Dec. 26, 1907. Pg. 7.

Chapter Nine

Severing Ties

At 3 p.m. on April 1, 1908,[1] while A.G. set sail on the *Mauretania*, Mrs. Elsie French Vanderbilt filed suit for absolute divorce, which, in the state of New York, could only imply adultery.[2] It was an adroit and carefully executed move, since Alfred's departure negated any further questioning by the press for the next week as he traveled aboard the ship. His wife's lawyers from the firm of Carter, Ledyard & Milburn appeared in court exactly one hour later, just as the court office was closing, and made an application on her behalf based upon statutory grounds, just as A.G., the plaintiff, departed from the dock.[3] Beguiled by reporters, Alfred Gwynne declined any comments, saying that he had "nothing to say about the matter"[4] and that it was a "personal affair and my lips are sealed."[5] Avoiding any discussion about a possible impending divorce, A.G. instead spoke about his coaching plans for the Brighton Road.

Sailing with him on the *Mauretania* was his cousin, the Duchess of Marlborough.[6] Consuelo didn't seem particularly friendly towards her cousin. While Alfred talked to the press before sailing, Consuelo boarded the ship. At first it "looked as though there was to be no salute exchanged" but the duchess soon noticed the press, so she "inclined her head a fraction of an inch and Vanderbilt touched the brim of his hat."[7] Consuelo's attitude, it seemed, was the overwhelming feeling of society.

Elsie departed from Oakland Farms two weeks prior.[8] She told the press that she was going down South, but it was soon discovered that this was a ruse so she could avoid doing any interviews.[9] She subsequently relocated to her uncle's luxurious estate at Tuxedo, New York, with her son and all of her belongings, bringing increased speculation about their separation. A French cottage in her uncle's Amos Tuck's residence, known charmingly as "Tuck's Eden," was being prepared for occupancy. At the time however, she

Frontal, half body view of Alfred Vanderbilt. Ca. 1907. Library of Congress. Bain Collection.

Alfred Vanderbilt on the cover of Town and Country, *April 20 1907.*

had declined any comments and, when pressed, had categorically denied any possible separation or divorce.

His cousin Willie K., who had accompanied his wife to the pier to send off A.G., denied any knowledge of these private affairs.[10] Elsie's suit was obviously planned well in advance; since the Court Justice was aware of the proceedings before as the lawyers representing both parties had contacted him earlier in the day to present their cases.[11] Yet the final decree was cloaked in secrecy and the council's action could not have been better orchestrated. By the time the comparing clerk received the actual divorce papers, it was too late in the day for the divorce proceedings to be officially recorded or even commented upon. Alfred Gwynne was able to escape on his boat, sailing the high seas, free of the moral reprimands that society would soon heap upon him.

In their divorce case, Elsie alleged that her husband had engaged in adultery with an unknown woman in Virginia aboard his private car the *Wayfarer* during a trip from Richmond to Norfolk in October of 1906.[12]

The referee David McClure, appointed by Court Justice O'Gorman, submitted an appeal of divorce to the court. The appeal would come before the Supreme Court for final approval and if the decree was signed, it would take another three months to become absolute.[13] During these proceedings, the fate of their only child, William Henry, would also be determined as well as alimony payments.

All individuals directly related to the case were either too busy or unavailable for comments.[14] Approached by curious reporters, David McClure, the referee, denied any previous knowledge of the impending divorce proceedings. Justice O'Gorman declined to discuss the case. Lawyers for Mrs. A.G. Vanderbilt categorically refused to share any information that would affect the privacy of their client. As the news reporters reached the *Breakers*, Alice issued her own statement declining to comment upon the affairs of her son. Friends of the couple expressed immediate surprise by the divorce proceedings with some of Elsie's friends even declaring that they had heard her say that she did not have the "least intention of applying for either a separation or divorce."[15] In fact, both parties denied any sort of separation until the day the papers were filed.[16]

Everything remained shrouded in mystery as the first divorce proceedings began. Only the findings were to be made public, while "all evidence was sealed"[17] for one hundred years according to statute and every effort was made to conceal the real nature of the suit.[18]

When Alfred set sail aboard the ship, despite taking possession of the most luxurious of suites, it was noticed that he was accompanied by only one servant and that his personal valet, Mr. Howard Kempster, was missing.[19] The reason for this lay entirely with the suit that his wife was presenting against him; Kempster testified in court against his employer. Interestingly enough, A.G. did not seem to protest this action at all, but agreed to the testimony in order to rush matters through and in fact, once the testimony was concluded, Kempster set sail for England to rejoin Alfred Gwynne as his valet. Kempster had enjoyed a long and confidential relationship with his employer, privy to all that happened within the family, and acting in a manner much larger than that of a typical body servant.[20]

Scandals of "beautiful young women and Vanderbilt grooms"[21] stirred up a mixture of mockery and gossip from both American and European society as Newport friends declared that the suit was the result of A.G.'s "loving his horses too well."[22] Initially leaders of their own social set, Alfred and Elsie apparently had drifted apart with a noticeable "lack of mutual good feeling between the young people."[23] An intimate friend of the family was quoted as saying that "Vanderbilt would leave a social function and the society of his wife anytime to look at a horse,"[24] while another added, "His horses have won him blue ribbons, but have lost a wife."[25] Friends of Mrs. Vanderbilt said that it was Elsie's desire to bring a speedy conclusion to the "anomalous relations"[26] she had with her husband in the past few months that had brought the case so quickly before Justice O'Gorman.

Apparently, in addition to his own "penchant"[27] for horsemanship and possible affair with an "unknown woman" strongly believed to be Mrs. Agnes Ruiz, Alfred Gwynne's entanglement with the Schenck affair had created a notoriety for the young man and his horse culture that was "extremely distasteful"[28] to his wife. The office of the County Clerk, which had carelessly misplaced some of the Vanderbilt divorce papers, emphatically denied any attempt to engage in secrecy.[29]

As rumors grew rampant, reporters stalked the entrance of Agnes' apartment on Grosvenor Street in London. Mrs. Ruiz refused to give interviews and to even discuss the Vanderbilt case.[30] Growing tired of incessant questions and of dodging interviews, Agnes asked the elevator boy William, "I wish that you would have this man go away,"[31] as reporters commented upon her "large blue eyes,"[32] "red cheeks,"[33] and general voluptuousness.

How much of the Vanderbilt millions would Elsie get through the divorce? She was a wealthy woman in her own right prior to her marriage to Alfred Gwynne Vanderbilt, being liberally bequeathed millions by her own father, Mr. Francis O. French, a wealthy railroad magnate and banker.[34] No reports were released at the suit. Not a single member of the Vanderbilt or French families attended the court proceedings. While no one in Newport society had foreseen the split, friends reported that A.G. had failed to call on his mother-in-law several times in the past two years and increasingly preferred the stables to the drawing room. His personal habits left much to be desired and displeased his wife, who would say that "Alfred has the instincts and breeding of a stable boy."[35]

Apparently Alice had reached out to her daughter-in-law in efforts to breach the gap and offer a way toward reconciliation, but the young woman had refused politely and only traveled to and from her lawyer's office, court room, and her uncle's residence, refusing to maintain her former relations with the Vanderbilt family. While her lawyers maintained a masterful silence and all matters relating to the entire affair were hushed up, Alice persisted, extending the olive branch to Elsie, and invited her to visit the *Breakers* for a luncheon. Mrs. Vanderbilt Sr. met with the young woman for several hours and after Elsie had left the mansion, Alice stated, "I still hope there will be no divorce."[36] While continuing to try to effect reconciliation[37] between her son and daughter-in-law, the elder Mrs. Vanderbilt also announced her immediate plans to travel to Paris and stay there for a while. With her daughter Gladys now a Countess in Europe and her son's affairs sordidly on display at home, Alice was eager to "abandon her native land"[38] because of the publicity that haunted the Vanderbilt name. A rumor also began to circulate that several of the detectives found spying on Madame Ruiz were said to be in the employment of Mrs. Vanderbilt Sr.

Other rumors as well began to surface about Elsie's relationships with other men such as Mr. Worthington Whitehouse;[39] all her male companions were apparently possible suitors in the imagination of the public. Soon after she obtained the public decree for divorce, the former Mrs. A.G. Vanderbilt would be free to enter a new matrimony. Mr. Whitehouse was a friend of Elsie's who had been in the party accompanying her on the fateful trip to the Adirondacks from Grand Central that had resulted in a calamitous wreck.

While Elsie gave her personal testimony before the referee behind closed doors,[40] with her statements based "upon information and belief"[41] and backed by strong witness accounts. It was believed that the entire testimony would provide sufficient evidence to win her case. No testimony was requested from the senior Mrs. Vanderbilt or from any other person in their social group.

There was a noticeable difference in the attitude of the respective counsels. While A.G. noticeably had no witnesses for his defense,[42] Elsie's lawyer, J.G. Milburn, from the firm of Carter, Ledyard and Milburn presented a strong case with five very convincing witnesses:

Harry Kempster, Alfred's personal servant, testified to the happenings aboard the *Wayfarer* during the Richmond and Norfolk Horse Shows. He also told the court about the sleeping arrangements aboard the *Wayfarer* as well as in the hotels they stayed in. He gave details of Agnes' New York apartment and attested to the couple's various inappropriate behaviors, including being seen often in their pajamas.

Thomas Benedict Clarke Jr., the Vice President of the Night And Day Bank, and a friend of Alfred's, discussed the half a dozen dinners and luncheons that he spent with Alfred and Agnes in the New York apartment on Lexington Ave. His testimony that he would often leave the two lovers alone at the end of the night, as well as the fact that he often saw them kiss in front of him, gave evidence of the affair.

William Pirie, the porter aboard the *Wayfarer*, verified the majority of Kempster's testimony as well as providing colorful stories such as finding a woman's nightdress in Mr. Vanderbilt's room.

William Wilkinson was the superintendent of Agnes' New York apartment and testified to the date that he sold it to her. He also revealed that she had procured the apartment under an assumed name and that Alfred was seen entering the apartment just two days after she initially rented it. He would visit several times a week, arriving around eight o'clock at night and not leaving until around nine o'clock the following morning.

Elsie offered two personal testimonies to McClure, despite the fact that her testimony was not actually necessary and her lawyers had not requested her to do so.[43] Her testimony was used only to prove the legitimacy of her case because at the time, New York law had three stipulations: the wife could not in any way be aware of or have procured the adultery; that she had not forgiven adultery in the past; and that she had not resided with her husband since she found out about said adultery. She verified all these requirements in her testimony.

Since the actual testimony was sealed to the public, the only sources available to newspapers were second hand accounts of the proceedings. Mrs. Vanderbilt was said to be a most compelling witness as she told the referee about a marriage broken by a sordid affair and how she had managed to maintain public appearances and prevent unwanted publicity for over a year. In fact, Elsie's testimony worked only to establish the required stipulations in New York State law. Elsie answered every question posed to her with a simple 'yes' or 'no'. Apparently, her discovery of her husband's infidelity resulted in a violent altercation at *Oakland Farm*, when she confronted him with stories she had heard, leading instantly to the joint decision to separate.[44] Though such a statement is not in the testimony at all, it is a curious one.

Many newspapers reported a fight at *Oakland Farms* previous to Elsie's departure, but in the testimony Elsie says that she hasn't spoken to Alfred since discovering the affair. She claims to not know the identity of the woman with whom her husband is "guilty of improper relations"[45] and she has not "cohabited with him as man and wife…since the discovery or knowledge of these facts."[46] She testifies that she was only convinced something was wrong when he sent word that he would not return home from Europe. At this time she says she went to her lawyer who said that he would find out "the real reasons of his neglect."[47] She states very clearly at the end of her testimony that there was absolutely no communication between she and Alfred after he sent word that "he wouldn't be returning from Europe."[48] If that's the truth, how could they possibly have had a row at *Oakland Farms* about his affair? Clearly there was something going on behind the scenes of the trial.

Another curious aspect of the trial was that Alfred's lawyer, Henry B. Anderson from Anderson & Anderson, barely put up a fight. He did not ask many questions, sometimes even waving his right to a cross-examination. It was obvious that Alfred had told him not to protest so as to extend the proceedings. When the time came for Anderson to present the defense, he asked for a "motion to dismiss the complaint on the ground that the evidence does not prove any act of adultery of my client."[49] The referee then asked, "You mean directly?" The motion was denied. The testimony offered was indisputable. The only evidence lacking was a witness actually catching Alfred and Agnes in the act, but even that wasn't necessary based on the other evidence provided. After the motion was denied, Anderson said, "I have no testimony to offer. Defendant rests."[50]

Elsie's complaint against her husband's infidelity mentioned only one person directly, with accusations of multiple deeds of misconduct at numerous places, to which his lawyers only offered a general denial. It seemed that Alfred was fully supportive of hastening proceedings as quickly as possible. Most assumed that he was complaisant largely due to Mrs. A.G. Vanderbilt's willingness to settle for a moderate financial arrangement proposed by his lawyers.[51] But for the amount of bad publicity that Alfred got for the divorce, it's odd that he was so cooperative throughout the whole process.

New details about the divorce case leaked out. Apparently, the depositions offered on behalf of Mrs. A. G. Vanderbilt exceeded the allowable limit[52] and Alfred had requested specifically that certain names be kept out of the case. It certainly was a well-oiled hearing.

Alice reacted with intense displeasure to not only the scandal and divorce proceedings, but also to Alfred. Two significant changes occurred: she forgave and accepted Neily, her eldest son, once again as the head of family, restoring his position, and offering him absolute forgiveness for marrying Grace Wilson. In comparison to A.G.'s union, theirs was considered one of the "happiest unions in the social set."[53] Alice also added a codicil to her own will, bequeathing a share formerly destined for Alfred to Cornelius and his wife, while removing Alfred Gwynne from the inheritance altogether.

Divorce apparently was the new rage. Alfred's cousin Willie Kissam Vanderbilt Jr., in the weeks to come, would separate formally from his wife Virginia Fair. His relationship had been rapidly deteriorating for months. Soon after his arrival from Havana on his yacht *Tarantula,* Willie K. was purportedly full of advice, waxing eloquently about the difficulties inherent in relationships:

> 'Men and women of to-day,' he said, 'live in the strenuous atmosphere that will not endure any one thing for long. Marriage is one of the things that can only continue pleasantly with the simple life.'[54]

As the reporter persisted in questioning and asked the impudent question whether A.G. was responsible for the tangled web of scandals and confusion surrounding his own divorce, Willie K. grew furious, demanding that the reporter leave the *Tarantula*, and allegedly pushing him down the gangway, nearly drowning him.[55]

Hot on the heels of this announcement, Florence Schenck also filed suit for divorce, against Charles Wilson for breach of promise of marriage in the amount of $100,000.[56] Wilson immediately denied all such allegations, proclaiming that he was already married and now was a subject of the King of England and therefore couldn't be tried in an American court.[57]

As for Madame Ruiz, or Flores as she was known in London circles, reporters had followed her every move so closely that she was forced to lead a different lifestyle, entering and exiting buildings from side and back entrances, jumping into cars parked away from her home to avoid suspicion, with her face swathed in numerous veils to conceal her appearance.[58]

In whose custody would the young boy William Henry be placed? Elsie insisted that her son be left in her charge and allowed paternal visits as deemed appropriate by the court.[59] Alfred conceded her right to gain parental control for their son, with visitation rights for Alfred.[60] A.G.'s response to his wife's anger was one of complacence. He did not refute her allegations nor did he try to compel her to stay in their sham of a marriage. The only substantial issue remaining was the financial settlement.

Alfred Gwynne proposed that his wife take possession of the original securities he had given her in the amount of $1,500,000. Though, with the bank failure in 1907, the value of the stocks had dropped, lowering the fortune to $1,000,000, A.G. proposed raising his offer to $2,000,000.[61] Elsie however would not accept his proposal, deeming it too low. She demanded no less than ten million dollars.

Mrs. Vanderbilt's future plans for occupancy were to alternate between *Tuck's Eden* and her mother's villa *Harbor View* in Newport.[62] She also planned to assist in the wedding of her niece Miss. Pauline O. French to Samuel Wagstaff[63] at Hallidan Hall.[64] She would never return again to *Oakland Farms*. As the taking of the testimony had been concluded with a resulting report drawn and the decision of Vanderbilt divorce case to be announced the following day, Elsie declared her own travels abroad. She would be taking her little son William Henry to the south of France[65] apparently for his health during the middle of the summer. Mrs. A.G. Vanderbilt also did not refrain from attending public events, serving as a patron of the workhorse parade for the *American Society for the Prevention of Cruelty to Animals.*[66]

Rumors continued to mill about that A.G. and Elsie would possibly reconcile. When she heard this, Elsie said to a personal friend:

> I know that there is talk of a reconciliation and separation instead of a divorce. It's all bosh. When I saw my husband with that woman, I felt that I had done all that a woman could do.[67]

Another week dragged on and Elsie was still waiting upon the judge's decision, after being informed for the fourth time that she would receive it any day. As she waited, she had to deal with her mother-in-law trying to convince her to hold off on a final divorce. Tired of speaking to the press herself, a man closely connected to her legal and business affairs indignantly addressed the press on her behalf:

> Mrs. A. G. Vanderbilt refused to abandon proceedings, and justly so. I think Alfred ought to be taught a lesson, and I have so advised members of the family.[68]

Newport society was turning against Alfred; they demanded that he receive his comeuppance for his outrageous behavior. His complaisance and the publicity surrounding his adulterous affair frightened many of the social elite. They were threatened by the scandalous nature of the divorce proceedings. Alfred's complaisance towards the process of divorce was now accepted and rapidly adopted by many members of their set.

Elsie too was not free from criticism:

> Time was when a society woman seeking a divorce also sought seclusion from social affairs. It was a state of mourning or semi-mourning state, and was observed rigidly by both parties. . . . But all this is relegated to the past. Nowadays the host or hostess infers that her guests speculate on the divorce only when they are reading the papers. Women in the inner circle of the most exclusive sets entertain as freely while waiting on their decrees as they did in the days when the domestic sky was clear and cloudless. Impending divorces is no longer considered a bar to entertainment these busy days. Mrs. Alfred G. Vanderbilt will give a dinner for fifty people at Newport next Saturday.[69]

The elder Mrs. Vanderbilt finally gave up trying to reconcile the marriage on May 10, 1908, declaring that she had failed in her mission:

> The quicker the matter is settled, the better it will be for all concerned. I regret my failure.[70]

Elsie offered her own comments about the situation:

> My mother-in-law has been everything to me during these trying times and she thinks that she can make Alfred see things in a different light. I did not have the heart to tell her that under no consideration would I ever live with Mr. Vanderbilt again. I consented to her making one more effort. She has failed in her effort, as I knew she would before she went abroad.[71]

Referee David McClure had delayed his report to Justice O'Gorman upon Mrs. Cornelius Vanderbilt's request but would now move forward to permit the final proceedings. By May 19th, McClure submitted his report to the judge and also turned it over to the attorneys for review as they made final arrangements for a money settlement agreeable to both parties.[72] New light was cast upon Elsie's supposed demand for a ten million dollar settlement as she sought the fortune for their child William Henry and not for herself.

However, A.G. did not want to put aside ten million dollars of his fortune at that date because it would drastically affect his own income at the time, which had been severely reduced in the bank failures and resultant stock market fluctuations of the prior year to $800,000.[73] Vanderbilt had apparently

Elsie French, in this post divorce photograph dated 1919 by Alman and Company, 500 5th Avenue, New York, Elsie appears to have aged beautifully. She was accepted by society immediately after the divorce, more than could be said for Alfred whose reputation would take endless blows precipitated by his conduct. Society feared that the Vanderbilt divorce might undermine the very institution of marriage.

also borrowed significantly, tying up use of his securities for up to ten years. Hence, he would lose access to immediate cash if he put aside that large a sum for his son. It was at the request of the attorneys for both parties that the final report from McClure was delayed for more than three weeks.[74] While Alfred tried to stall, directing his lawyers by cablegram, Elsie traveled to New York[75] and issued a warlike decree through her attorneys the following day to fight to secure her child's right to the Vanderbilt fortune:

> Mrs. Vanderbilt will go on with the matter to the end. She will not be satisfied with what the court might agree to settle on her. Justice O'Gorman might offer her a million. This Mrs. Vanderbilt does not want and will not take. It is agreed among those who know that Alfred will marry again. Mrs. Vanderbilt is not going to have her child denied his rights to a proper share of the Vanderbilt millions.[76]

Alfred countered, "Ye agreed not to agree two years ago and that being true, I am willing to settle $1,500,000 on my wife. But the settlement must be in the shape of securities and based on the valuation at the time our differences started."[77] At the time the offer was made, New York Central stock had sunk to $93 from $156 which would bring the settlement to an unacceptable $900,000. The next day the referee's report was delivered to Justice O'Gorman and "all the papers in the case were at once sealed and filed."[78] Mrs. Vanderbilt's attorneys immediately moved that the report be confirmed, implying a favorable outcome for Elsie.[79] Without the finality of a financial agreement, Supreme Court Justice O'Gorman granted Elsie an interlocutory decree of divorce in her favor. As the verdict was announced to the public two days later, A.G.'s financial arrangements, while not involving the transfer of ten million dollars, were considered "extremely liberal."[80]

Not everyone was sympathetic to Alfred's predicament, as evidenced by this popular statement frequenting the press: "Alfred G. Vanderbilt says his income is less than a million a year; but some of us have been known to pull through on a little less than that."[81]

The ultimate financial settlement was revealed; Elsie received $5,000,000 in trust for her son.[82] Elsie now had regained her freedom[83] along with a personal victory over her husband, while securing the financial fortune of her young son. Soon after the final divorce proceedings were announced, Miss French began to renovate her mother's villa at *Harbor View,*[84] while acquiring a farm outside of Newport with the intention of raising horses for competition as rumors ran rampant that she would go head to head in competition with her former husband on the tanbark.[85]

The divorce was almost over. Alfred seemed to be in the clear, but everything that had occurred seemed to have greatly altered the young Vanderbilt.

Those around him noticed a great character change over recent years. They hypothesized that living so long in the coaching world had changed him, corrupting the very core of the gentleman that he was:

> Even Vanderbilt's most intimate friends, who have long tried in vain to make him break away from his debauchery, frankly admit that Alfred Gwynne's reckless dissipation has changed him utterly.
>
> From a shy, pleasant, courteous, youth, whose polish and perfect manners at first made him a favorite among older men, Alfred Vanderbilt has degenerated to a mere husk of his former self. His face is heavy and scared; his jaw and mouth have become hard, and in every way the present head of the Vanderbilt house and chief controller of the greatest fortune in America, reflects in his exterior the brutalizing effects of a hard fast life.[86]

NOTES

1. *The Chicago Daily Tribune*. "Mrs. Vanderbilt Sues for Divorce." April 2, 1908. Pg. 4.
2. *The Washington Post*. "Vanderbilt Is Sued." April 2, 1908. Pg. 1.
3. *The Chicago Daily Tribune*. "Mrs. Vanderbilt Sues for Divorce." April 2, 1908. Pg. 4.
4. Ibid.
5. Ibid.
6. *The Hartford Courant*. "Vanderbilts Part; Wife Brings Suit." April 2, 1908. Pg. 1.
7. *Oakland Tribune*. "Mrs. Alfred Gwynne Vanderbilt Sues for an Absolute Divorce." April 2, 1908: 16.
8. *The Hartford Courant*. "Vanderbilts Part; Wife Brings Suit." April 2, 1908. Pg.1.
9. *Oakland Tribune*."Mrs. Alfred Gwynne Vanderbilt Sues for an Absolute Divorce." April 2, 1908. Pg. 16.
10. Ibid.
11. *The New York Times*. "Mrs. A. G. Vanderbilt Sues for Divorce." April 2, 1908. Pg. 1.
12. *The Washington Post*. "Mrs. Ruiz A Suicide." June 11, 1909. Pg. 5.
13. *The Washington Post*. "Vanderbilt Is Sued." April 2, 1908. Pg. 1.
14. *The Chicago Daily Tribune*. "Mrs. Vanderbilt Sues for Divorce." April 2, 1908. Pg. 4.
15. Ibid.
16. *Oakland Tribune*. "Mrs. Alfred Gwynne Vanderbilt Sues for an Absolute Divorce." April 2, 1908. Pg. 16.
17. Ibid.
18. *The Los Angeles Times*. "Vanderbilt to Give Wife Five Millions." April 3, 1908. Pg. 11.

19. *The Atlanta Constitution.* "Mrs. Vanderbilt in Hurry to Secure Her Divorce." April 3, 1908. Pg. 1.
20. *The Washington Post.* "$10,000,000 for Wife." April 4, 1908. Pg. 3.
21. Ibid.
22. Ibid.
23. Ibid.
24. Ibid.
25. Ibid.
26. *The Washington Post.* "$10,000,000 for Wife." April 4, 1908. Pg. 3.
27. *The Los Angeles Times.* "Vanderbilt to Give Wife Five Millions." April 3, 1908. Pg. 11.
28. Ibid.
29. *The New York Times.* "Vanderbilt to Defend Suit." April 3, 1908. Pg. 9.
30. *The Chicago Daily Tribune.* "Vanderbilt Stand Scares Society." April 3, 1908. Pg. 2.
31. *The Los Angeles Times.* "Vanderbilt to Give Wife Five Millions." April 3, 1908. Pg. 11.
32. Ibid.
33. Ibid.
34. *The Chicago Daily Tribune.* "Referee Shields Mrs. Vanderbilt." April 5, 1908. Pg. 3.
35. *Oakland Tribune.* "Mrs. Alfred Gwynne Vanderbilt Sues for an Absolute Divorce." April 2, 1908. Pg.16.
36. *The Chicago Daily Tribune.* "Mrs. Vanderbilt Gives Testimony." April 4, 1908. Pg. 3.
37. *The Los Angeles Times.* "With the Four Hundred: Vanderbilts May Make Up." April 22, 1908. Pg. 11.
38. Ibid.
39. Ibid.
40. *The Los Angeles Times.* "Dame Gossip's Tongue Wags." April 4, 1908. Pg. 12.
41. *The Chicago Daily Tribune.* "Mrs. Vanderbilt Gives Testimony." April 4, 1908. Pg. 3.
42. *The Chicago Daily Tribune.* "Vanderbilt Troubles Old." April 11, 1908. Pg. 5.
43. *The Chicago Daily Tribune.* "Vanderbilts Part When Cash Fails." April 7, 1908. Pg. 5.
44. *The Washington Post.* "Money Halts Divorce." April 11, 1908. Pg. 3.
45. *Ellen F. Vanderbilt Vs. Alfred G. Vanderbilt.* No. 1908-2273. Supreme Court of the State of New York, New York County. 2 April 1908. Pg. 45.
46. Ibid. Pg. 46.
47. Ibid. Pg. 47.
48. Ibid. Pg. 46.
49. Ibid.
50. Ibid. Pg. 90.
51. *The Chicago Daily Tribune.* "Referee Shields Mrs. Vanderbilt." April 5, 1908. Pg. 3.

52. *The Chicago Daily Tribune*. "Breakers Ahead for Vanderbilt." April 6, 1908. Pg. 11.
53. *The Chicago Daily Tribune*. "Referee Shields Mrs. Vanderbilt." April 5, 1908. Pg. 3.
54. *The Washington Post*. "Suggests Simple Life: W.K. Vanderbilt Says It's Way to be Married Happily." April 23, 1908. Pg. 1.
55. Ibid.
56. *The Washington Post*. "Denies Promise to Wed Her." April 8. 1908. Pg. 9.
57. *Boston Daily Globe*. "Wilson Denies All." April 8, 1908. Pg. 11.
58. Ibid.
59. *The Los Angeles Times*. "Dame Gossip's Tongue Wags." April 4, 1908. Pg. 12.
60. Ibid.
61. *Boston Daily Globe*. "Mrs. Vanderbilt to Get Divorce." April 10, 1908. Pg. 1.
62. *Boston Daily Globe*. "Returns to Newport." April14, 1908. Pg. 13.
63. *The Washington Post*. "Money Halts Divorce." April 11, 1908. Pg. 3.
64. *The New York Times*. "A.G. Vanderbilt Returns in Summer." April 12, 1908. Pg. 11.
65. *The New York Times*. "Mrs. A.G. Vanderbilt is Going Abroad." April 19, 1908. Pg. 6.
66. *The New York Times*. April 17, 1908. Pg. 6.
67. *The Washington Post*. "Mrs. Vanderbilt's Rival." April 26, 1908. Pg. 3.
68. *The Washington Post*. "Chat of Well-Known People." April 28, 1908. Pg. 7.
69. *The Washington Post*. "Chat of Well-Known People." May 1, 1908. Pg. 7.
70. *The Los Angeles Times*. "Son Will Not Listen to Her." May 11, 1908. Pg. I1.
71. *The Washington Post*. "Social Gossip." May 12, 1908. Pg. 7.
72. *The Chicago Daily Tribune*. "Vanderbilt Divorce Sure?" May 19, 1908. Pg.1.
73. Ibid.
74. *Boston Daily Globe*. "Money Delays." May 19, 1908. Pg. 6.
75. *The New York Times*. "Mrs. A.G. Vanderbilt Here." May 20, 1908. Pg. 1.
76. *The Washington Post*. "Will Fight for Child." May 20, 1908.
77. Ibid.
78. Ibid.
79. *The Washington Post*. "Vanderbilt Papers Sealed." May 22, 1908. Pg. 1.
80. *The Los Angeles Times*. "Favors Divorce of Vanderbilts." May 22, 1908. Pg. 12.
81. *The Atlanta Constitution*. May 23, 1908. Pg. 6.
82. *Boston Daily Globe*. "Settles for $5,000,000." May 23, 1908. Pg. 7.
83. *The Washington Post*. "Mrs. Vanderbilt Free." May 26, 1908. Pg. 3.
84. *The New York Times*. "Mrs. Vanderbilt's Plans." May 29, 1908. Pg. 7.
85. *The Washington Post*. May 25, 1908. Pg. 7.
86. *Oakland Tribune*. "Mrs. Alfred Gwynne Vanderbilt Sues for an Absolute Divorce." April 2, 1908. Pg.16.

Chapter Ten

The Brighton Road

Growing tired of incessant reporters badgering him about his impending divorce, Alfred plainly stated that he had no intention of discussing his private affairs for them to publish.[1] He did offer to share information about his new coaching venture along the Brighton Road. A.G.'s arrival in London had evoked tremendous interest from the English public[2] who were curious about his latest pursuit of driving a coach from the Victoria Hotel at Charing Cross in London south to the quaint village of Brighton by the sea, more than fifty odd miles away.[3] Londoners expressed interest in visiting Brighton to witness his triumphant arrival on the first leg of his journey. A seat next to the young man was appealing not only for the inspiring views of the countryside, but also for the close companionship with a peculiarly interesting millionaire. The public was fascinated that A.G. revealed a "hint of atavism"[4] in his actions by returning to a slower and antiquated method of transportation when he was the heir of an expansive empire built upon speed. Unlike his native land, where his name stewed in a quagmire of scandal and gossip, England offered Alfred a refreshing friendliness mingled with some respect. In general, the feelings towards him, while skeptical at times, were positive and even admiring:

> We are all greatly interested in young Mr. Vanderbilt's business experiment. The English people themselves frequently say they need an infusion of new, vigorous young blood in their public life. . . . Very few men would care to drive six horses a day more than sixty miles every day. It is a good test of patience and endurance, and requires both nerve and skill, and we hope Mr. Vanderbilt when he balances his books at the end of the coaching season, will find a profit.[5]

Steeped in history and English traditions, the Brighton Road has long captured the imagination of many a record-breaker and outdoor enthusiast, who enjoys the diverse landscape and picturesque towns from London southward to the sea. The main route begins at the south side of the Westminster Bridge and continues past the towns of Croydon, Redhill, Horley, Crawley, and Cuckfield, covering 51.5 miles in length.[6] Winding lanes past medieval churches, quaint villages, historic residences, and town squares lead the traveler to the Sussex coast. As a new member of the prestigious Four-in-Hand Coaching Club of England, A.G. Vanderbilt was eager to restore interest in the glorious tradition of coaching along the Brighton road[7].

> The spirit of all these whips is part and parcel of Vanderbilt's enthusiasm in his British experiment, but he scores over all other American whips in being the first amateur to take the English road with American horses and an American coach.[8]

In 1821, forty coaches were running daily to and from London to Brighton and by 1826, the tidy sum of £40,000 was the yearly profit from passenger fares.[9] At the pinnacle of the coaching era in 1833, 480 people rode as passengers on one day;[10] a trifle sum in comparison to rail travel but a significant number for coaching, more than triple the number from a few years back. However, in just six years, new developments in technology, such as the steam engine, radically altered public opinion. Stock in coaches dropped significantly and coaching as a practice began a steady decline. Railroads dominated transportation and as the nineteenth century drew to a close, the beginning of a new era without horses dawned in England.

While most Londoners embraced the speed of the new rail lines, there were some such as John Ruskin, the prolific writer, who opposed what they viewed as the destruction of the countryside:

> There was a valley between Buxton and Bakewell, once upon a time as divine as the vale of Tempe; . . . You enterprised a railroad through the valley – you blasted its rocks away, heaped thousands of tons of shale into its lovely stream. The valley is gone and the Gods with it, and now, every fool in Buxton can be at Bakewell in half-an-hour, and every fool in Bakewell at Buxton; which you think a lucrative process of exchange – you Fools everywhere.[11]

Full-blooded sportsmen, however, continued to be drawn to the Brighton Road, whose length at approximately fifty miles offered alluring opportunities for competitions and for testing out new theories and modes of transportation. The Prince of Wales set the first record for horseback riding, making it from London to Brighton and back in ten hours. Other records included walking the entire distance and travel via bicycle or Hobby Horse. It made perfect sense then that the Brighton Road, clothed in rich history and tradition, would evoke the interest of someone like Alfred Gwynne Vanderbilt. A.G. could relate to the English coaching tradition on many levels. He admired their love of form and tradition, as well as the inviting historic journey through time along the Brighton road. Alfred's coaching efforts revived interest[12] in the equestrian pursuit.

A battered old milestone with the inscription "Horseguards Whitehall" marked the beginning of the trip to Brighton from London by the Westminster Bridge.[13] A circuitous road at times, the path wends its way past churches of often "decadent Gothic delicacy,"[14] medieval castles, winding over a suspension bridge, traversing switchbacks,[15] and through tunnels. The remnants of Anglo Saxon tradition filled these areas[16] and London coaches passed by tiny and picturesque villages unspoiled in their beauty and rustic silence. The road widened generously by the larger town of Crawley[17], known more for its hotels and pubs than private cottages till it reached Hand Cross, a village of numerous houses where several roads intersected in a "delightful land of forests."[18] At Hand Cross, the road split, offering two routes; one called the Bolney and Hickstead course and the other by Cuckfield down to Staplefield Common.[19]

A.G.'s plan of action followed the antique path by Cuckfield, a pleasant town with lovely hills and romantic residences, ending in Jacob's Post,[20] an area shrouded in mystery and legends of Gothic ghosts. From there, the winding road went past Friar's Oak to South Downs via the Clayton tunnel and past sheep farmers with their Pyecombe crooks tending sheep in Clayton Hills. As the coachman came upon the Clayton Hill, the Sussex region was in panoramic view and from there, the last leg of the journey to Brighton was relatively quick.

By the time A.G. decided to embark upon his new coaching venture in England, the last coach still operating on the Brighton Road, the *Vigilant*, ceased service.[21] In April of 1908, Alfred embarked upon a series of trial runs along the Brighton Road in his four-in-hand coach *Venture*, painted a rich royal red with white spoke wheels; all of which were followed enthusiastically by thousands of locals with a "veritable ovation"[22] of seven hours, almost the entire journey from the Berkeley Hotel in London to the Metropole in Brighton.[23] Leaving at eleven a.m. sharply, pulling his team of grays at a "spanking trot," A.G. attired fashionably in a fawn coaching coat with pearl buttons and a silk hat. Seated next to him was the coaching guard Walter Gadden, famous in coaching circles for accompanying James Selby during his historic record-breaking trip to Brighton aboard the *Old Times* coach.[24] The thousands of thronging spectators blocked traffic, resulting in policemen shutting down Piccadilly Street until the coach passed through, while enormous cheers broke out amidst the crowds.

Vanderbilt dispelled rumors that he would attempt to break Selby's record of 3 hours and 54 minutes along his return journey from the southern coast

Charles Wilson (left) and Alfred (right) Published in the Bystander, April 29, 1908.

Vanderbilt at the ribbons on his first London to Brighton trip. He is atop the Meteor in April 1908 apparently in Piccadilly. He had not yet instituted regular service and this was a trial run. He made eight team changes in the course of the trip. To provide teams he had brought over some sixty horses.

back to London. Instead, he spoke to the British and American press about his interest in reviving coaching practice in England. When asked why he chose the Brighton road, A.G. replied at length:

> "The distance between London and Brighton, fifty-two miles, makes a nice day's run, and that is why this route has been selected. In addition, it runs through one of the prettiest sections in England, and the driving will be all the more attractive.
>
> "I shall drive for about six weeks, and as I have accepted the invitation of the Olympia Horse Show management as a judge, I shall discontinue the driving a couple of days before the show opens. I am anxious to show the English horsemen that the American-bred trotters are the best for coaching purposes, and I am sure I can do so with the horses I have over there."[25]

Alfred also announced a thorough schedule as well as advertisements in local British papers with pictorial representations, fees, timetable, and a sketch

Alfred in top hat with unknown hand at stables. He was caught in a nether world between the responsibilities of phenomenal wealth and the life of his stable community. He seemed to settle in neither place trapped in a world where his stable hands knew enough to keep him at bay while he rejected the responsibilities bestowed upon him by his inheritance.

of a four-in-hand going at a swift, steady pace. Beginning at the Victoria Hotel in London and ending at the Metropole in Brighton, the Venture would harness sixty horses changing at eight stops along its course, stopping at fourteen inns in between and seating up to twelve passengers at a time.[26] A.G.'s coach also introduced the powerful American trotting horse to England, a development which horse merchants were eager to exploit. The Vanderbilt millionaire also announced that his horses would be sold at Tattersall's on June 25th.[27]

The young Vanderbilt's coaching efforts did not go unappreciated. Many Brits expressed their encouragement, with encomiums such as:

> "That a millionaire should come over to this country to revive an Old World method of traveling for the sheer pleasure of it is a high tribute to the fascination of coaching. Mr. Vanderbilt's arrangements are on a scale so complete that little is left to chance as concerns the running of the Venture. . . . Whether Mr. Vanderbilt's generous lead will be taken up on other old coaching roads remains to be seen. It is to be hoped that more enthusiasts, even in these hustling times, will be found with the wealth, leisure, and interest necessary to help to bring back the glories of the English road."[28]

On the 1908 and 1909 London to Brighton trips Vanderbilt provided miniature copies of the a book entitled "The Brighton Road" "Souvenir of The Venture" By Charles G. Harper (published by Anthony Treherne and Co., Ltd., 1906) complete with maps and illustrations. Within its 2 ¼ and 3 ½ inches a folded map with 324 pages of instructions detailed the 51 ½ miles "... measured from the south side of Westminster Bridge to the Aquarium."

Two of Alfred's horses being delivered to England. Some said that the horses were better housed on the ship than the people.

Vanderbilt's famous greys. This photograph was part of a souvenir photograph album given by Alfred Vanderbilt to his passengers from 1910 to 1914. Each included his photograph and a changing selection of images along the London to Brighton route. This particular photo volume and the others that are included here (16A-D) were included in a volume provided to May Barwell.

Two of Alfred's horses becoming acclimated at the farm in England.

Beginning in May of 1908 Alfred launched a regular service from London's Victoria Hotel to the seaside village of Brighton.

Coach on the road "twixt Dorking and Horsham" with Alfred at the whip. This photograph was part of a souvenir book given by Alfred Vanderbilt to May Barwell.

Coach Venture, Walter Fodden, Guard and Alfred Vanderbilt, Proprietor-whip. May 1908 on the Brighton Road after the initial trial runs. Library of Congress. Bain Collection

Alfred Gwynne's test runs along the Brighton Road were successful, and with delight he told a New York Times reporter:

> "In making my test trial over the route we shall travel with the coach, I could well appreciate how delightful were the old English coaching days. Sitting upon the seat of the phaeton and driving a pair of horses, even without the picturesque buglers, really proved a pleasure hard to surpass when one is on the old Brighton road."[29]

He also offered the *Venture*'s daily schedule, leaving the hotel Victoria promptly at 11 a.m. and reaching Brighton by 5:30 p.m. giving passengers enough time to catch a train if they wished fifteen minutes later back to London. A.G. expressed also his desire to drive the coach every day if he could and if he could not, his manager would drive instead.

Alfred Gwynne's first test on the Brighton Road was deemed a success and heartily cheered from its beginning right to the very end.[30] He would begin regular passage by the end of May. Great crowds enthusiastically crowded the route, cheering the resuscitation of heritage at every hitching post where horses were exchanged, as they encircled A.G. as a champion driver, akin to the former days of coaching glory.

Waiting outside the Victoria Hotel, Alfred was mistaken by a passenger for an attendant, who handing him his umbrella, requested, "Here my good man hold my umbrella until I get up, will you?"[31] Politely, the young millionaire accepted the umbrella as the passenger comfortably took his seat in A.G.'s coach, and then handed it back to him.

From its conception, the Coaching Club in London consisted of young full-blooded amateur whips, part of the "coterie of the Prince Regent"[32] who drew up plans for coaching and held regular meets in Hyde Park by the Marble Arch. Two years later, one of the first Americans to ride a coach in England, Mr. George William Tiffany, ran two coaches along the Brighton Road. It made perfect sense, in keeping with tradition, that Alfred, as a new member and active whip, would choose the same route.[33]

By the time A.G. came upon the scene, road coaching was a summer pastime of gentlemen and had lost the interest of the public, more fascinated with speedier modes of transportation.[34] Yet, the announcement of two intriguing foreign coaches, Alfred Gwynne's *Venture* from Piccadilly along the Brighton Road, as well as Señor Martinez de Hoz's *Reliance* coach on the Guilford route, breathed fresh life into the ancient sport. The induction of these two men into the Coaching Club at the Ritz Hotel was followed with great interest by the press and the public turned out in record numbers to all the coaching meets,[35] in hopes of meeting the foreigners.

Martinez de Hoz was not a contestant to easily forget since he was known for being the greatest stockbreeder in his native country. Unlike A.G. who insisted upon driving his own coach, having shaved off his mustache and attired in severe clothes, "horsy"[36] tie, silk hat, and driving coat, resembling a typical coachman, Martinez de Hoz had selected Ernest Fownes, a son of a famous whip Edwin Fownes, and a coaching celebrity in his own right. Of the two men, the young Vanderbilt millionaire again had the upper hand, because of the familiarity of his name and availability as an eligible bachelor once again, enjoying popularity with his coach greater than that accorded to the royal family's processions. Sitting next to A.G. in the box seat was considered the "ambition of a good many London society women;"[37] a position that charged an extra fee and was sold a "considerable time in advance."[38]

It was not just the English public who flocked to his coach; the *Venture* attracted his younger brother Reginald and his wife during their summer trip abroad to Europe and Newport friend James R. Deering with his new bride. Attired in a pale blue costume, Mrs. Reginald Vanderbilt occupied the box seat next to Alfred Gwynne, looking as "pleased as punch"[39] as Reggie helped her up the ladder to her spot. Other guests included Mrs. J.C. King and Craig W. Wadsworth, an embassy secretary based in London. It was a full convoy of American guests that day and enthusiastic, cheering crowds greeted every changing of the horses. Deering was ecstatic about the ovation greeting their coach:

> "My wife and I have been in Europe on our honeymoon ever since our wedding in March, but we haven't seen an American arouse so much enthusiasm as Alfred Vanderbilt with his coach since our departure. I am sure other Americans on the coach the day we made the trip were, with myself, proud of Mr. Vanderbilt's all-American turnout."[40]

While London's metropolis continued to expand at an exponential rate, Brighton remained a small, quaint town. The coaching experience would be historic for Alfred and he was keenly aware of it, as well as the timeless quality of the region:

> But Brighton itself is eternal. It suffers change, it grows continually; but while the sea remains and the air is clean and the sun shines on it, and the road to it, will be the most popular resorts in England.[41]

NOTES

1. *The Washington Post*. "Americans in London." April 12, 1908. Pg. 19.
2. *The New York Times*. "Vanderbilt Coach on Time." May 5, 1908. Pg. 4.
3. *The New York Times*. "American Industry Abroad." May 6, 1908. Pg. 6.
4. Ibid.
5. Ibid.
6. Harper, Charles G. *The Brighton Road: The Classic Highway to the South*. London: C. Tinley & Co. Ltd. Third Edition. 1922. Pg. 1.

7. *The New York Times*. "Alfred Vanderbilt Will Drive Coach." March 29, 1908. Pg. S3.
8. *The Washington Post*. "Vanderbilt to tool Trotters to His Coach on Famed Brighton Road." March 15, 1908. PG. S3.
9. Ibid. Pg. 34.
10. Ibid. Pg. 37.
11. Ruskin, John. *Praeterita*.
12. *Boston Daily Globe*. "While Piccadilly Halts." April 22, 1908. Pg. 4.
13. Harper, Charles G. *The Brighton Road: The Classic Highway to the South*. London: C. Tinley & Co. Ltd. Third Edition. 1922. Pg. 128-9.
14. Ibid. Pg. 140.
15. Ibid. Pg. 148.
16. Ibid. Pg. 148.
17. Ibid. Pg. 184.
18. Ibid. Pg. 199.
19. Ibid. Pg. 200.
20. Ibid. Pg. 235.
21. Carder, Tim. *The Encyclopaedia of Brighton. Lewes: East Sussex County Council.*1991.
22. *The New York Times*. "Thousands Cheer Alfred Vanderbilt." April 23, 1908. Pg. 4.
23. Ibid.
24. Ibid.
25. *The New York Times*. "Alfred Vanderbilt Will Drive Coach." March 29, 1908. Pg. S3.
26. *The Washington Post*. March 22, 1908. Pg. R19.
27. *The Washington Post*. Feb. 19, 1908. Pg. 3.
28. *The Washington Post*. "Vanderbilt Coach Welcome in England." May 22, 1906. Pg. C2.
29. *The New York Times*. "Alfred Gwynne Vanderbilt, His Horses, and His Coach." April 19, 1908. Pg. C1.
30. *The New York Times*. "Vanderbilt Coach on Time." May 5, 1908. Pg. 4.
31. *The Washington Post*. "Social Gossip." May 2, 1908. Pg. 7.
32. Ryder, Tom. "The History of the Coaching Club: 1871-2000." London: J.A. Allen. 1999. Pg. 3.
33. Ibid. Pg. 4.
34. Ibid. Pg. 71.
35. Ibid.
36. *The Washington Post*. "Social Gossip." May 2, 1908. Pg. 7.
37. *The Chicago Daily Tribune*. "Yankee Girl May Get a Rothschild." May 24, 1908. Pg. A2.
38. Ibid.
39. *The Washington Post*. "Social Gossip." May 6, 1908. Pg. 7.
40. *The New York Times*. "London Greets Many American Visitors." May 10, 1908. Pg. C2.
41. Ibid. Pg. 272.

Chapter Eleven

A Reputation to Defend

While A.G. was in the full swing of his coaching schedule, Elsie, despite her first enthusiasm for hosting events, withdrew from the public eye. She purchased a home in Chester, N.H. and planned on visiting New York and Newport only to see family. Her friends declared that Elsie was becoming a recluse, and was "bitterly disappointed in life"[1] and "was not resolved to marry again."[2] Since the man she had known and trusted since childhood had "proved false to her, none other was to be trusted."[3]

Madame Ruiz was stirring up controversy in her own right. Her husband sought divorce and an entire column of the *Washington Post*[4] became devoted to discussion of her social entanglements. Señor Antonio Ruiz had employed the services of a high profile Park avenue attorney George Young Bauchle on his behalf to pursue divorce on statutory grounds,[5] bearing a striking resemblance to the former Mrs. A.G. Vanderbilt's suit that was granted one month prior.

Mary Agnes Ruiz however could not be found. Apparently, she occupied apartments all over New York, London, and Paris. Considered highly skilled among equestrian society, Mrs. Ruiz was seen riding her fine horses through Central Park. She had been separated from her husband for no less than three years and Señor Ruiz had no idea where she was. However, in the aftermath of the Vanderbilt divorce case, Señor Ruiz pursued his own divorce proceedings against his wife, demanding also that action be taken against an unknown man of high social standing, who he alleged, had alienated the affections of his wife.[6]

A few days after the divorce proceedings began, Bauchle and his team of lawyers found Agnes in a villa near Port Chester on Pelham Bay about twenty-five miles from New York City.[7] Waited upon by a coachman, footman, and maid, with six full-blooded thoroughbreds at her disposal, she appeared to be happy, outgoing, and social; attending parties and riding her horses. The contents of the divorce papers were also revealed: absolute divorce based on statutory grounds for events that occurred at her residence, 596 Lexington Avenue.

The tables were reversed: Who was the man with whom Mrs. Ruiz had an affair during her marriage? Mr. Ruiz proclaimed that his wife's deception about her identity as the principal reason he was pursuing divorce. Agnes used many different aliases. Her stage name was Ruth Hamilton but in London she was known as Adelaide Flores; the same name used to rent the apartment for her in New York City. In addition, she was also known as Belle O'Brien and Belle Baudoin. Apparently, Mr. Antonio Ruiz was unaware of her various pseudonyms. This was the reason he stated for their prompt separation. However, at the time of their separation, it was widely known that Agnes was the famous mystery woman responsible for Alfred and Elsie's divorce. Antonio Ruiz did finally concede to divorce due to an affair. When asked by the press, "Is that person a millionaire?" George Bauchle replied, "I believe the man is a millionaire."[8]

Señor Ruiz was infuriated by the publicity and the idea of an alienation suit, declaring in distress, "All I want is an absolute divorce; I wish I had never seen this woman. Money would not compensate me for all the trouble and distress this continuous notoriety has brought me."[9]

While yet another scandal with Alfred's name threatened to explode all over New York society, A.G.'s friends came to his rescue, booking his coach *Venture* for the entire season. One ride with his friend R.P. McGrann of Philadelphia, along with British nobility, resulted in a "veritable furor"[10] in Brighton as most of the town gathered to watch the celebrated team of grays.

Alfred Gwynne's preference for judging over competing and his noticeable absence from the four-in-hand event was discussed greatly in the press.[11] He gained notoriety for renting a luxurious flat on Piccadilly Avenue for $10,000 a year without including taxes or extra fees. The building itself only housed six flats and each flat contained "ten large bedrooms, three bathrooms, a number of smoking, billiard and drawing rooms, cloak rooms, kitchen, halls, a boudoir and a great ball room."[12] Unlike most British subjects who entertained guests at various places around London, A.G. was set up to entertain quite comfortably at home.[13]

Displaying a remarkable penchant for advertising, Alfred Gwynne promoted his coaching schedule all over the city with liberal use of newspaper ads and "gorgeous posters"[14] that also advertised the sale of his stud trotting horses at Tattersall's at the end of June in bold font. When asked about the sale of his horses at the horse show, A.G. adroitly replied: "I can't be accused of neglecting my coaching as I have driven all but four trips in the season; say roughly, over 2,000 miles. The season of coaching has been the most delightful experience of my life."[15]

However, the Vanderbilt millionaire's relationships came under more scrutiny as news of his divorce hit London. The beguiling French woman in whose company he was frequently seen was soon discovered to be a woman other than his wife.[16] Who then was this companion seated next to him on the box seat and fashionably attired from head to toe? She was a singer and very outgoing, chatting nonstop as Alfred would lead his "prancing grays through traffic".[17] Names of other women cropped up in society gossip columns,[18] vying for the attention of the eligible bachelor. Yet A.G.'s affection for his former childhood sweetheart and his son was still evident, despite parting ways. A locket attached to his watch chain, held a picture of his son William Henry on one side and one of Elsie, his former wife, on the other.[19]

In uncharacteristic fashion, Alfred withdrew from social circles entirely, isolated from London's elite who considered him "depressed"[20] and deviant. Instead, A.G. chose to spend the majority of his time at the International Horse Show[21] and in the company of a few American friends such as Craig Wadsworth. He also acquired a houseboat *Miranda* on the Thames River,[22] where he was noticed, "sitting in solitary state on the upper deck of the *Miranda* looking neither at the races nor at the brilliant water carnival."[23] Contradiction marked his path wherever he went and it was more evident than ever that society could not fully grasp all that was going on within Alfred Gwynne. Just as he was described as shunning English society, A.G. was discovered at the Kings Way Theater as a frequent guest, enjoying the performance of the brilliant young actress Lina Ashwell in the play, *Diana of Dobsonis*.[24]

The press was none too gentle:

> Don't suppose we want to criticize little Mr. Vanderbilt or any unpleasant things to him or about him. Not for a minute. We have seen many a squirrel dashing madly around in his little wheel. We have felt sorry to see his energy wasted, wished that he might be stuffing nuts into his little fat cheeks, or jumping from tree to tree. We have never been tempted to pull his tail or call him a foolish squirrel.
>
> There is no temptation to be unkind in the case of the other little squirrels—hereditary little American millionaires—dashing around in their little squirrel cages—helpless, busy doing nothing.
>
> Think of a young man who could, if he had it in him, add to and direct the prosperity of a nation. Then think of the poor child going over to England to drive 'favorite gray horses,' and try to get excitement out of that.[25]

His fall from grace was readily apparent in the sharp criticism he received from the *Boston Daily Globe* when he shared his feelings about coaching:

> 'I love to drive,' says Mr. Alfred g. Vanderbilt, whose seven-weeks' coaching trips between London and Brighton have cost him about $1000 a week. 'It's my hobby, my fad, and why should I not drive a coach if I want to? I do not care for golf. I do not care for bridge, I do not care for many things which interest English people and Americans, but I do care for horses.' Considering how many ways there are in which Mr. Vanderbilt might make his wealth profitable to the world, what a pity it is that he should be thinking only of amusement.[26]

This criticism immediately brought focus as to why Alfred had left his native land for England. A.G. thought England was a place where wealth was accepted and could be enjoyed, unlike America where the wealthy were always consumed with acquiring more power and riches.

Elsie threw a grand charity fête at *Oakland Farms* for St. Mary's Church in Portsmouth, assisted by her former sister-in-law, Mrs. Reginald Vanderbilt.[27] Soon after the event, she sailed on the *Kronprinz Wilhelm* with her son to France. Her mother, Mrs. F.O. French, had already bequeathed her Newport villa, *Harbor View,* to Elsie[28], and had taken up permanent residence in France. Attired in a "fetching black gown" with a white bodice and a black hat, Elsie appeared relaxed as she spoke to the press: "Please don't ask me to talk. I am going away to rest and to forget my family troubles, and I hope the newspapers will forget them too."[29]

As Elsie's fortunes rose, Alfred's fell. Soon after A.G. had broken in his newly acquired American trotting horses via his daily coach runs, of which mainly the English middle class and his own friends participated in, he offered fifty-six horses for sale at Tattersall's in a private auction. The local English horsemen known as "gyps" took matters into their own hands. Creating a rumor that the millionaire was only going to sell the horses for which he had no use and would retain all the champion studs himself, the gyps were successful in perpetuating this false belief among the public, forcing the prices to drop at the actual sale. Each horse sold at $250 a head and was promptly acquired by one of the gyps and resold again for double or more, making them a tidy profit of at least $15,000.[30]

His manager Charlie Wilson, under heat already for his bigamy with Florence Schenck, tried to make his case: "The British dealers played a clever trick on us when we sold the horses, but the same thing will not happen next year when Mr. Vanderbilt sells his next lot…They best us out of about $15,000 by their clever trick, but it will be a lesson for us."[31]

A.G. participated in the Long Branch horse show at which the four-in-hand event garnered the attention of a special feature,[32] and despite putting up a good showing, was prevented from a victorious finish by railroad trains that slowed his progress at crossings, as C. Watson breezed home as the clear winner.[33] While reports issued that Mrs. Agnes Ruiz[34] was present at the event, her husband's lawyers remained frustrated, since all their attempts to lodge a formal complaint and serve her with a subpoena had been thwarted by her unavailability. The referee in the case at White Plains had accepted Senor Ruiz's request in favor of an interlocutory decree for absolute divorce on the first of August.[35]

When a prominent social figure from Newport, who declined to be named, was asked about her attendance at the charity fête earlier in the summer at the Vanderbilt estate, she angrily insisted that she was not present, and would not ever expect to "set her foot on the farm again"[36] and asked the reporter to be far more careful in using her name in conjunction with anything related to Alfred G. Vanderbilt.

Despite being rejected by a colony of former social companions, when Vanderbilt returned to Newport, he entertained at a feverish pitch and hardly an evening went by without company or social events that he planned or participated in, acquiring a new name for himself as his parties swirled with wild exhilaration and crazy events such as taking one of the guests, General Whitehouse, prisoner and throwing him into the pool as spectators gasped and others giggled with excitement. Headlining news stories described his parties in dervish detail with titles such as "Weird Doings at Vanderbilt Ball,"[37] "Alfred G. Celebrates Divorce with Function Full of Excitement,"[38] and "Cotillion Leader Hurled into Swimming Pool while Women Cheer."[39]

Already rumors began to circulate about new suitors for Elsie, ranging from the American bachelor William Whitehouse[40] to William Spencer, the handsome president of the Pennsylvania Railroad; expectations of a formal announcement of engagement grew imminent.[41] Spencer had been a friend of A.G. at Yale[42] who apparently had a disagreement with Alfred when he admonished Vanderbilt for his tone when speaking to Elsie at a dinner party. Elsie had no knowledge of the affair until an eavesdropping maid confided what she had overheard[43] between the two men who had come too close to blows. Alfred Gwynne was believed ill prepared to hear about his wife's new liaison with Spencer:

> It is no secret to Alfred's friends that he still possesses a good deal of love for the woman who will soon get a final decree of divorce from him. It is also known that he has long been jealous of Willing Spencer, and the story that Mrs. Vanderbilt is soon to announce her engagement to Spencer is causing him no end of annoyance. I am satisfied that if Willing Spencer's name had not been coupled with Mrs. Vanderbilt's Alfred would never have appeared publicly with a woman who is not accustomed to visit horse shows with him.[44]

Mrs. Cornelius Vanderbilt was now returning to Newport, with plans of opening up the *Breakers* to summer entertainment.[45] She had nothing to say about her son's divorce and was apparently ready to move on to other discussions. A.G continued to throw elaborate parties[46], inviting the notable restaurant Sherry's to bring its entire traveling kitchen to his estate for a masque ball[47] for one evening of entertainment. A supper on the lawn for two hundred guests with an accompanying fire drill[48] to test out his new equipment. It was a brilliant event for more than two hundred and fifty guests[49] with dancing, dining, and live entertainment. He even threw last minute parties to entertain his brother Reggie and his wife, while telling tales about attending sumptuous parties in Europe on the eve of the Grand Prix.[50]

Elsie was not to be undone. Stories abounded about her visit to Berlin, attending the Kaiser's events such as the annual review of the guard at Tempelhof and the Royal Opera House, as well as being entertained by Mr. and Mrs. Robert S. Hitt of the American embassy in Berlin.[51]

Alfred Gwynne's coterie of associates continued to make waves in the press. His chauffeur John Sante was imprisoned for five days for speeding at forty miles an hour, the judge severely reprimanded the driver for recklessly engaging in repeat offenses as his rich employer continued to pay his fees.[52]

Large crowds gathered to watch the four-in-hand class at the Newport Horse Show. Alfred Gwynne's reputation had preceded him and spectators were eager to witness him driving a coach after hearing about his tooling the *Venture* for most of the summer in England. Mr. Vanderbilt placed third after C. Watson and William H. Moore.[53] A.G. charmed the crowd as his niece, Reginald's daughter, rode one of his ponies and secured the first and fourth prizes on a day of perfect weather and a picturesque turnout of prominent citizens.[54]

There were noticeable absences that were commented upon, such as that of his brother Neily and his wife Grace, Elsie and her mother Mrs. F.O. French, and the Tuck, Spencer, Belmont, Fish, Taylor, Oelrich, and Deerham couples. Definite sides were being drawn up in the aftermath of the divorce case. Most of Elsie's friends among their mutual acquaintances deferred to her side, and yet the separation was quite amiable:

> Socialists will please take notice that the head of the house of Vanderbilt---one of the owners of America---has set this new fashion of broad high-mindedness in divorce ethics. The exclusive coteries who were wont to enjoy the affairs at Oakland Farm when Mrs. Alfred Vanderbilt was the hostess, the Vanderbilt family in all its ramifications and even Alfred's chums have been, since the break, openly constant to both parties.[55]

By the eighteenth of September, the final decree for absolute divorce was filed with Justice Garay of the Supreme Court, finalizing the split between

Elsie and Alfred. Elsie regained her freedom as a single woman, with no opposition from A.G.[56]

On the very same day, A.G. brazenly appeared at the White Plains Horse Show with Agnes Ruiz at his side, noticed by everyone, and definitely invoking the ire of Elsie through this flamboyantly public display. All attention was diverted from the display of fine stallions to the young pair who appeared at ease and in high spirits.[57] The curiosity of everyone present was satiated and all eyes followed the young couple, watching their every move from their arrival in a large touring automobile to their departure together. Speculations surfaced that this was tit for tat: Alfred wanted to declare his own freedom as a single bachelor again with the notorious Madame Ruiz as rumors circulated further about Willing Spencer and Elsie. However as more rumors spread, Elsie vehemently denied any such possible union between them, declaring that she "had no idea of marrying again."[58]

Willing Spencer was abroad and despite rumors, Elsie showed no signs of any impending matrimonial engagement. Instead, she settled comfortably into her new life at *Harbor View*, taking loving care of her son William Henry. Now seven years old, the young boy was turning out to be a fine horseman in his own right, enjoying riding into town to complete errands for his mother.[59] Elsie displayed her parental authority in discipline and generosity by acquiring him the finest stallions available and every educational opportunity. She began to build up a horse coterie that was only rivaled by her former husband. Making his first visit to *Oakland* since the divorce, A.G. devoted every waking hour to his son[60], enjoying horses and a new electric motorcar[61] capable of going as fast as eighteen miles per hour.

The Wilson and Schenck battle reared its ugly head once again, as the Virginia beauty refused to let go of the suit. She demanded that her case be heard even though her lawyers, whom she had not paid in over a year and a half, were now eager to drop the case and move on.[62] It was yet the third in a series of sensational divorce cases where A.G. Vanderbilt's name would crop up. It was ascertained that through a genuine marriage the action could be ended. Wilson, however, denied the charges of breach of promise of marriage as well as bigamy and refused to pay the punitive damages. Schenck brought up an incident aboard the *Wayfarer* on October 27, 1906, just a week after the events outlined by Elsie in her own suit for divorce, where Wilson had lured her with the promise of marriage.[63]

With such a whirling abyss of confusion surrounding his close associates, it would appear that Alfred Gwynne Vanderbilt would be a social outcast. Yet amazingly, his notorious reputation only seemed to bring him increased attention from the fairer sex. He was pursued heavily at horse shows, coaching trips, and parties. He was, in particular, highly sought after by numerous Southern belles:

> 'One can never tell what will happen after one of these delightful affairs of Alfred Vanderbilt,' said a delightfully pretty girl in Kentucky when Alfred Vanderbilt wandered among the blue grass on the lookout for horses.
>
> 'Just to think of it, out of our immediate intimate party he has played Cupid to three of us…'[64]

Women sighed about him languorously, deeming that, "where he is, there is Cupid."[65] The young attractive women came not only to capture his eye but to languish in "air about him" since being near him, was considered fortuitous: "'It may mean great luck,' said a sweet languorous girl."[66]

As the cold winter set in, Elsie made plans to sail for Europe with young William aboard the Cunard liner *Lusitania* for four months. Little William almost caused his mother to miss the departure of the ship when he grew fascinated by a time-clock hand stamp, refusing to go until he could "see the insides." A hotel porter explained the workings of the machine and when the little man was satisfied, he said, "Thank you, very much," nodding his head, and departed for the pier.

Despite his son's departure, Alfred Gwynne displayed his love for children when he participated at the gift-giving ceremony at the Thames Street Methodist Church, attired in a Santa Claus outfit with "long white whiskers and hair, and a long, loose robe trimmed with fur and besprinkled with a glisten powder resembling snow."[67] Giving away sleds and dolls among other toys, he invited the same group to *Oakland Farms* the following summer.

As the New Year dawned, plans were revealed to the public for the construction of a new nineteen-storey hotel on Alfred Gwynne Vanderbilt's property in New York city on the west side of Park Avenue, estimated at $2,000,000 in building costs at a site two hundred by eighty feet in size, that was formerly the home of the Princeton Club.[68]

A month later, A.G. was ready to sail for Europe again. Sending him off at the pier was the Boston society athlete Miss Eleanor Sears.[69] Apparently, the taxi driver taking Vanderbilt and Sears to the dock was arrested for speeding and the beautiful Miss Sears was able to charm the police officer in allowing the driver to take them to the pier first. The policemen proceeded to arrest the driver after they had got out of the vehicle, holding him on a $300 bond.[70]

Before leaving, Vanderbilt had agreed, along with William H. Moore and a third millionaire patron, that the importance of the Madison Square Garden required their backing. Through their sponsorship the horse show would be again offered in the fall. The three millionaires generously proposed to cover any losses through their largesse.[71] However, the arrangement was not satisfactory enough to suit A.G.'s taste and nine days later he announced that he would be taking control over the entire show. Having acquired the majority of the stock, A.G. suppressed all rumors that the show would be closed down.[72] He was greeted with positive acclaim for his efforts to save the Madison Square Garden show, and "earned the gratitude of every horseman in the country."[73] Headlining several papers, A.G.'s action was deemed commendable and exhibiting a "truly sportsmanlike spirit."[74]

In London, Alfred Gwynne was out inspecting and working with his ninety-nine horses from Maine daily. He was confident and enthusiastic as always, stating:

> I expect a good season on the road. I was very well satisfied from a sporting point of view last season, and have determined to run two coaches this year instead of one. The arrangement is for the Venture and Viking to start daily at opposite ends of the road, meeting half way for luncheon. The season will open on the first Monday in May.[75]

His manager Wilson was busy getting the fifty-one teams ready. It would take roughly two entire months for the horses to get used to the different climate and culture. As Wilson put it:

> The English climate has a peculiar effect on American bred horses...American horses generally land in England fresh and well, and they remain so from ten days to a fortnight. By this time the more humid English climate seems to get hold of them and they become slack and sluggish, so that they have to be pulled along, so to speak.[76]

As stories of impending conflict among the Balkans and dissent in the Austrian-Hungarian empire spread, more attention was put upon Americans abroad such as Elsie, whose travels in Paris evoked numerous comments as well as her occupancy in Berlin, where she had spent the winter, apparently "on the verge of plighting troth to a titled heir of the famous Anglo-Dutch-German house of Bentinck, a continental branch of the duke of Portland's family."[77] The Count William Frederick Chirres von Bentinick was frequently seen by her side and the pair often attended carefully to each other. However, her brother Amos Tuck French denied all rumors.[78]

While Alfred Gwynne was enthusiastically engaged in the promotion of his horse events and coaching schedule in great style in London, another case of matrimonial estrangement was brought to the public attention; that of a young woman Margaret Emerson McKim from her husband, a chemist Dr. Smith Hollins McKim. Rumors circulated that she would soon be marrying a recently divorced New York millionaire, whose identity remained a mystery.[79] The *Chicago Tribune* called it a "Sea Romance" that "Hits Shoals".[80] While no person was named, society papers noticed how the young wife was not seen in the company of her husband but rather was an active socialite, often the guest of "Mr. and Mrs. Reginald Vanderbilt at their farm entertainments and also at Oakland Farm when Mr. Alfred G. Vanderbilt entertained."[81] It appeared that Alfred was courting again.

NOTES

1. *The Washington Post*. "Social Gossip." June 9, 1908. Pg. 7.
2. Ibid.
3. Ibid.
4. *The Washington Post*. "In Fashion's Realm." June 13, 1908. Pg. 7.
5. *The Washington Post*. "In Fashion's Realm." June 13, 1908. Pg. 7.
6. *The Washington Post*. "In Fashion's Realm." June 13, 1908. Pg. 7.
7. *The Chicago Daily Tribune*. "Madame Ruiz Found Close to Gotham." June 14, 1906. Pg. 10.
8. Ibid.
9. Ibid.
10. *The Washington Post*. "Americans in London." June 14, 1908. Pg. 15.
11. *The New York Times*. "Few American Entries." June 15, 1908. Pg. 8.
12. *The Atlanta Constitution*. "Finest Flats in London." June 21, 1908. Pg. 6.
13. Ibid.
14. *The Washington Post*. "Gossip of Society." June 23, 1908. Pg. 7.
15. Ibid.
16. *The Atlanta Constitution*. "Alfred Vanderbilt Cut by Smart Set of London." Aug 9, 1908. Pg. D5.
17. *The Chicago Daily Tribune*. "English Snub Vanderbilt." June 28, 1908. Pg. A2.
18. *The Washington Post*. "A.G. Vanderbilt to Wed?" June 5, 1908. Pg. 1.
19. Ibid.
20. *The Los Angeles Times*. "Vanderbilt Shuns Society." June 28, 1908. Pg. 12.
21. *Boston Daily Globe*. "Shuns English Society." June 28, 1908. Pg. 26.
22. *The Los Angeles Times*. "Vanderbilt Shuns Society." June 28, 1908. Pg. 12.
23. *The Chicago Daily Tribune*. "Few Americans at Henley." July 5, 1908. Pg. 15.
24. *The Los Angeles Times*. "Vanderbilt Shuns Society." June 28, 1908. Pg. 12.
25. *The Hartford Courant*. "Coachman A.G. Vanderbilt." June 29, 1908. Pg. 8.
26. *The Boston Daily Globe*. "Editorial Points." July 7, 1908. Pg. 6.
27. *The New York Times*. "Gay Charity Fete at Oakland Farm." July 9, 1908. Pg. 7.
28. *The Washington Post*. "Deserts Newport." July 23, 1908. Pg. 7.
29. i "Gossip of Society." July 16, 1908. Pg. 7.
30. *The New York Times*. "Vanderbilt Loses $15,000 on Horses." July 21, 1908. Pg. 1.
31. Ibid.

32. *The New York Times*. "Best Show Horses for Long Branch." July 26, 1908. Pg. S1.
33. *The New York Times*. "Judges Make Final Awards." Aug 2, 1908. Pg. S1.
34. *The New York Times*. "Ruiz Sues for Divorce." Aug 2, 1908. Pg. 2.
35. Ibid.
36. *The New York Times*. "Social War at Newport." Jul 25, 1908. Pg. 1.
37. *The Los Angeles Times*. "Dancer Ducked! Weird Doings at Vanderbilt Ball." September 12, 1908. Pg. I1.
38. Ibid.
39. Ibid.
40. *The Atlanta Constitution*. "London Society Women Dancing like Maud Allen." Aug 8, 1908. Pg. D5.
41. *The Washington Post*. "Social Gossip." Sept 19. 1908. Pg. 7.
42. *The Los Angeles Times*. "Mrs. Vanderbilt to Wed Alfred's Chum?" Sept. 19, 1908. Pg. 12.
43. *The Washington Post*. "Madame Ruiz with Him." Sept 19, 1908. Pg. 1.
44. Ibid.
45. *The Washington Post*. "Chat of Well Known People." June 6, 1908. Pg. 7.
46. *The Washington Post*. "Domino Ball at Newport." Sept 3, 1908. Pg. 7.
47. *The Washington Post*. "Chat of Well Known People." Sept 5, 1908. Pg. 7.
48. *The Washington Post*. "Will Have Supper on Lawn." Sept 4, 1908. Pg. 7.
49. *The Washington Post*. "Vanderbilt Gives Ball." Sept 6, 1908. Pg. 12.
50. *The Los Angeles Times*. "Good Short Stories." Sept 6, 1908. Pg. IM309.
51. *The Chicago Daily Tribune*. "Berlin Filled with Visitors: Americans are in the Lead." Sept. 6, 1908. Pg. A1.
52. *The New York Times*. "Chauffeur Sent to Jail." Sept 2, 1908. Pg. 2.
53. *The New York Times*. "Newport Society Flocks to Horses." Sept. 9, 1908. Pg. 9.
54. *The New York Times*. "Moore's Radiant Loses at Newport." Sept. 8, 1908. Pg. 9.
55. *The Washington Post*. "Gossip of Society." Sept 22, 1908. Pg. 7.
56. *The Atlanta Constitution*. "Vanderbilt Divorce Suit." Sept 19, 1908. Pg. 4.
57. *The Washington Post*. "Madame Ruiz with Him." Sept 19, 1908. Pg. 1.
58. *The Boston Daily Globe*. "Mrs. Vanderbilt Denies." Sept. 20, 1908. Pg. 13.
59. *The New York Times*. "Simple Life at Newport." Sept 27, 1908. Pg. X10.
60. *The New York Times*. "Son with A.G. Vanderbilt." Oct. 14, 1908. Pg. 1.
61. *The Washington Post*. "Gossip of Society." Oct. 20, 1908. Pg. 7.
62. *The Chicago Daily Tribune*. "Marriage Fails to Halt a Suit." Oct. 18,1908. Pg. 6.
63. *The Washington Post*. "Miss Schenck Delays Suit." Oct. 18, 1908. Pg. 2.
64. *The Washington Post*. "How One Charming Romance after Another Has Followed in the Wake of His Jolly…" Oct. 24, 1908. Pg. M10.
65. Ibid.
66. Ibid.
67. *The Washington Post*. "Gossip of Society." Dec. 20, 1908. Pg. 7.

68. *The New York Times*. "19-Story Hotel Planned." Jan 1, 1909. Pg. 8.
69. *The Boston Daily Globe*. "Vanderbilt to Run Two." Feb. 4, 1909.
70. *The Washington Post*. "Social Set of Other Cities." Feb. 5, 1909. Pg. 7.
71. *The Washington Post*. "Social Set of Other Cities." Feb. 5, 1909. Pg. 7.
72. *The New York Times*. "Sponsors Plan to Save Horse Show." Feb 10, 1908. Pg. 1.
73. *The Los Angeles Times*. "Vanderbilt Saves Horse Show, Wins Plaudits." March 7, 1909. Pg III 16.
74. Ibid.
75. *The New York Times*. "Vanderbilt Sees Horses." Feb. 10, 1909. Pg. 4.
76. *The Washington Post*. "Vanderbilt Horses Arrive." Feb 21, 1909. Pg. 11.
77. *The Chicago Daily Tribune*. "Rumor Links Count Name with Mrs. A. G. Vanderbilt." Mar. 21, 1909. Pg. A1.
78. *The Boston Daily Globe*. "Not to Wed Count." Mar 22, 1909. Pg. 6.
79. *The New York Times*. "Dr. Smith H. McKim and Wife Separate." May 22, 1909. Pg. 2.
80. *The Chicago Daily Tribune*. "Sea Romance Hits Shoals." May 22, 1909. Pg. 2.
81. *The New York Times*. "Society at Newport." May 30, 1909. Pg. X2.

Chapter Twelve

The Alibi

A loud gun shot echoed through the apartment and as Miss Caney made her way frantically up the stairs of the large suite, she found her close companion, a breathtaking blonde beauty, unconscious on the floor of her bedroom. Shot right through the heart, Mary Agnes O'Brien, formerly the wife of Cuban attaché Don Antonio A. Ruiz y Olivares, was found dead in her London apartment[1] on May 19, 1908. Arriving at the door of the apartment, where Mary's horse waited patiently for its usual routine, Miss Caney, an American friend, heard a distinctly loud gun shot from upstairs and rushed forward to find Mary Agnes O'Brien lying on the floor, revolver clasped in her hand. Despite rushing her instantly to the hospital, Mary died that night.

It was an entire three weeks later that the news of her death was actually discovered by the press on June 11. The inquest details remained a secret except the coroner's jury verdict of suicide as a result of temporary insanity. She was described as being "depressed" and "melancholic." A "well known American friend"[2] was legally represented during the inquest held before the coroner D. Danford Thomas. Apparently, the inquest was public, yet no news of it reached the people. Were the reporters present at the time bribed to suppress information?[3]

The press questioned why it had been a secret. Newspapers started to inquire as to why the information was kept from the public. It quickly became more than a "newspaper sensation", rising to "a matter of state." Though the British Parliament "cares nothing about the life of Mary Agnes O'Brien Ruiz", the government had to question "why the fact that Mrs. Ruiz died by her own hands in a splendid house in Grosvenor street was concealed; why the report of the Coroner's inquest was kept out of the papers; why the funeral was a strange and secret ceremonial, and why all those connected with the affair make a mystery out of what was only a plain, sordid tragedy." All of

London, and much of the world, began to wonder if "some very rich outsider—some say a very rich American—has interfered with British Institutions and has suppressed the reports of officials by the plain process of bribery."[4]

The investigation led to the discovery of this mysterious American woman's identity. It was ascertained that she was the daughter of a simple Missouri farmer. She had been an actress with the stage name of Ruth Hilton when she met her husband-to-be during a Broadway performance where she was a chorus girl.[5] Mr. Antonio Ruiz was the attaché to the Cuban ambassador stationed in Washington D.C. After a quick courtship, they married, traveled to Cuba and then England, finally returning to America. Her love of horses grew soon apparent, and she spent a lot of time riding through Central Park with her fine stallions. It was in Central Park that she met Alfred Gwynne Vanderbilt who assisted her when she was "tugging helplessly at an obstinate saddle buckle."[6]

Three years later, she parted ways with her husband, who left Washington after their divorce was finalized and took up an apartment in the Waldorf-Astoria. Her name, which had remained concealed from the press, resurfaced

Agnes Ruiz—from the 1908 divorce files, Old Archives, New York City. The entrancing beauty was brought to Alfred's attention by Charles Wilson. The wife of the Cuban Attaché, she fell deeply in love with Vanderbilt. The image was sealed for 100 years according to statute.

during the divorce case of Alfred Gwynne Vanderbilt. Mary O'Brien shunned the publicity surrounding the divorce.[7] Whatever had been concealed for the last few years was being dug up and explored by a hungry press eager to feed the insatiable appetite of the public about one of Newport's most celebrated sons.

Every detail that could be found surrounding the death of this mysterious woman was revealed. Apparently, she was in possession of a fine automobile purchased for $11,000 by Alfred Gwynne's notorious employee, Harry Brenchley[8], who ran off with the wife of Alfred S. Dietrich, and lived in excellent style at her luxurious London apartment for the last year. Her arrival in London was quiet and unnoticeable; yet A.G. too was in London increasingly, having forsaken temporarily his coaching routine in New York as he pursued a new London circuit. Coincidence? Probably not.

More details began to pop up: Alfred Gwynne had called upon the former Mrs. Agnes Ruiz at her apartment on Grosvenor Street several times. The record at the inquest described her intense depression when Mr. Vanderbilt's visits grew "less frequent and finally ceased"[9] early in May. Withdrawing from her friends, she only was seen in public with her friend Miss Caney and occasionally indulged in her favorite pastime of cantering through Hyde Park. The newspapers speculated and even friends of the family wondered whether the divorce of the Vanderbilt couple was linked to an affair with Mary Agnes O'Brien.

As the shock of her death reverberated through society, with paper after paper describing in sordid detail any and all knowledge of the circumstances around her death, one can only imagine the frustration shaking the house of Vanderbilt. Alice had safeguarded her family reputation with such assiduous care only to have glaring and sensational scandals ripple throughout Newport society as the gossip columnists speculated about her son Alfred's numerous affairs.

Hardly a year had passed since the divorce proceedings for Vanderbilt were finalized and the Western world had just started to embrace Alfred Gwynne once more as their social favorite, when the news of Mary Agnes O'Brien Ruiz's death in a London apartment hit the streets.[10] All eyes turned towards A.G. once again as the name that appeared in his own divorce proceedings, resurfaced in the press.

As surprising new facts came to light, it grew apparent that the actual suicide had occurred three weeks prior and that the entire case had been buried from the public, suppressing all details pertaining to the case. As the *Los Angeles Times* reported, "The facts brought out at the inquest were suppressed in some manner, and it did not become definitely known until to-day that Mrs. Ruiz was dead. The feature of the case is being investigated."[11]

Alfred Vanderbilt in top hat with trademark white corsage. States on reverse, "P.S. Rogers, Photographs, 254 West 39th St., New York. "Dated September 1, 190(9)?"

According to her friend Miss Caney, Agnes Ruiz was morose and depressed in the weeks prior to her suicide[12], taking pills for insomnia, and her only caller had been Alfred G. Vanderbilt. The record at the inquest described her intense depression when Mr. Vanderbilt's visits grew "less frequent and finally ceased"[13] early in May. Withdrawing from her friends, she only was seen in public with her friend Miss Caney and occasionally indulged in her favorite pastime of cantering through Hyde Park. A.G.'s behavior was highly scrutinized: "...but for some time recently it had been noticeable that he had been giving less attention than usual to his favorite pursuits and much surprise has been expressed at his rare visits to the International Horse Show at Olympia."[14]

The role that the young man had to play in the death of Agnes Ruiz was a mystery and remained to be seen. All information from the inquest held on May 19th was hidden for three weeks, as newspapers slept in a vacuum of information. Editors then feverishly tried to find every detail about the story and investigations were launched to find out if local reporters had been bribed to "suppress any mention of the proceedings."[15]

A.G. was represented at the inquest by his legal counsel. The physician in attendance revealed that, after shooting herself in the chest, "the bullet had perforated her stomach and glanced upward toward the spine. It had severed an artery and she died a few minutes later from internal hemorrhage."[16] Servants had rushed her into a carriage, which immediately left for the Fitzroy Square Hospital where, despite frantic attempts by an emergency team, they failed to save her life. Agnes Ruiz died on the night of May 19th. The coroner's jury offered a verdict of suicide by temporary insanity. Her attorney Hymes, who was in charge of Agnes Ruiz's personal affairs, offered no factual information to the press about her death, while adding, "but you can draw your own conclusions."[17]

A mysterious man named Williamson appeared at the inquest and claimed to be Ruiz' Parisian counsel. He took charge of everything in front of reporters and the court. Apparently, it was "easy to secure suppression of police and coroners' court cases in London."[18]

Why had Agnes Ruiz taken her own life? Like a pendulum, conjecture vacillated from one extreme to the other. Some suggested the suicide occurred because she was so severely depressed, but others attributed her mental breakdown to stress from learning that the object of her affections, A.G. Vanderbilt, actually loved another woman. The latter case appears to have been the strong belief among the echelons of the horse show circles.[19] Another woman had vied with Ruiz for Alfred Gwynne's affections and won. As Ruiz "found herself practically supplanted,"[20] she had given up all hope, taking her own life in grief. Another rumor circulated that the doctor attending Ruiz found her conscious[21] and confused, admitting to shooting herself before being hurried away on a stretcher to the local hospital.

As Agnes Ruiz's body was lowered into the ground at the Kensai Green Cemetery[22] in London, only those closest to her were present: her companion Miss Caney, the housekeeper at the Grosvenor street mansion, her servants, and the man called Mr. Williamson who declared that he was Mrs. Ruiz's business associate from Paris. A noticeable addition to the gravesite was a "marked profusion of beautiful flowers from some anonymous friend."[23] Soon after the ceremony, all the servants were dismissed after being paid by Williamson. The grave marker did not mark the site with the name of Mary O'Brien or Agnes Ruiz. Her grave was marked by a name that prevented anyone from finding her except those that already knew where she was buried. Her gravestone blended seamlessly into row after row of gray, bleak stones.

Reporters were frustrated. No information could be gleaned since there were no known participants to question. Approaching the hospital where Mrs. Ruiz was brought in her final hour, the press soon learned that the surgeon that brought her home, Dr. Bland Sutton, paid her doctor's bill. On questioning the surgeon about the unusual practice, the doctor replied:

> I seldom respond when asked to act in such capacity but a man who came to me to attend to Mrs. Ruiz said that the woman probably was dying: consequently I lent assistance, though I never heard of Mrs. Ruiz before. No, I won't say who paid me, though it was the proper person.[24]

The press rallied around the story of a woman who lost the love of the man she so desperately loved. He had forsaken her for another and she had taken her life in despair. Ruiz no longer appeared as the adulterous woman who had broken up a marriage; the press now painted her as an unfortunate victim of failed relationships. A.G., as was his wont, when asked if he had something to say about the death of a woman he had apparently been involved with, replied, "No nothing at all."[25]

His failure to comment made him look bestial to the public. The timing could not have been worse as the press uncovered more unsightly clues to the bribing involved in hushing up the story. Cash had been lavishly thrown around and, not too long ago, seventeen dollars could "suppress a scandalous divorce case."[26] Corruption in London courts was well known at the time but in the case of an actual death, knowledge of such bribery created a furor: "It is a notorious scandal that cases in the minor courts of London, including the coroner's can be kept from the public by the judicious use of a little money."[27]

Again and again the same story circulated. With each round, Alfred Gwynne's silence drew further comments and innuendos, as his "debonair"[28] and "nonchalant" attitude increasingly invoked the ire of the press. The amount of money that had been freely distributed in bribing the press aroused suspicion, resulting in an investigation.[29]

The press connected the dots; it was obvious that the secrecy involved in covering up all knowledge regarding her suicide was the act of a wealthy patron who had enough money to throw around. All roads pointed to Vanderbilt. Despite his silence, the golden boy had fallen so far from grace that his every expression was deemed sinister and foreboding.

The scandal was even seeping into the high levels of equine society where questions arose about possible investigations at the International Horse Show in London to determine Vanderbilt's role in the affair and any information that could be garnered about Ruiz. Due to strong English libel laws, A.G. was not implicated directly and while "none of the London papers ha[d] dared to name Mr. Vanderbilt in connection with the suicide, they refer to him in such a direct manner that none can mistake whom they mean."[30]

The town of St. Louis, Missouri mourned the loss of one of their own, with editorials about her life. With simple origins, Mary O'Brien was famous in her hometown for her "escapades and extraordinary beauty."[31] Known for hopping freight trains to New Orleans and back, the young woman married twice: first to a man called Hilton, from whom she borrowed the last name as she made her first stage appearance on Broadway, and second to the Cuban diplomat Ruiz. Mary had taken care of her younger brother after marriage made her comfortable.

As rumors were confirmed about the bribery of reporters and the secrecy surrounding Mary Agnes Ruiz's death, a storm of protest issued forth from

London society against the existing system of the courts, reaching up to the House of Commons.[32] The Daily Mail reported that the coroner, Dr. Danford Thomas, at the inquest would be questioned. Apparently a sum of $1,500 was given to a reporter of *The Washington Post* to suppress his report, along with cases of other reporters being "similarly influenced."[33]

Instantly, society abandoned its formerly favorite son: "It is a matter of speculation as to whether Alfred Vanderbilt...will long find London to his liking. As a matter of fact London long ago decided the young man was best left to himself and his mixed crowds of satellites and parasites with whom he has consorted."[34] Disapproval extended from the highest echelons of society when King Edward noticeably avoided the American millionaire and "anything that is derogatory to the royal influence for good."[35] While A.G. was not banished, "the prediction is freely made that this particular Offender will ere long find Paris more to his taste."[36]

More drama ensued. A woman formerly employed by Mary Agnes Ruiz told reporters that Ruiz was consumed by jealousy and that she had tried two times previously to end her life using morphine. A year prior to the actual suicide, Mary Agnes Ruiz had upbraided Alfred for being with another woman, crying bitterly, "I'll show you!"[37] Ruiz had witnessed A.G. driving his coach with a beautiful female companion, whom she had met on a steamer sailing to Europe. The woman was not easy to dismiss; she was able to hold her own in Vanderbilt's society and her presence discomfited Ruiz so deeply that her mind was tormented by thoughts of Alfred with this other woman. After "flying into a rage"[38] followed by a "prolonged fit of jealous weeping,"[39] Agnes Ruiz had fallen at his feet soon after consuming the drug and Alfred Gwynne had rushed her to the hospital, where a physician restored her to consciousness. Sweltering with inner resentment, Agnes Ruiz had also threatened in the presence of all of her servants, "I'll shoot him if he doesn't do what I want him to do."[40] She had even kept a loaded pistol by her side at the dinner table despite remonstrations from her servants.

A description of Agnes' suicide attempt may have accidentally found its way into the testimony for Alfred's divorce. During his testimony, Harry Kempster, Alfred's personal servant, was asked about his first time seeing Agnes' apartment at 596 Lexington Ave in New York City. His first time at her apartment was "about the 10th"[41] of November. Alfred asked Kempster to come to the apartment because Agnes was sick. When he arrived, Kempster noticed she was in "a state of coma".[42] Alfred and Kempster stayed with Agnes until five in the morning. They had to keep her awake until "she got right . . . and was able to speak intelligibly."[43]

The prosecutor was going to breeze over the subject, asking questions merely about whether Alfred and Agnes were ever left alone, but the referee was curious about Kempster referring to Agnes as being in "a state of coma".

If he hadn't let that small phrase slip, the story wouldn't be in the testimony at all. Kempster revealed more details than perhaps A.G. would have preferred to share. Whether or not Kempster knew what truly happened cannot be discerned from his testimony. Without divulging any more details, he merely said that "she had taken a tablet, I suppose for some pain."[44]

As Parliament received notice of the Ruiz case, a member of the House of Commons, Pete Curran, put forth a question to Home Secretary Gladstone regarding the facts that had been suppressed during the suicide case of Mrs. Antonio Ruiz on May 16. He inquired why the inquest was held in private. Court officials came under close scrutiny while at the same time care was taken to avoid calling A.G. directly by name, referring to him instead as a "well-known millionaire."[45]

More details surfaced. Neighbors shared their tales, including one about a "violent quarrel"[46] between Ruiz and A.G. in January of 1908 that had spewed out into the street. Agnes Ruiz had run out on to the street in a "loose wrapper and house slippers",[47] rushing directly into the path of a trolley car, and narrowly escaped death as Alfred chased her down and pulled her away. He calmed her down and brought her back into the apartment. After that dramatic scene, Vanderbilt's visits were subdued and "not remarkable for anything save frequent orders to the boys to fetch domestic cigarettes and whisky from nearby saloons."[48]

Hot on the heels of this announcement, a bombshell fell on June 15th, 1909, as shocking revelations of yet another woman who had purportedly committed suicide for the love of Alfred Vanderbilt. An American society patron, a friend of Elsie's, declared that Agnes Ruiz was not A.G.'s real paramour and that, in fact, she was only a ruse to conceal his true affair:

> She after all, was only a 'blind' behind which he conducted his real love-affair—with the first woman who killed herself, a young matron of a splendid New York family.[49]

Furious, the woman continued:

> If a woman loves Alfred Vanderbilt she might as well make up her mind to take poison or blow her brains out. Why there isn't a woman in the younger set in New York who doesn't believe that he has the evil eye. Two women have killed themselves for him already and we are all asking each other which one will be the next.[50]

She declared that Ruiz was a blind, a pawn in the game of love, nicknamed "Ruis" or "The Alibi" in the New York social set, accordingly.[51] This high society woman who declined to be named publicly, but was a well-known figure in New York and Newport circles, had a lot to say, unleashing a torrent of information that purportedly had hitherto been cleverly concealed:

> The only woman with whom he ever was really in love was a young matron prominent in New York. But he was married and so was this woman and their meetings might have caused unpleasant comment. Therefore this girl who killed herself in London was induced to pose as his inamorata.[52]

The society matron claimed that Agnes was forced to marry Antonio Ruiz upon the insistence of Alfred. She then "began to pose as his favorite and he allowed his association with her to become known." The mystery matron suggested that Agnes killed herself only partially because of Alfred's neglect; the true reason was that Agnes realized her affair with Alfred "had destroyed all her chances of ever winning an honest love."[53]

Ruiz, who posed as A.G.'s true love, accompanied him to midnight suppers, drove his horses, and accepted his visits so that scandal would be "placed upon her and not upon the other woman."[54] While almost everyone was deceived by this hoax, Elsie was "never fooled for a minute."[55] Apparently, she was completely aware of Alfred Gwynne's devotion to this other woman even though she claimed during the divorce proceedings that she didn't know the identity of any of Alfred's mistresses. Purportedly Elsie "went to the other woman and told her she knew. Within a few days the other woman killed herself. Her death was followed not too closely to arouse any suspicion, by Mrs. Vanderbilt's successful suit for divorce."[56] Vanderbilt maintained his association with Madame Ruiz for a short period after to keep up appearances after the woman he truly loved, had died by her own hand.[57]

Who was this woman that Newport society so confidently described as A.G.'s true paramour? If the woman was of the same social stature as Elsie and a regular in Newport society, it could only suffice to conclude that the two women knew each other and possibly, were even friends. This could only mean that the woman's identity was concealed intentionally from the divorce proceedings and that both Elsie and Alfred had consciously chosen to place all the blame on Agnes. Elsie could get her divorce and hopefully, A.G. would not be linked to the suicide of his real mistress.

Everything remained shrouded in a veil of mystery. Even Agnes' family members were silent at her funeral and her butler, who was privy to everything that happened in her household, was quietly relocated to his home in Scotland and no one would reveal his address. While newspapers in the Eastern United States failed to report on the matter at all, some Western newspapers persisted, despite the apparent lack of adequate information. They anxiously sought to find the truth. Some even began to conjecture that "some expert hand with an abundance of money at command is at work to prevent all the details of the tragedy becoming public."[58]

Just as loudly as the cry had risen in Parliament to investigate the secrecy that surrounded the Ruiz inquest, it fell, subsiding quietly and fading away; encountering more obstacles that prevented the airing of the entire affair in public as though some "powerful occult influence was still at work."[59] Pete Curran's query to reexamine the case was rejected by the Clerk of Commons upon the grounds that it was improperly framed. The Clerk postulated that under their current law, the judge held power in deciding whether the issue was public or private, and that in the future, under new legislation, all Coroner hearings would be public. Despite Curran's determination to renew his question every day, court officials confirmed that the case facts had been accepted as those provided at the inquest: death by suicide due to temporary mental illness. The case was considered closed.

On March 25, 1909, the lovely wife of Mr. Pierre Lorillard V, committed suicide by asphyxiation in her Dupont home of Washington D.C.[60] The death of Mrs. Caroline Lorillard struck an unexpected blow to the Lorillard family and all of her close friends who were completely taken aback by the news. While the coroner's official verdict was death by suicide, the family attributed her death to heart failure and her husband called it an accident.[61]

Known for her charming personality, Caroline was highly accomplished in arts and traveled extensively abroad.[62] Family members said that she would get depressed and morose when left alone as she grew older, exacerbated by years of suffering from her heart condition.[63] According to her family physician Dr. Cuthbert, Mrs. Pierre Lorillard Jr. had a heart condition that had caused her to suffer greatly[64] and required some care but did not leave her an invalid by any means or affect her mortality, repudiating the claims of her family upon her death. Her husband was Pierre Lorillard V, the son of the famous tobacco magnate and thoroughbred owner, Lorillard IV.

The Lorillard family had close ties to the Vanderbilts. Cornelius, Alfred's father, had purchased the thirteen-acre tract in Newport from Pierre Lorillard IV,[65] Caroline's father-in-law, and built the colossal Beaux-arts mansion the *Breakers* on that property overlooking the ocean. Part of the exclusive Jekyll Island club privy to only millionaires such as Morgan, Vanderbilt, and Rockefeller. Pierre Lorillard was also a real estate developer who established a luxurious private retreat at Tuxedo Park in New York.[66] Lorillard IV had also gained a reputation for being an avid horseman, with his prized thoroughbred *Saxon* winning the Belmont Stakes and another American trotter *Iroquois* taking home the Epsom Derby cup in Europe. His son Pierre Lorillard V was a fashionable socialite in a more subdued fashion, winning gardening competitions against Neily.[67]

Pierre Lorillard with dog. Lorillard's wife unexpectedly committed suicide by gas asphyxiation. Library of Congress. Harris and Ewing Collection.

Caroline had left notes that were kept private at her request. The notes, while not addressed to anyone in particular, were deeply personal. Over the next few days, it came to light that there were two notes: one written by Caroline and the other by someone else addressed to Caroline. Mrs. Lorillard, when planning her own death, had enclosed both notes in an envelope with the words, "Bury this with my body – unopened" scrawled on the outside.[68] The envelope was found next to her body the morning after her suicide and was opened by the coroner Dr. Nevitt. Found on her body, in addition to the notes, were small trinkets apparently of some personal value to the deceased and possibly gifts from a loved one. It was Caroline's wish that the notes and the jewelry be kept private and never revealed again to the human eye. Dr. Nevitt was sworn to secrecy by Pierre and did not reveal the details of this discovery to anyone.

On the night of her death, Mrs. Lorillard had attended a dinner party at the residence of Mr. and Mrs. Richard Townshend on Massachusetts Avenue with her husband. A few hours later, the couple returned home apparently in high spirits and retired to their separate quarters.

At eight-thirty the following morning, the butler detected a strong pungent odor of gas and found her lifeless on the floor, clothed in her dressing gown with the previous night's diamond adornments still fastened in her hair. Two doctors were immediately summoned but despite their best efforts, Caroline Lorillard was beyond help. The coroner Dr. Nevitt, who visited the home and investigated the circumstances, issued a certificate of suicide by gas poisoning. Her funeral party consisted only of her husband Pierre and her son by the same name. While the coroner refused to make public the contents of the note, it became public knowledge that both notes were informally written by hand many days prior to her sensational death.[69] There was no doubt that her death rippled through society and affected the Vanderbilt clan. Her funeral service was attended by intimate friends of the family, among who was Mrs. Chauncey Depew, the wife of the Vanderbilt attorney. Akin to the funeral of Agnes Ruiz, carriages of flowers were brought out in a stately procession.

Why this vivacious woman committed suicide when she enjoyed such an esteemed position in society remained shrouded in a veil of mystery. The conclusion could be that the notes were of deep significance to her and contained information that she wished to communicate, despite her request. Had she wanted the contents of the letters to remain secret she would not have drawn intense attention to them. The trinkets held a cherished and intimate memory, and it was likely that Caroline Lorillard was longing and missing something in her life that these notes and trinkets reminded her of. Did Elsie write that note that forced Caroline into taking her own life? Knowing her husband was with another woman would undoubtedly infuriate a spouse, but one from within her own social realm would be far worse.

Caroline was forty-nine years old when she took her own life. At the time, Alfred was only thirty years old. One could say Alfred was into older women - Agnes Ruiz was thirty-two years old at the time of her death– but perhaps Caroline was a bit too old for Alfred. Then again, maybe Caroline's beauty and wit transcended her age. The mystery matron who had spoken to the newspapers said that the woman who was Alfred's true lover had killed herself using gas, which was Caroline's cause of death. She also died in the correct time frame that the society matron described. But the story has yet to be fully revealed.

Three years later, another woman who had married into the Lorillard family, Kathleen, also committed suicide in her hotel bathroom at the *Holland House*, hanging herself with a strap.[70] Married to Beekman Lorillard, the young uncle of Pierre Lorillard V, Kathleen was a mere twenty-eight years old and an active horsewoman known for her literary aspirations and as a distinguished Southern belle. The doctor who examined her dead body was certain that her nervous condition had temporarily brought on a fit of madness, inducing her to take her own life.

Were these two deaths related? Were these women in love with Alfred G. Vanderbilt? With the layers of secrecy that enshrouded the deaths of these two women of the Lorillard family, nothing would be revealed without prying open the family vault.

NOTES

1. *The New York Times*. "Mrs. Antonio Ruiz A Suicide In London; Was Mentioned in Connection with the Divorce Case of Alfred G. Vanderbilt. June 11, 1908. Pg. 4.
2. *The Chicago Daily Tribune*. "Cast off by Vanderbilt; Dies." June 11, 1909.
3. Ibid.
4. *Chillicothe Constitution*. "Ruiz Death is a London Scandal." 14 June 1909: 3.
5. *The Washington Post*. "Mrs. Ruiz A Suicide." June 11, 1909. Pg. 5.
6. *The New York Times*. "Mrs. Antonio Ruiz A Suicide In London; Was Mentioned in Connection with the Divorce Case of Alfred G. Vanderbilt." June 11, 1908. Pg. 4.
7. Ibid.
8. *The New York Times*. "Mrs. Antonio Ruiz A Suicide In London; Was Mentioned in Connection with the Divorce Case of Alfred G. Vanderbilt." June 11, 1908. Pg. 4.
9. *The Chicago Daily Tribune*. "Cast off by Vanderbilt; Dies." June 11, 1909.
10. *The Chicago Daily Tribune*. "Mystery Shrouds Report Mary Ruiz Is Dead Abroad." May 30, 1909. Pg. 4.
11. *The Los Angeles Times*. "Mrs. Antonio Ruiz A Suicide in London." June 11, 1909. Pg. 4.
12. *The Chicago Daily Tribune*. "Cast off by Vanderbilt; Dies." June 11, 1909. Pg. 7.
13. *The Chicago Daily Tribune*. "Cast off by Vanderbilt; Dies." June 11, 1909.
14. Ibid.
15. Ibid.
16. *The Chicago Daily Tribune*. "More Mystery in Ruiz Suicide." June 12, 1909. Pg. 5.
17. *The Chicago Daily Tribune*. "Mystery Shrouds Report Mary Ruiz Is Dead Abroad." May 30, 1909. Pg. 4.
18. *The Chicago Daily Tribune*. "More Mystery in Ruiz Suicide." June 12, 1909. Pg. 5.
19. *The Chicago Daily Tribune*. "More Mystery in Ruiz Suicide." June 12, 1909. Pg. 5.
20. Ibid.
21. Ibid.
22. *The Los Angeles Times*. "Secret Burial of Mrs. Ruiz." June 12, 1909. Pg. II4.
23. Ibid.
24. Ibid.

25. *The Washington Post*. "His Love Lost to Her." June 13, 1909. Pg. 1.
26. Ibid.
27. Ibid.
28. *The Chicago Daily Tribune*. "Madame Ruiz Suicide Stirs All London." June 13, 1909. Pg. 4.
29. Ibid.
30. Ibid.
31. *The Chicago Daily Tribune*. "St. Louis Remembers Woman." June 13, 1909. Pg. 4.
32. *The Chicago Daily Tribune*. "Mme. Ruiz Stirs All London." June 13, 1909. Pg. 4.
33. *The Washington Post*. "Ruiz Case To Parliament." June 14, 1909. Pg. 3.
34. *The Chicago Daily Tribune*. "Exile Through Ruiz Case." June 14, 1909. Pg. 5.
35. Ibid.
36. Ibid.
37. *The Los Angeles Times*. "Mrs. Ruiz Twice Tried Suicide." June 15, 1909. Pg. 11.
38. Ibid.
39. Ibid.
40. Ibid.
41. *Ellen F. Vanderbilt Vs. Alfred G. Vanderbilt*. No. 1908-2273. Supreme Court of the State of New York, New York County. 2 April 1908.
42. Ibid.
43. Ibid.
44. Ibid. Pg. 27.
45. *The New York Times*. "Ruiz Case Brought Before Parliament." June 15, 1909. Pg. 1.
46. *The Washington Post*. "Vanderbilt Escaped." June 16, 1909. Pg. 3.
47. Ibid.
48. Ibid.
49. *The Los Angeles Times*. "Mme. Ruiz Second to Die for Alfred." June 16, 1909. Pg. I1.
50. Ibid.
51. Ibid.
52. Ibid.
53. *Oakland Tribune*. "Another Woman In Ruiz Scandal." June 16, 1909. Pg. 9.
54. *The Los Angeles Times*. "Mme. Ruiz Second to Die for Alfred." June 16, 1909. Pg. I1.
55. Ibid.
56. Ibid.
57. Ibid.
58. *Oakland Tribune*. "Two Nations Enmeshed In A Woman's Suicide." June 13, 1909. Pg. 13-14.
59. *The New York Times*. "Clerk of Commons Bars Ruiz Inquiry." June 17, 1909. Pg. 7.

60. *The Chicago Daily Tribune*. "Mrs. Lorillard Jr. Commits Suicide." Mar. 26, 1909. Pg. 1.
61. Ibid.
62. Ibid.
63. *The New York Tribune*. "Gas Fumes Kill Mrs. Pierre Lorillard. Jr." Mar. 26, 1909. Pg. 1.
64. *The Chicago Daily Tribune*. "Mrs. Lorillard Jr. Commits Suicide." Mar. 26, 1909. Pg. 1.
65. Tschirch, John. *The Breakers*. NPS Report. The Preservation Society of Newport County. Feb 22, 1994. Pg. 6.
66. Hutto, Richard. *Their Gilded Cage: The Jekyll Island Club Members*. Macon: Indigo Custom Publishing. 2005. Pg. 100-2.
67. *The New York Times*. "Newport's Chrysanthemums." Nov. 12, 1893. Pg. 17.
68. *The New York Times*. "Notes Put in Coffin with Mrs. Lorillard." Mar. 27, 1909. Pg. 3.
69. *The Los Angeles Times*. "Secret in Shroud." Mar. 27, 1909. Pg. I1.
70. *The Atlanta Constitution*. "Hanged Herself with a Trunk Strap." Mar. 17, 1912. Pg. 1.

Chapter Thirteen

In the Dark

With remarkably poor taste, the same day that the Ruiz suicide appeared all over the press, a rumor circulated out of Baltimore that Miss Margaret McKim would marry Alfred G. Vanderbilt[1] after her divorce was finalized. While one woman's death was being discussed in lurid detail, another's social triumphs were being heralded. One woman may have died from a broken heart for A.G., but his marital plans would continue unabated. Sarcasm dripped from reporters, even attacking Maggie directly: "Mrs. McKim may marry Alfred Vanderbilt if she likes, but if she were the sister of some men we know she would have a fine horsewhipping coming to her."[2]

Beautiful Maggie Emerson was known both for her charming social manners and the high society "400" that she so naturally became part of. The New York matriarch Mrs. William Astor[3] adored the pretty girl and brought young Maggie under her wing. The daughter of a chemist, Isaac E. Emerson, who had made millions selling bromo-seltzer to treat headaches, she had grown up in Baltimore, Maryland and quickly grew accustomed to the grandiose lifestyle of her father. Mr. Emerson doted upon Margaret, his favorite child, bestowing her with a valuable estate close to New York City at Irvington-on-the-Hudson[4] soon after her marriage to their physician Dr. Smith Hollins McKim.

Despite her simple origins, Maggie was adroitly adapting to social mores, quickly becoming well known for her lavish gowns and parties that "have hardly been surpassed in exclusiveness and display."[5] The young woman was on board her father's yacht *Margaret* (named after her), traveling all over the world with McKim who acted as the family physician and surgeon. After a whirlwind romance at sea, the two had happily wed when they reached shore at the tail end of December of 1902.[6] The couple had made their home in New York, occupying both the Irvington-on-the-Hudson property as well as a

7,000 acre plantation near Georgetown, South Carolina.[7] Her generous father purchased both homes.[8]

Maggie's family strongly denounced any allegations that Margaret was leaving her husband for a millionaire.[9] The Emerson family itself was no stranger to marital discord as Maggie's elder sister Daisy was divorced and her former husband T. Mitchell Horner had stirred up quite a scandal in his suit, claiming alienation of affection in 1907. It was less than two years later, and another Emerson woman was again embroiled in a separation that whispered of a possible affair. As Newport buzzed with the news of their separation, Maggie continued to be socially active, frequenting the residences of Reginald and those of Alfred.[10]

Maggie's divorce had not yet gone through but rumors sparked again that Mrs. Margaret McKim would soon be marrying Alfred.[11] Just as the papers started to run with the story, the startling news came out that Alfred Gwynne Vanderbilt had been shot. As the coroner's office relayed the news to the police, newspaper reporters dispersed as frantic editors sent them packing over to the *Union Hotel*. Stirring up New York,[12] the news sent paper after paper in hot pursuit of the story, sending reporters on a wild goose chase to numerous locations where A.G. had been sighted: the Bellevue Hospital, the Plaza Hotel, and other hot spots. Just as the press got ready to release what would be the biggest story of the year, a phone call came in that there was no story to report at the Union. The reporter then confirmed this again over at Bellevue Hospital. In desperation, the editor called the Plaza Hotel to find out that Alfred G. Vanderbilt was there, in perfectly good health, and in fact had never left his suite. The associated press issued a report that stated that Mr. Vanderbilt, "or a man who said he was Mr. Vanderbilt," had called up the Coroner's office forty minutes after noon and said dryly, "I hear I'm shot."[13] All the locations where A.G. had apparently been sighted or found shot, were swarming with policemen and reporters, and as reporters pushed for a response from A.G. at the Plaza Hotel, Alfred gave the manager this message: "Go away and do not disturb me again with such foolish rumors."

Reginald and his wife threw a costume party a week later, at which both Alfred Gwynne and Mrs. Margaret Emerson McKim were present. Interestingly, both were fashionably attired in matching clothes; A.G. sported his white flannel coaching jacket that he had worn during his coach runs along the Brighton road that summer, and Maggie was dressed in a magnificent costume of gray and white as *Marguerita*.[14]

At the onset of November, amidst a whirlwind of rumors, Maggie arrived with her father in Reno, Nevada, also known as the divorce capital of the Americas, to meet with the best divorce lawyer in a two-hour strategy session in preparation for her divorce from Dr. Mckim.[15] Separation was now final; the couple would no longer entertain any hopes of possible reconciliation.

With her father's devotion and financial assets, Margaret was confident and secure that she would ascend favorably in society's ranks. Dr. McKim came from a wealthy and well established family from Baltimore and her connection to him had only improved her social ranking. In less than three years, she had moved seamlessly up the social ladder, and even her divorce from her physician husband was not necessarily cast in a negative light by the press.[16]

Now that she was moving forward, possibly into the wings of the Vanderbilt fortune, she would have to prove her case. When her divorce suit was filed in Reno, Maggie stated that while she did not request any alimony payments or lay claim to any property, she was leaving her husband because of the "gross drunkenness and physical cruelty"[17] she had experienced for the last seven years at his hands. On the "advice of her physicians, she was compelled to leave her husband to avoid becoming a physical and mental wreck."[18]

The divorce proceedings were definitely unpleasant as Mrs. McKim alleged that her husband was so drunk and incapacitated that he could not fulfill his business pursuits or promises and had failed to supply her with the basic necessities of life, forcing her to depend upon her father for sustenance. Maggie was afraid of his violent outbursts and his abusive tongue that would agitate innocent bystanders and excite friends.[19] She had feared that he would burn the house down by knocking down lamps. In a violent temper in January 1908, he had "hurled her across a room"[20] with tremendous force, and on another occasion had twisted her arm, causing her enormous pain and suffering as he dug his nails into her flesh, disabling use of her arm for several weeks. She was horrified and embarrassed by his "helpless intoxication"[21] in public places.

By August 17th, her divorce suit had taken hold and triumphantly, Maggie set sail for Japan along with her friend, the Baroness de Chaboulon, while a handsome young man, Ray Baker, who had worked extensively on her divorce case, blew kisses at her from the pier.[22] Apparently, the former Mrs. McKim had quite the effect on her companions, a trait that she shared easily with Alfred.

The Chicago Daily Tribune devoted an entire section to reviewing the history of divorce among the Vanderbilts, calling it their "curse"[23] and categorically stating that the "possession of money does not guarantee happiness is again proved by the somewhat startling number of Vanderbilt kin who have separated from their mates."[24] Listing eleven examples, the article detailed the contradictory statements made by members of the Vanderbilt clan about money and marriage, with considerable sympathy for the children affected by such divorces, namely William Henry, the son of Alfred Gwynne and Elsie.

As rumors circulated that both A.G. and Elsie, now "irrevocably divorced"[25], would marry and beget other children, questions arose about how and to whom Alfred would decide to allocate the bulk of his fortune. In the winter, Elsie, along with her son William Henry, moved officially to Berlin.[26] She sold her favorite sloop, *Caprice,* that she had enjoyed sailing in Newport harbor. After visiting her sister Lady Cheyslemore in Windsor, Elsie was seen attending the theater with her suitor, the dashing Count Berham,[27] who frequently left flowers at her door at the Ritz hotel.[28]

A.G. may have thought he was finally free of scandalous rumors now that he was home, but scandal pursued him and his associates once again. Out of the blue, his manager Charles Wilson was arrested in public at the Madison Square Garden horse show.

The Wilson-Schenck drama, quiet now for a few months, again reared its ugly head. Charlie's wife Mrs. Elizabeth A. Wilson had filed a suit of divorce against her husband and won alimony income of $125 enforced by Justice Thomas. Arrested as a scofflaw, Wilson had to post $5,000 bail in cash. Wilson's former wife declared that during his stay in England, Charles had paid her $200 less than her due. Even after seizing his bank accounts, she was not able to secure the funds since they had been drained in what she deemed luxurious living to support Wilson's new wife, Florence Schenck.

When lawyers pressed Wilson to get his employer to bail him out, he appeared uncertain and pleaded that Vanderbilt not be involved in the matter. However, the bond was posted by early evening and Wilson was back at the show immediately. A.G. was furious when the press badgered him with questions, refusing to discuss both the arrest and the bond payment.[29]

Wandering penniless along the streets of London was a sad and familiar face: Florence Schenck, the formerly sassy Virginia beauty and horse whip. After repeated failed attempts to locate Charles Wilson, Florence Schenck came knocking at Vanderbilt's door in desperation. Alfred Gwynne refused to meet with her and when he ran into her on the street, again showed no interest in participating in her affairs. Schenck was a mere twenty-two years old when her life completely spiraled out of control. Evicted out of the *Metropole* Hotel for failing to pay her bill, she fled to another hotel on the west end of London and wrote desperately to Wilson, "I've no one but you to turn to. All the world is against me. Failing to hear from you by tomorrow I will let the lights go out, and in the dark will be my heart for you."[30]

Ruiz's death had cast a dark shadow over Florence Schenck. Contention had seeped into stable life and after Ruiz' suicide, Vanderbilt wanted his stables cleared of anything that reminded him of Agnes Ruiz. Schenck, who had been present at the time of Agnes' suicide and was good friends with the deceased, was made to leave. The young woman found herself stranded in London, penniless, without friends, and the object of ridicule and scandal. Soliciting the services of lawyer John B. Enever to restore her conjugal rights, Schenck soon found out that Wilson considered the marriage certificate invalid. Visiting old acquaintances, she was unable to secure enough money. In a fit of melancholy, Florence took an overdose of chloral.[31] Crying in pain, hotel staff found her at three o'clock in the morning and working with a physician, struggled to keep her alive, as she teetered on the threshold of death, suffering excruciatingly.

While the papers ate up the next story of an affair gone sour, Alfred exhibited no signs of involvement or caring. He was reported as being on the verge of engagement with Maggie,[32] followed soon after by donating $100,000 to Yale,[33] within days of denying Schenck any assistance.

Less than a week passed before Schenck spoke to a reporter about her life with Charlie as she recovered at the Midland Grand Hotel, comparing herself to Mary Agnes O'Brien Ruiz, and describing all the "fine times" she had enjoyed at the Vanderbilt farm in Newport, in London, and in Paris.[34] The reporter described her: "Her great mass of golden hair flooded a cool pillow as she talked. Beneath it was a face of almost deathly pallor---a face marred by black circles under eyes which stared out wistfully through long dark lashes."[35]

Schenck was depressed, angry, defiant, and remorseful. She declared her life a mess and her own willingness to "pay in full" for her actions, explaining her own craving for the high life:

> Do you know what hurts most? It is the fact that I can't control myself. I recently read a book called *The Danger Mark*. In which the story girl is born with a longing for liquor. She fought it down, and in the end married and was happy. Well, I was born with the same craving. I fought it: God knows how I fought it. The girl in the book had strong men to stand in and help her fight. I didn't have a helping hand. I knew nothing but callers who urged me to drink.[36]

Wistfully remarking upon a friend who had managed to control her desires and had found love, feelings about her own failed attempts at love overwhelmed her, and she grew hysterical:

> 'Florence.' She said to me, 'it is beautiful to live for love---real, true love.' Heaven knows it is beautiful. But Hattie has some one to love and some one loves her. What have I?[37]

A nurse had to calm her down, ending the interview abruptly.

NOTES

1. *The Los Angeles Times*. "Beauty's Tragedy." June 11, 1909. Pg. 1.
2. *The Los Angeles Times*. "Editorial Pen Points." June 12, 1909. Pg II4.

3. *The Washington Post*. "Social Sets of Other Cities." May 25, 1909. Pg. 7.
4. Ibid.
5. Ibid.
6. *The Los Angeles Times*. "Separation Climax of McKim Romance." May 22, 1909. Pg. 12.
7. Ibid.
8. *The Washington Post*. "McKims Agree to Part." May 22, 1909. Pg. 3.
9. *The Los Angeles Times*. "Separation Climax of McKim Romance." May 22, 1909. Pg. 12.
10. *The New York Times*. "Society at Newport." May 30, 1909. Pg. X2.
11. *The Atlanta Constitution*. "Mrs. Smith Hollins McKim May Marry Vanderbilt." Aug. 22, 1909. Pg. A3.
12. *The Boston Daily Globe*. "A.G. Vanderbilt was not Shot." Aug. 26, 1909. Pg. 2.
13. *The New York Times*. "Vanderbilt Yarn Agitates the Town." Aug. 26, 1909. Pg. 1.
14. *The New York Times*. "R. C. Vanderbilt Gives Costume Dance." Aug. 28, 1909. Pg. 7.
15. *The Washington Post*. "Mrs. M. E. McKim in Reno." Nov. 2, 1909. Pg. 4.
16. *The Atlanta Constitution*. "Gossip about Mrs. McKim Occupies New York Society." May 15, 1910. Pg. E6.
17. *The Washington Post*. "Mrs. McKim's Plaint." June 1, 1910.
18. Ibid.
19. Ibid.
20. Ibid.
21. Ibid.
22. *The Washington Post*. "Mrs. McKim Off to Japan." Aug. 18, 1910. Pg. 7.
23. *The Chicago Daily Tribune*. "Divorce the Vanderbilt Curse." Oct. 24, 1909. Pg. G1.
24. Ibid.
25. Ibid.
26. *The New York Times*. "Quits Newport for Berlin." Nov. 22, 1909. Pg. 9.
27. *The Washington Post*. "Seek Hand of Miss Gould." Dec. 12, 1909. Pg. 14.
28. *The Washington Post*. "Mrs. Vanderbilt May Marry." Dec. 19, 1909. Pg. 12.
29. *The New York Times*. "Vanderbilt Man Arrested in Garden." Nov. 12, 1909. Pg. 1.
30. *The Boston Daily Globe*. "Deserted, She Tries Suicide." Feb. 7, 1910. Pg. 1.
31. Ibid.
32. *The Washington Post*. "Society Outside the Capital." Feb. 9, 1910. Pg. 9.
33. *The Atlanta Constitution*. "Vanderbilt Gives to Yale." Feb. 11, 1910. Pg. 7.
34. *The Washington Post*. "Life Palls on Beauty." Feb. 11, 1910. Pg. 11.
35. Ibid.
36. Ibid.
37. Ibid.

Chapter Fourteen

Indiscreet Romance

As the final curtain lifted, a crowd of eager spectators jumped to their feet, clapping loudly and yelling enthusiastically. Among them was a young American millionaire up in the balcony seat of the Daly Theater who also rose to applaud the fine ensemble. The main attraction, a young woman attired splendidly from head to toe in delicately flowing Grecian robes, fastened with satin ribbon at the waist to reveal a girlish figure, bowed to thunderous applause. Her eyes were large and doe-like, her mouth wide and generous, and as she smiled radiantly, Lily looked around the audience and up to the balcony, catching Alfred's eye as he stared intensely.

Just as New York society was spinning with tales about an impending betrothal between McKim and Vanderbilt, Alfred surprised everyone by his adoration of an entirely different kind of woman: Miss Lily Elsie. Night after night, the attractive actress performed as the *Guardsman's Goddess* in a musical comedy production in London. With a neoclassical Italian façade, the Daly Theatre was exquisitely decorated and seated 1,200 spectators in a three-tiered amphitheater setting. Considered one of the most bewitching women in all of England, Lily fascinated her audiences, with numerous suitors eager to shower her with gifts. Alfred Gwynne lavished attention on the voluptuous beauty, filling Lily's dressing rooms with lovely blossoms and sending her expensive jewelry.[1]

In 1910, Lily Elsie enjoyed being at the height of her popularity, having performed in George Edwardes' beloved *Merry Widow*, *Dollar Princess*, the *Gaiety Girl* series of plays, and numerous other shows in the Strand, Apollo, and Daly theaters of London's West End. Winston Churchill, a beloved patron of the dramatic arts, said, "It is inconceivable to me that anyone should wish to see the *Merry Widow* without Lily Elsie."[2] Acting since she was eleven years old, Lily was a natural on the stage, losing herself wholeheart-

The beautiful theatrical performer Lilly Elsie captivated Alfred while he was courting Margaret McKim. Vanderbilt sent the young beauty an abundance of flowers and jewels, but to no avail.

edly into her roles and emerging triumphantly transformed into a wealthy heiress, princess, Grecian goddess, or other character with seemingly little effort. Her winsome personality combined with her charming appearance, made her one of the most envied and frequently imitated actresses of her time. Just as the burlesque and vaudeville traditions were delighting audiences across the country, Lily appeared on the stage, with an innocent beauty and seductiveness of a more lasting appeal.

Neily, once spurned by society, had now regained his social stature and, if anything, was painted, in the most pleasing of terms, as a man who had sacrificed his fortune for the "lips of a pretty woman"[3] to whom he had remained faithful and devoted. Society resurrected him as the true leader of the Vanderbilt family despite his father's dictum, recognizing his fidelity to his wife and his inventive ability that had created a sizable fortune of $25,000,000 through his own work. Neily also patented thirty different inventions for locomotives,[4] ten or twelve of which "were of serious importance. They reversed long-established methods of locomotive building."[5]

The Washington Post wrote an article with the witty title "Why It's Lucky for a Millionaire's Son to be Disinherited." With a scathing opinion of Alfred, they claimed that "Every time a new scandal concerning Alfred was reported, a new and useful invention by Cornelius was announced."[6] Society had clearly chosen their favorite son.

Despite his reconciliation with his mother, Neily did not reveal any intimacy with his brother Alfred with whom he expressed cold and cordial relations. Instead, he displayed strong disdain in a private letter to his wife, where he enclosed a clipping from the paper *Town Topics* about A.G.'s "indiscreet romance"[7] with a "much married"[8] woman.

But it seemed, at the moment, Alfred was not as focused on Maggie as Neily thought. Cupid had struck the heart of Alfred, whose devoted attentions to Miss Lily Elsie, nicknamed the "Merry Widow of England,"[9] garnered tremendous attention and noticeably agitated New York society. His affection for the young actress displayed a love of pleasure and social drama that was out of character with the more safe and conventional methods known to the Vanderbilts. Sensational notoriety followed the movements of A.G. whose relationships with women were considered dubious.

Considered "sweet and unspoiled,"[10] with a "sunny and transparent"[11] disposition, Lily Elsie was beloved on the stage for her acting prowess, apparent innocence, and her magnetic personality. Alfred Gwynne was obviously seduced by her charms and exhibited a devotion to the stage beauty that made social companions in Newport circles nervous. His admiration of her was obvious and "flowers, jewels, bonbons, and everything else that the heart of a woman could desire" lay at her feet.[12] Her stage manager George Edwardes rebuked Lily for wearing too many diamonds, which he found distracting from the music and scenery of the set. By early June, Alfred gave up coaching on the weekends, preferring to enjoy the company of Miss Lily Elsie in London.

While in London, Alfred's preparation for the London Show at Olympia was underway. A.G.'s finesse was discernible at every level: he exhibited his ability to both create the space and revive interest in an ancient sport while whetting the appetite of the public who eagerly anticipated every news tidbit that was revealed about the event. Exquisite floral arrangements decorated the stalls of all the exhibitors. A.G. had only twenty stalls while Judge William H. Moore had forty of his own. Every detail of Vanderbilt's entourage was impeccable from the silver fittings to plush curtains of his stalls with white enameling and crimson frieze. Even the walkway was covered with fine Turkish carpets.[13]

Through his influence, Alfred Gwynne Vanderbilt had left an "ineradicable impression on all English equine matters"[14] as he brought horse shows under his "protecting wing"[15] and attracted numerous American visitors to London events. Another coaching event also was announced, the coaching Corinthian for private coaches driven by amateurs only. Military teams from England, France, Spain, Belgium, Sweden, and Greece entered jumping events with prizes over $25,000 and the American and German contingents considered participating as well.

More American tourists flocked to London and the London Opera,[16] which enjoyed record attendance numbers as British royalty mingled with American millionaires. Finding suitable accommodations within the metropolitan area also grew exceedingly difficult. Landlords demanded and received exorbitant rental fees: wealthy Americans were willing to pay anywhere from between $5,000 and $15,000 for three months.[17] As the International Horse Show approached, anticipation was high and hotels filled up quickly in advance.

Exhibitors were wildly enthusiastic about the London show where the judging was improved and the competitors represented greater quality and precision. Resembling a gorgeous glass conservatory with a large closed amphitheater, the Olympia venue was particularly appealing for its attractive floral displays and panoramic view of the exhibitors. Judge W. H. Moore called it the "best managed horse show in details."[18] Displaying his good sportsmanship, Vanderbilt was delighted with the performance of the harness horses, which he called the finest collection of "high class horses I've ever seen."[19]

The Americans set the lead in the coaching competitions.[20] Moore secured first place in the Coaching Corinthian event.[21] Alfred G. Vanderbilt placed third in the new coaching event, while taking first place in the four-in-hand event as well as the Coaching Marathon, excelling at events that he was most familiar with. By winning the marathon event again, Alfred Gwynne retained his cup that he had won the previous year.[22]

As the International Horse Show came to a rapturous finale, A.G. hosted a late-night party to celebrate. Initially a stag party for all the men, the event changed to encompass a few women and included musical comedy artists from all over London, going into the wee hours of the morning. Every guest received fine souvenirs of gold and enamel[23] and the night was one of revelry and merriment akin to a Bacchalian fete.

Outside the equine world, Maggie's divorce case dragged. Her husband sought to rectify what he considered false charges of intoxication and cruelty against him, and hiring detectives to follow his wife on her social escapades.[24] Deftly avoiding the heap of criticism landing on him, Dr. McKim challenged the authority of the Reno courts to invalidate a marriage for a couple who were residents in other states, bringing in his own powerful legal counsel to back up his claim. Revealing a hitherto unknown steely determination, the physician announced that he would take it up to the Supreme Court.[25] While Maggie swore on oath that her husband had mistreated her and had been violent, jealous, and drunk constantly, McKim took his appeal to the higher courts. Despite his legal maneuvers, the Supreme Court in Nevada did not support his efforts to block a district court hearing of his wife's divorce petition.[26] Maggie was gaining ground.

She was quick to capitalize on it:

> Now the case can be tried on its real merits, and I am sure I will get my divorce. All I wanted was a fair trial and he did not want me to have it. Now I can go to trial and prove my case.[27]

By August,[28] in a swift decision made by Judge Pike, after her moving testimony against her husband's cruelty and drunkenness, Maggie triumphantly received her full divorce decree on the grounds of non-support[29] as the court accepted her story alleging mistreatment. Ecstatic, the new divorcee hugged and kissed her attorneys,[30] delighted by the verdict. Her trip to Japan[31] soon after temporarily quelled any further discussion about her relationship with A.G.

With Maggie on the other side of the world, Alfred G. Vanderbilt took the opportunity to engage in a business venture. A.G. capitalized on the example provided by Uncle Willie, who had championed the development of "air rights" buildings over the approach ways to Grand Central Terminal. A.G's first significant real estate investment came as the appropriately named *Vanderbilt Hotel* at Park Avenue and 34th street, as well as joining a hotel

Alfred's second wife, Mrs. Margaret Smith H. McKim the daughter of the man who invented Bromo Seltzer. She obtained a messy divorce from McKim and moved onward to her relationship with Alfred. Library of Congress digital collection.

chain called the United Hotels Company organized by J. P. Morgan. Prior to this investment, his only business venture had been the acquisition of stock in horse shows such as Madison Square Garden and the Olympia event in London.[32] Dr. Isaac Emerson, Maggie's father, who was building an Emerson hotel in Baltimore, helped Alfred with the hotel merger that would consist of the new *Vanderbilt Hotel* in New York City along with a new hotel to be built in Chicago.[33] This decision, coupled with the opening of an important subway station nearby, offered the promise of adding to family coffers.

Alfred was also busy working with other equine supporters to make the Madison Square Garden event more international in scope, inviting British cavalry officers as well as the Belgian war department.[34] He rushed home from Europe aboard the French liner *La Provence* and the steam yacht *Adroit*[35] to see his brother Reggie who had developed typhoid. After suffering for several months,[36] Reginald began to recover and he came to New York along with his wife to take up residence at Alfred's luxurious new digs[37] at 11 East Sixty-Second Street, a spacious residential property near Fifth Avenue, and the former home of Ernesto G. Fabbri.

When Alfred purchased the home of Fabbri in New York,[38] he fueled rumors of an impending marriage, since previously he had sworn that he would not take up residence in New York unless he planned to marry and settle down a second time. Maggie's name resurfaced again in unison with A.G. Society was hopeful that Alfred and Maggie would marry because she was "charming and brainy enough to assume the social leadership in New York which no one seems clever enough to capture since the death of the late Mrs. Astor."[39]

Despite her father's denial, Margaret's own behavior only fed the fire. When asked by reporters, she had said, "I will not deny it. Just don't bother about it."[40] While she often appeared at the *Plaza Hotel* where Alfred was frequently sighted, she also had taken up residence at *The Orchard*, a quaint cottage on Narragansett Avenue in Newport, dining frequently with Mrs. Reginald Vanderbilt along with traveling to the Adirondacks with Alfred upon his return from Europe.

It would be in the equine world, however, that the pair would be best suited; Maggie revealed an uncanny ability at horsemanship. A remarkable athlete in her own right, she was considered a "crack shot"[41] that could participate in "every branch of sport that appeals to the wealthy." She had already dazzled the British with her beauty and her exquisite gowns, taking "London by storm"[42] with her presence at the London Horse Show. Alfred G. Vanderbilt had devoted himself in the last two years exclusively to horse shows and coaching. Maggie was equipped to handle both sides of his personality and the ease with which he moved from social events to horse circles.

Refusing to comment upon her marriage plans for the future, Maggie vehemently denied all statements that had been attributed to her since her divorce, calling them "entirely without foundation, ridiculous in the extreme, and exceedingly distasteful."[43] Yet despite her denials, the gossip did not abate. Maggie's appearance at Madison Square Garden in Alfred's box 13 fueled intense rumors. The National Horse Show was the most anticipated social event of that year and her presence in Vanderbilt's luxurious box could not be ignored. The woman definitely attracted considerable attention in her "gown of white brocaded satin, made with an empire bodice of gold net, and wearing a large black velvet hat with white plumes"[44] that painted "a pretty picture."[45]

Despite all that, Maggie failed to impress the matriarch of the Vanderbilt family. When Alice arrived, she entered the garden and walked towards her son Alfred's box. Tongues wagged as Mrs. Cornelius Vanderbilt consciously ignored Margaret McKim: "she deliberately turned her back and walked on."[46]

Maggie was no easy force to quell, being a "strong, restless woman."[47] She was "dark-haired, opinionated, and self-sufficient,"[48] as well as an expert rider and athlete, who had traveled the world on her father's yacht. She was seasoned, nimble, and adroit: the "perfect match for Alfred."[49] Perhaps she was more than a match; she was clearly capable of reigning in his wandering eyes, if not by strength of character then by her constant policing. She was seemingly always by his side.

Charlie Wilson was also busy courting. He had met a beautiful young woman, Miss Jane Delahanty, at a horse show in New York. After a swift courtship, the pair was wed with the blessings of Jane's parents in Boston. Wilson declared himself rapturously in love:

> After the introduction Cupid actually took the bit in his teeth and would not be guided. We are both very happy and I consider myself the most fortunate of men.[50]

Wilson was fifty years old and his bride only nineteen. At the ceremony, he lied and said he was forty-five.

Not everyone was as happy as Wilson. In a fit of rage, Maggie's former husband, Dr. McKim, threatened to sue them all: his former wife, his father-in-law Dr. Emerson, and even Alfred G. Vanderbilt, her supposed lover. Yet his suit of alienation did not hold up in the Nevada courts. His indignant voice was subdued after a legal agreement was reached at the law office of Hayes and Hershfield, where a settlement of $50,000 was granted to cover his fees incurred as well as an additional $7,500 a year, the product of a $150,000 trust fund created by Alfred.[51]

As the physician linked Alfred Gwynne romantically with his former wife in the suit, the public's attention was riveted upon an impending engagement between the pair. Dr. McKim was reported as saying, "I am absolutely done with this matter. This settlement ends all relations between my wife and myself."[52] Whatever their relations prior to Dr. McKim's request, A.G. and Maggie were forced to address the situation. Maggie refused to comment while a woman speaking on behalf of A.G. replied to reporters, "That's too funny. Mr. Vanderbilt has nothing to say about it."[53] Their lawyers stepped in, announcing that the pair would soon be sailing together in March. Questions about Margaret possibly paying McKim alimony as the wealthier spouse arose: "Have not the sexes reached a plane where equal privileges ought to be shown them?"[54]

As was his wont, Alfred Gwynne remained silent, refusing to comment upon his personal affairs. Instead, he offered a private showing of a new ambulance he had built for disabled horses, named *Venture* after his coach, and generously presented as a gift to the Dumb Friends League.[55]

By April, all of England was caught up in the coronation of King George V. Americans flooded the London metropolis, eager to witness the grandiose ceremony. Among them were Alfred G. Vanderbilt and Margaret McKim, who both arrived separately. London was soon overwhelmed by tourists. To escape the crowds, Alfred and Maggie went on a holiday in Paris.

Maggie acted "under the impression" that everyone present "was a reporter in disguise."[56] Occupying a suite in a small Parisian hotel, she quietly retired to her stateroom and remained there until A.G. appeared in the French capital. She met him at the station and greeted him "effusively."[57] Maintaining appearances, if not their reputations, Alfred Gwynne occupied his own garconnière along the Avenue Victor Hugo, a quieter residence than his luxurious apartment in Bristol. Apparently his apartment at the *Hotel Bristol* had not been occupied by him for the previous three years, but during his stay in Paris he brought Maggie to his "once historic apartment."[58] They "entered the dusty, deserted apartment"[59] at eight o'clock. They emerged at eleven o'clock the same evening, but the press wanted to know what had gone on inside that apartment for three hours.[60]

The press persisted in asking why the pair had not yet issued a marriage license. Vanderbilt had nothing to say on the matter. Rather than speaking to the press herself, Maggie sent her friend Miss McCormick to speak for her. McCormick told the press that "Mrs. McKim…is here and is going to stay here indefinitely." When the press asked about the wedding, McCormick responded, "There's not going to be one. Mrs. McKim had no intention of getting married anyway."[61] While A.G. returned to London, Margaret, along with her friend Miss McCormick, left for Berlin.[62]

While London exploded with millions of visitors eager to witness the king's coronation, rental prices shot through the roof. Alone, Alfred enjoyed the luxurious space of his 14,000 square-foot elaborate apartment priced at $15,000: a price that no Englishmen would fork over. The privileged bachelor, A.G. emerged fresh as a daisy every day, with his signature rose in the buttonhole of his suit.[63]

As American cavalry prepared to enter the jumping competitions, wealthy Americans, such as Harriman, Whitney, Vanderbilt, and Moore, offered their own high quality equines to the soldiers to replace the horses issued by the army. Immediately, the English expelled a tirade of criticism:

> We are apparently to be treated to a contest between American dollars and British skill. It is very regrettable that we are to have another example of the degradation of sport, which is so unsatisfactory a feature of American life. We are apparently not to have a competition between men who have trained their own horses and will exercise their own skill, but the American officer will have little to do on his $5,000 Virginian jumper.[64]

Along with the feverish excitement generated by the coronation, the country geared up for the International Horse Show, which again promised to be a fine event. Prices soared as Americans paid more for the best views, real estate owners made veritable fortunes renting out apartments and residences, new decorations were acquired for the show, and a full spectacle of royal entertainment, from bugles to wagons, was offered.

As bonfires encircled the city, the royal family proceeded to the *Crystal Palace*, while members of the church lit candles and prayed for His Highness. Every pub celebrated the coronation as taverns overflowed with tipsy guests and drunkards in a lavish party that extended into the early morning. Capitalizing on the event, Alfred threw a magnificent party at his residence in Gloucester House. A.G. had a view of the entire procession from his penthouse; he could see the royal entourage emerge out of *Buckingham Palace* and wind its way from the *Ritz Hotel* to Hyde Park and down Constitution hill back to the palace gates.[65]

Ten days later, in honor of the new British monarch, Alfred offered guests at his supper party a commemorative souvenir of cigarette, match, and card cases made of solid silver with the names "George V and Mary" in blue enamel. As usual, his attention to fine detail was immaculate and guests were awed by the Coaching Club decoration placed at the center of the dining table. The arrangement consisted of a complete coaching model in silverware of the Coaching Club meet in Hyde Park, replete with full promenades, railings, lamp posts, five exquisite four-in-hand coaches, and numerous little figurines ranging from nursemaids to gowned society folks, dogs, and soldiers. Dwarf trees and miniature grass turf complemented the gleaming silver, creating a "perfect work of art."[66]

On December 17, 1911, a wet and grey Sunday only five months later, Alfred Gwynne Vanderbilt and his secretary and lawyer, arrived in the small town of Reigate, one of A.G.'s favorite watering holes along the Brighton Road. A trio met his entourage: Margaret McKim, her friend Ethel McCormack, and her lawyer Roy Gasser. Maggie was attired in a modest black silk gown with a brimmed black hat trimmed with cord.[67] In a small secret ceremony that took only a few minutes, Mr. Handsotone, the registrar, wed the young pair. A.G described himself as a man "of independent means"[68] and listed his residence as the "*Gloucester House.*"[69]

Maggie's betrothal was so well concealed that none of her servants at her residence *The Stream* in Botchworth, three miles from Reigate, had any knowledge of her wedding, and were completely taken by surprise when she returned soon after to offer gifts and a luncheon.

Not a single member of the Vanderbilt clan was present at the wedding, a radical departure from Alfred's previous marriage conducted with fastidious attention and a large guest list of family and friends. A.G. sent a telegram to his mother with the news of his marriage, which Alice conveyed to the public without emotion via a footman:

> Vanderbilt-McKim-On Dec 17, at Reigate, Surrey, Eng, Alfred Gwynne Vanderbilt, son of the late Cornelius Vanderbilt of New York, to Margaret Emerson McKim, daughter of Capt I. E. Emerson of Baltimore.

All attempts to draw forth her opinion on the union failed miserably. Mrs. Cornelius Vanderbilt Sr. valued her family's privacy above all and even if she did not approve of her son's marriage no one in the public would ever know. No one was prepared to hear the news and Grace, in surprise, refused to comment instantly. She would not say whether she or Neily approved of the match.

The Emersons responded quite differently, expressing joy at their daughter's union. The Captain had divorced his wife, who now occupied a residence in Druid Hill Park. Both of them, however, expressed similar emotions of approval and surprise at the announcement.

While the wedding itself had been a sedate ceremony of a few minutes, the honeymoon promised adventure and romance, as the couple embarked upon a month-long motorcar tour of the continent. They also announced their intention to create their own flat, occupying the top and adjacent floors of the *Vanderbilt Hotel*, in New York. These luxurious accommodations were undoubtedly among the most attractive properties in the entire city and speculated to be $40,000 a year in rent alone.[70]

Opulent and stately, the *Vanderbilt Hotel,* with twenty-three stories, had cost more than four million dollars to build and followed many specifications precisely laid out by the young millionaire. A.G. had missed most of the fanfare accompanying the hotel's opening in January, but looked forward to occupying a grand penthouse flat with a commanding view. It was unfortunate for Alfred that within a few days of its grand opening, through one person's careless action of throwing a lighted match on the ground, the insulation and then furniture on the third floor would catch fire, resulting in heavy water damage as fire trucks rushed to put out the flames.

NOTES

1. *The Los Angeles Times*. "Vanderbilt Wealth Spent on Stage Beauty." Jun 6, 1910. Pg. 11.
2. Wickham, Glenn. *A History of Theatre*. London: Phaedon Press, 1994.
3. *The Washington Post*. "Paid High for their Kisses." Nov. 27, 1910. Pg. MS1.
4. *The Washington Post*. "Why It's Lucky for a Millionaire's Son to be Disinherited." 10 June 1910.
5. Ibid.
6. Ibid.
7. Vanderbilt Jr., Cornelius V. *Queen of the Golden Age: The Fabulous Story of Grace Wilson Vanderbilt*. New York, NY: McGraw-Hill Book Company. 1956. Pg. 224.
8. Ibid.
9. *The Chicago Daily Tribune*. "The Imp, the Merry Widow, and the Millionaires." Jul 3, 1910. Pg. G1.
10. Ibid.
11. Ibid.
12. *The Atlanta Constitution*. "Alfred Vanderbilt to Wed 'Dollar Princess.'" Jun 12, 1910. Pg. D7.
13. *The New York Times*. "Arena at Olympia A Mass of Flowers." June 5, 1910. Pg. C3.
14. *The Washington Post*. "Alfred Vanderbilt's Influence." March 20, 1910. Pg. 14.
15. Ibid.
16. *The New York Times*. "London Opera Prospers." April 3, 1910. Pg. C2.
17. *The New York Times*. "Americans Pay High for London Houses." March 20, 1910. Pg. C2.
18. *The Chicago Daily Tribune*. "Horse Show Best Ever Held, Says Americans in London." Jun 19, 1910. Pg. A1.
19. Ibid.
20. Ibid. Pg. 95.
21. *The New York Times*. "Moore Beats Vanderbilt." Jun 14, 1910. Pg. 15.

22. *The Christian Science Monitor*. "A.G. Vanderbilt Defends Trophy." Jun 11, 1910. Pg. 3.
23. *The Chicago Daily Tribune*. "Vanderbilt Gives Late Party." July 3, 1910. Pg. A2.
24. *The Washington Post*. "Sidelights of the Smart Set." Jun 7, 1910. Pg. 7.
25. Ibid.
26. *The Chicago Daily Tribune*. "Mrs. McKim Wins Point." Aug. 5, 1910. Pg. 3
27. Ibid.
28. *The Washington Post*. "Mrs. M'Kim Gets Divorce." Aug. 4, 1910. Pg. 7.
29. *The Los Angeles Times*. "Divorce Makes Her So Happy." Aug. 14, 1910. Pg. 12.
30. Ibid.
31. *The Washington Post*. "Mrs. M'Kim Off to Japan." Aug. 18, 1910. Pg. 7.
32. *The Wall Street Journal*. "A. Vanderbilt Experiment." Sept. 15, 1910. Pg. 1.
33. *The Chicago Daily Tribune*. "$50,000,000 Hotel Merger: A.G. Vanderbilt as Backer?" March 31, 1910. Pg. 3.
34. *The Chicago Daily Tribune*. "Alfred G. Vanderbilt Head of New York Horse Show." Aug. 14, 1910. Pg. C3.
35. *Boston Daily Globe*. "Newport, R.I. Sick Improve." Sept. 5, 1910. Pg. 4.
36. *The New York Times*. "Newport Patients Do Well." Sept. 5, 1910. Pg. 7.
37. *The Washington Post*. "Fashion's Fads and Fancies." Nov. 6, 1910. Pg. E8.
38. *The Washington Post*. "Fashion's Fads and Fancies." Nov. 11, 1910. Pg. 7.
39. *The Evening Post*. "A Baltimore Beauty." July 2,1911. Pg. 7.
40. *The Washington Post*. "Social Set of Other Cities." Sept. 23, 1910. Pg. 7.
41. Ibid.
42. Ibid.
43. *The Washington Post*. "Mrs. M'Kim Silent on Plans." Oct. 24, 1910. Pg. 3.
44. *The Washington Post*. "Snapshots at Social Leaders." Nov. 18, 1910. Pg. 4.
45. *The Washington Post*. "Snapshots at Social Leaders." Nov. 18, 1910. Pg. 4.
46. *The Washington Post*. "Society at the Show." Nov. 19, 1910. Pg. 11.
47. Ibid.
48. Ibid.
49. Ibid.
50. *Boston Daily Globe*. "East Boston Girl Bride of Vanderbilt's Whip." Jan 20, 1911. Pg. 11.
51. *The New York Times*. "McKim Agrees Not to Sue Vanderbilt." Feb. 22, 1911. Pg. 1.
52. *The Washington Post*. "McKim to get $7,500 a year." Feb. 23, 1911. Pg. 2.
53. *The New York Times*. "Alfred Vanderbilt Silent." Feb. 26, 1911. Pg. 11.
54. *The Chicago Daily Tribune*. "Shall Rich Wife Pay Alimony?" Mar. 26, 1911. Pg. G1.
55. *The New York Times*. "See Vanderbilt Ambulance." March 12, 1911. Pg. 14.
56. *The New York Times*. "Vanderbilt-McKim Wedding Expected." Apr 23, 1911. Pg. C1.
57. Ibid.

58. *Oakland Tribune.* "A. Vanderbilt Meets Mrs. M'Kim." 23 April 1911: 18.

59. Ibid.

60. Ibid.

61. Ibid.

62. *The New York Times*. "A.G. Vanderbilt Leaves." Apr. 24, 1911. Pg. 4.

63. *The Atlanta Constitution.* "$15,000 Flats too Rich for the Blood of Englishmen." ENGLISHMEN. May 7, 1911.

64. *The New York Times*. "Olympia, London, to be Transformed Into an Elizabethan Village for the Coronation Year Horse Show." May 7, 1911. Pg. C2.

65. *The Boston Daily Globe*. "London is Jammed for the Coronation." Jun. 22, 1911.

66. *The Atlanta Constitution*. "Horse Show in London Centers World Interest." Jul. 2, 1911. Pg. A4.

67. *The Boston Daily Globe*. "Marry In London Under a License." Dec. 18, 1911. Pg. 1.

68. *The New York Times*. "Bride Cables Her Parents." Dec. 18, 1911. Pg. 1.

69. Ibid.

70. *The Boston Daily Globe*. "In Luxurious Flat." Dec. 19, 1911. Pg. 9.

Chapter Fifteen

A Rising Tide

Eager to put aside their mutually "stormy marital careers"[1] behind them, Alfred and Maggie embarked upon a new life together. While the Vanderbilt family itself expressed surprise and refused to comment upon the union, Newport society was not surprised.[2] Avoiding the harsh winter, the couple stayed in Europe, taking a trip in February down to Naples, Italy from where they set sail on the yacht *Maud* to tour Egypt.[3] Away from the magnifying lens of American reporters, Maggie relaxed in the company of her new husband as papers compared him to a Roman reveler Marcus Antonius Crassus from centuries ago, whose love letters had recently been found in Pompeii:

> Crassus was a gay young millionaire from Rome, a sort of Alfred Vanderbilt of that period. He was a sportsman, a connoisseur of wine, and had a remarkable number of sentimental affairs.[4]

Soon after that flattering comment was made, the *Titanic* departed from the port of Southampton in London on April 10th, 1912. Measuring eight hundred and eighty-two feet in length and ninety-two feet in width, and capable of carrying more than three thousand and five hundred passengers, the *Titanic* was the second in the family of luxurious Olympic cruisers for transatlantic journeys from America to Europe. With one thousand and three hundred passengers on board[5], the *Titanic* embarked upon its maiden voyage across the Atlantic a little after noon.

The White Star liner *Titanic* invited disaster from the moment of its departure. As she pulled out of port, the suction issuing from the *Titanic* passing through the water, pried the smaller liner *New York* loose from the pier. As the *New York* drifted helplessly, stern first, towards the looming *Titanic*, breathless spectators watched[6] as the harbor pilot and captain, acting quickly and decisively, halted the *Titanic*, putting its engines in reverse while catching the *New York* with ropes, tugging her away and avoiding a dreadful collision.

Continuing along without any major incidents to Cherbourg, France[7] that evening, as new passengers boarded and others disembarked, the *Titanic* called at Queenstown, Ireland the following morning with more than two thousand passengers on board.

As she left the shores of Ireland and made her progress westward, the Titanic picked up speed, despite receiving warnings about icebergs in the surrounding waters. Twenty minutes before midnight on the fifth day of the journey, the ship slammed into a colossal iceberg, ripping its front immediately. The captain estimated that the ship would stay afloat for another two hours so the crew and passengers frantically lowered lifeboats into the freezing waters. Over seven hundred passengers were evacuated before the mighty ship sank at 2:20 a.m. The Titanic, described as an "unsinkable vessel,"[8] would go down in history as the largest passenger ship to sink in one of the world's greatest maritime disasters. More than one thousand and five hundred passengers perished that night. Reports of the first-class passengers on board surfaced in newspapers such as *The Atlanta* and the names of Colonel and Mrs. Astor, Benjamin Guggenheim, and others were announced, including that of Alfred G. Vanderbilt.[9]

Despite rumors, A.G. was not on board the *Titanic* and any anxieties his mother Mrs. Cornelius Vanderbilt experienced were allayed when she received a cablegram from Alfred in London that he was safe and had not traveled aboard the sinking liner.[10] Alice read the note to her dinner guests, dispelling all fear and anxiety.[11]

Completely unaffected by his near death experience, Alfred Gwynne resumed his coaching trips from London to Brighton once again,[12] with Maggie occupying the box seat next to him. His attention was split among his equine pursuits, life with Margaret, and his new real estate investments that included a new railroad Y.M.C.A.[13] adjacent to the Grand Central Terminal. Unable to give up his coaching, A.G. alternated his time again between London and New York with Maggie faithfully by his side.

On September 23, 1912, they welcomed their first child. Joyful telegrams, sent to Mrs. C. Hazeltine Basshor, the mother of Margaret, Captain Emerson, and Alice Vanderbilt, announced the birth of a son Alfred Gwynne Vanderbilt II in Betchworth, Surrey in England.[14] A new heir to the Vanderbilt millions had been born.

On October 20th, 1912, Alfred celebrated his thirty-fifth birthday, receiving the second half of his estate inheritance while in London.[15] A.G. and Margaret had created a new life for themselves in England that both enjoyed very much.[16] It would make sense that while they intended to return to New York

Alfred began construction of the Vanderbilt Hotel in 1910. The top two floors were dedicated to a private penthouse for the new Vanderbilt family. Unfortunately for Vanderbilt on the day he planned to move in a fire claimed the third floor. Everything has a beginning and here we see the new foundation on the west side of 4th Avenue between 33rd and 34th Streets. Foundation of Vanderbilt Hotel under construction. Culver Pictures. April 1910.

The Vanderbilt Hotel, New York. Period postcard with no identification or origin.

Alfred Vanderbilt at the whip. His wife Margaret McKim Emerson is next to him. 1913. The International News Service, 200 Williams St., N.Y.

Unidentified nurse holding baby son, Alfred Gwynne Jr., ten months old, with Margaret McKim center and Alfred on right. 1913. International News Service.

within a few weeks and occupy their suite at the *Vanderbilt Hotel*,[17] they also looked forward to having a more permanent English residence. Leaving their baby son behind because he was too young to travel, the young couple arrived in New York on the French liner *Provence* in fine health and good spirits. Vanderbilt attended to his duties as the director of the National Horse Show[18] and called upon his mother. Alfred Jr. would be christened in England,[19] fueling rumors that A.G. planned to live there permanently because of the many ties he had formed abroad, and the spacious accommodations he possessed at the corner of Park Lane and Piccadilly Street.[20]

After a short visit, the couple returned to England for the winter. In April, when the couple returned for another visit, America welcomed the prodigal children home. Unusually chatty with the press, Maggie revealed friendly and spontaneous warmth within her personality in an interview with Mary Isabel Brush, sharing her desires for a large vegetable garden and sewing, revealing a far more domestic side to the millionaire's wife than expected. Sharing pictures of her newborn, Margaret tenderly declared that the child was "exactly like his father."[21] The news reporter wrote however:

> It was almost humorous that a little scrap of a thing could be so like the handsome, buoyant, clean shaven, square jawed, husky looking young man who had left the room a few minutes previously.[22]

Mary Isabel's personal interview gave a favorable impression of a happily married young couple that "derived genuine amusement from small incidents"[23] together and were "excellent companions."[24] Maggie's warmth worked wonders, reaching even into the austere realm of the *Breakers*. To the surprise and envy of friends and family, the young woman succeeded in melting the frigid haughtiness of her mother-in-law Mrs. Cornelius Vanderbilt when she accompanied her husband, baby in tow, to meet Alice at the *Hotel Majestic*.[25] As the ice between the two women broke, they began to spend more time together, enjoying each other's company as they shopped, sipped tea, and tenderly admired Alfred Jr.'s every action. They were apparently "on the most intimate of terms."[26]

Maggie also accompanied Alfred whenever possible, traveling with him to Brighton as he prepared for his next coaching run and also to Paris for the horse show events.[27] The 1913 coaching line from London to Brighton and back had more passengers than ever before.[28] Maggie was always at his side, occupying the seat next to him "in case anything should happen to him, so that it might also overtake her."[29]

Everyone present noticed their love for each other as the couple exuded a particular vivacious enthusiasm.[30] As A.G. reaped in the honors in London, triumphantly winning the coaching marathon in the presence of Queen Alexandra,[31] Maggie was there to celebrate his victory with him. Wisely, the couple kept to themselves during the 1913 London horse show. Sometimes it seemed they should just stay away from society indefinitely.

A cold social war raged in Newport, where society debated which Mrs. Alfred Vanderbilt should receive their favor: Margaret or Elsie. For most of these women, their loyalties lay with Elsie French whom many had known intimately. Previously, the two women had taken great efforts to avoid seeing each other, leading entirely separate social lives, but now as they both occupied the same town, this avoidance now extended to their friends who chose alternately to entertain one while slighting the other. In most cases, Elsie won easily; Margaret and Alfred Gwynne were ostracized.

If Alfred were to encounter Elsie on the streets of Newport, it instantly became obvious who held the power in the situation. Whenever Alfred saw the "recognized Newport leader,"[32] he would look at her but she would "look at and beyond him without as much as a sign of recognition of his presence on the road."[33] Alfred's old friends would acknowledge him, but "their greetings have lost the old time cordiality."[34] When the women in Newport see Alfred walking with his new wife, they would "turn to look the other way, or are so engrossed in conversation they cannot see her at all."[35]

When the newlyweds arrived in Newport at the beginning of the summer season, they expected a friendly welcome. Even if society was against their marriage, they assumed everyone would at least want to meet their new son. However, when they arrived, the only person there to greet them was Reginald Vanderbilt. All of the other Vanderbilts had fled Newport. Even Alice, Alfred's mother, had left to sail for Europe.

> 'But didn't they know we were coming?' Mrs. Vanderbilt No. 2 inquired petulantly of her brother-in-law.
>
> 'Oh, yes; they knew all right," stammered Reginald in reply. But he did not need to finish, Mrs. Vanderbilt understood.[36]

When Elsie was invited to a particular social function such as Mrs. Stuyvesant Fish's[37] annual ball, the A.G. Vanderbilts were ignored. Three hundred acquaintances of the couple were invited to the ball as well as to dinner with Mrs. Hermann Oelrich before the ball.[38] Alfred instead took the family up to *Sagamore* in the Adirondacks aboard the *Wayfarer*, bringing along all the horses, men, and equipment necessary for the Syracuse show[39] that would follow soon after. Entertaining far less than he had just after the marriage, Alfred Gwynne instead took his wife and family from one horse show to another.[40]

Margaret Vanderbilt was remarkably different from other Vanderbilt women in her embrace of simple living, surprising socialites and reporters with her love of fresh air, as she walked along fashionable streets such as the posh Rue de la Paix in Paris, pushing her baby stroller at a dignified pace, revealing a down to earth and sweet motherly affection that was unexpected of the wife of a Vanderbilt millionaire. With a nurse following quietly behind, Maggie charmed locals, as she ventured into shops, whose owners delighted in having her as a customer.[41]

Uncle George, brother to Alfred's father, died unexpectedly, without a male heir and leaving behind his stately Vanderbilt mansion at Fifth Avenue in New York, numerous artworks, real estate, and cash totaling $6,000,000, all of which was bequeathed to Neily.[42] Fifteen years after his own father's death, Neily would be redeemed in every possible manner: society accepted him as the true heir to his father's legacy, his mother and wife were reunited, and he established himself as one of the greatest inventive geniuses of his family. Now his uncle bestowed upon him a large portion of his grandfather's fortune. The tide had definitely changed in his favor.

Open criticism of Alfred's lifestyle filled the papers at home when he embarked again upon his coaching endeavors in London the following summer. While Maggie was described as a "good wife"[43] who accompanied her husband in the "horsiest of expeditions, into the wildest of countries,"[44] A.G. was painted far less positively:

> What if the practice, the interest, the ardor, the talent which have gone on to perfect this good looking American in his accomplishment had been directed to something more practical, more serviceable, or more intellectually distinguished?[45]

Alfred Gwynne's accomplishment as a coaching whip, taking his customers to and from London for three pounds, was the pursuit of a man who had money, time to spare, and "skill at something which is no good to anybody."[46]

Weak and destitute, Florence Schenck was a pitiful alcoholic. Her desire for freedom and curiosity for what lay beyond the modest white home in Virginia that she knew, had compelled her to follow the path Charlie Wilson had enticed her to follow. Little did she know how deep she would fall and how, in her desire to escape society's narrow definitions of what she could be, Florence had lost who she was. Despondent and hopeless, her pleas for assistance and for common decency had fallen upon deaf ears.

At seventeen with "beauty of an unusual order,"[47] Florence was graceful, slender, and lovely; a remarkable blonde beauty that turned heads wherever she went. Hailing from a good Southern home, she had longed to expand her horizons beyond the limits of her small town. Charlie Wilson was almost thrice her age but he was prosperous. As a favored employee of Alfred G. Vanderbilt, Wilson was constantly traveling to London and Paris with his employer and enjoying a high life that Florence could only dream of. Wilson stirred up deep, dormant desires in her and when he offered her the opportunity to join aboard the *Wayfarer* during the Norfolk Horse Show, she agreed instantly without a moment's hesitation. It was a call of the wild[48] and unfamiliar, as the bright city lights of New York, Paris, and London beckoned and the young woman was entranced, her mind filled with ideas of romance, gaiety, and the high life.

She was Broadway bound, like so many dreamers. In 1907 she briefly appeared in the play *Hip! Hip! Horray!* as a member of the chorus, one "Dottie Fisher" pitifully indicated as "of the swell set."[49]

Telling her mother she was going to church, Schenck instead accompanied Wilson to the *Wayfarer*. The trip severed her family bonds and changed her life inextricably forever. In a heartrending letter to her friends in April of 1912, after she had been moved from one sanitarium to another, Florence recalled, "I have never seen my home since we went away on the *Wayfarer*. What a fitting name for that car! It made a wayfarer out of me."[50]

Initially when Florence left with Wilson aboard the *Wayfarer*, she was happy and in high spirits. Florence had given her body and heart so freely to Wilson: "The whole of me, forever, what more the woman can."[51] She was in love with him but she was also beholden to the relationship. Florence could not go home to her parents as the woman that she was now; the only possibility of redemption in society existed through marriage. Wilson had promised to wed Florence and though she married him in private, things soon began to unravel.

Schenck discovered Wilson's prior marriage and she took him to court because he denied marrying her. When her own betrothal to Wilson came under question in the courts, she was hysterical. Florence grew exceedingly frustrated as all attempts to take her case seriously failed. Apparently, Alfred G. Vanderbilt had assisted in conducting legal negotiations to "hush up the matter."[52] Wilson's wife soon divorced him, yet Charlie showed no sign of taking Florence as his new wife. He ignored her desperate cries for acceptance. Her rebellion from her own dull Southern lifestyle and the expected mores of society imploded. Schenck was helpless, bereft of any support; disowned by the only family she had ever known and a horse crowd that now turned its back on her.

After the death of Agnes Ruiz in 1909, Florence's depression took a darker turn, sliding into a downward spiral. Florence's lawyer told the press that Schenck reminded Alfred of Agnes, so "he ordered Wilson to get rid of her on peril of losing his place."[53]

Penniless, rejected by Wilson, and ignored by Alfred Gwynne, she turned to heavy drinking and grew suicidal herself. Frequently arrested in Paris for drinking too much, "Florrie" had lost the will to live, immediately reverting back to her old ways, crying, "What's the use, anyhow? My family doesn't want me, and as nobody cares for me, I will have to go on the best I can."[54] The death of Ruiz was particularly painful because of the memories of "jolly parties"[55] Schenck had enjoyed with Agnes, Charlie, and Alfred.

Florence confided in a friend that Agnes had a large painting of Alfred Vanderbilt in a solid gold frame right by her bed and was paranoid that A.G. would leave her. Blaming it on her perceived weight gain, Ruiz went crazy trying to lose weight. Schenck said, "She had the idea that Vanderbilt did not love her any more…The first thing I knew she shot herself and tumbled Vanderbilt's picture, the stand and herself over on the floor in a mess. Ugh!"[56]

The cold hard truth of death hit Florence hard. She found Alfred Gwynne was "never the same man"[57] after Ruiz's suicide. Charlie grew distant, refusing to see her after Agnes' death. Heartbroken and isolated, Schenck tried but could not forget. After a failed suit of betrayal against Charlie, Florence attempted suicide by overdosing on chloral. She tried again to make Wilson accountable in the courts, failing miserably. Charlie instead offered a miniscule alimony payment of $10 a month.

When Wilson wed another young woman, Miss Jane Delahanty, in January of 1911,[58] all of Florence's hopes of reconciliation were crushed. The woman was only nineteen years old and her parents from Boston had approved the match. The couple was very smitten with each other and there was no going back for Schenck as the new Mrs. Wilson accompanied her husband on all of his coaching trips and transatlantic journeys.[59]

As her spirits sunk further, her health, which had deteriorated from malnutrition, stress, and her suicide attempts, grew worse. The young beauty was hardly recognizable, as the color had faded from her cheeks and her eyes now lay sunken in a face terrifying in its hopelessness and despair. Begging for remorse, in desperation she pleaded in letters:

> And I am, only twenty-one. Since I ran away from home four years ago I have lived sixty years of humiliation and heartbreak. When I discovered my mistake I would have gone back home if they would have let me. I would have crawled back on my hands and knees, my head in the dust, but my father forbade me to ever cross the threshold of our home or ever communicate with my sisters. Oh, if I could only communicate with them. I would warn those lovely girls of what a monster the world is; how it waits, coiled in the heart of what we call the 'gay life,' to strangle their souls. I would warn them against the weakness and folly that have been my downfall.[60]

On December 8, 1913, it was revealed in the press that Florence Schenck was fatally sick with a tumor near her heart and was dying.[61] A patient at the private sanitarium of Miss Alston, the Virginia beauty who had brought two suits of defamation against Charlie H. Wilson, was not expected to live past the morning.[62]

Three weeks prior on November 20th, Schenck had filed suit against Wilson for $50,000. She claimed that she had married him believing that he had already divorced his first wife. Citing breach of contract, fraud, and deceit, Florence had also attached a certified copy of the marriage certificate between Schenck and Wilson to prove her claim and refute Charlie's contention that they were never married. In her legal suit, Schenck also stated:

> I have endeavored not to bring in members of the Vanderbilt set but it may be necessary to subpoena a large number of fashionables. By persons well known in society I can prove the chief contentions I make.[63]

While Wilson admitted to having received notice of her lawsuit, he declined to make any comments. As Florence lay on her deathbed, her father was immediately contacted while the doctor in attendance, Dr. E.P. Teague, warned that the young woman would not likely recover from the devastating illness. Resentment still raged within her father, Dr. Powhatan Schenck, who declined to leave immediately, waiting an entire day before coming to see her. He had telegraphed earlier in the day and heard that his daughter seemed to be better.[64]

As clergymen offered to call upon her, Florence refused to see them, growing more hysterical, pleading and praying to live: "I feel certain God will let me live. I don't want to die. I must live."[65]

According to Dr. Teague, the poor woman had "the slightest change of recovery"[66] and "death could come at any moment."[67] While she waited for death's arrival, Schenck dictated a letter to warn other girls who might be lured to the "gay primrose path"[68], sharing her own folly of leaving what she thought was a humdrum, respectable life in Norfolk to see the world in a journey that instead of leading her to "potter's field"[69] led to the morgue.

It would take an additional three weeks before Florence's father would actually arrive to his daughter's bedside, finally listening to her heartrending pleas for forgiveness and acceptance. Despite being warned that moving her body could possibly kill her in her delicate condition, Dr. Schenck carried his daughter in her comatose condition away from the sanitarium back to a Baltimore hospital by stretcher. Dr. Schenck hoped that his daughter would recover sufficiently from the trip to be moved back to her home to die in peace.[70] The very next day January 5th, 1914, Florence Schenck died in her parent's home.

The court gave its decree as Justice Gavegan rendered his decision on Florence Schenck's lawsuit against Wilson, taking into full consideration all of Schenck's claims about a "promise of marriage"[71] that had induced her to leave her family home while the plaintiff Wilson was already married and planned to divorce his previous wife but in actuality, had not commenced any such legal actions for divorce. While the Judge did not provide a definitive judgment on the case, he did hold that Schenck's allegations, while not yet validated, still had to be answered and that denying this process would not only be an "error of law"[72] but would also be "denying justice to a woman"[73] while "placing a premium on the perfidy and infamy of a man."[74]

Judge Gavegan did not know as he handed out his decision that the young woman was already dead. Once her death was confirmed, it grew uncertain whether the case would be heard at all. It seemed she would never get justice for the wrongs done to her. Florence Schenck had fallen; the fourth victim of Alfred's depravity.

NOTES

1. *The Chicago Daily Tribune*. "A.G. Vanderbilt Weds Mrs. McKim." Dec. 18, 1911. Pg. 1.
2. *The New York Times*. "No Surprise for Newport." Dec. 19, 1911. Pg. 13.
3. *The New York Times*. "Gives Dinners in Paris." Feb. 25, 1912. Pg. C2.
4. *The Atlanta Constitution*. "How a Pompeian 'Alfred Vanderbilt' Wrote Love Letters to His Chloe 1900 Years Ago." March 31, 1912. Pg. C7.
5. *The New York Times*. "Titanic in Peril, On Leaving Port." April 11, 1912. Pg. 1.
6. Ibid.
7. Ibid.
8. *The Atlanta Constitution*. "'Horrible Loss of Life,' Says White Star Officials." April 16, 1912. pg. 2.
9. Ibid.
10. *The Atlanta Constitution*. "Alfred Gwynne Vanderbilt." April 16, 1912. Pg. 2.
11. *The New York Times*. "Social Notes." April 16, 1912. Pg. 13.
12. *The New York Times*. "Venture Coaching Season." May 19, 1912. Pg. C6.
13. *The Atlanta Constitution*. "Vanderbilts to Erect Fine Y.M.C.A. Building." Jun. 2, 1912. Pg. C12.
14. *The New York Times*. "Mrs. A. G. Vanderbilt Gives Birth to Son." Sept. 23, 1912. Pg. 1.
15. *The New York Times*. "30,000,000 to Vanderbilt." Oct. 20, 1912. Pg. 1.
16. *The New York Times*. "Vanderbilt Likes London." Nov. 23, 1912. Pg. 4.
17. *The New York Times*. "A. G. Vanderbilt Coming." Oct. 26, 1912. Pg. 9.
18. *The Christian Science Monitor*. "Horse Show is opened in New York." Nov. 16, 1912. Pg. 22.
19. *The New York Times*. "A. G. Vanderbilts Here." Nov. 3, 1912. Pg. 6.
20. *The New York Times*. "Vanderbilt Likes London." Nov. 23, 1912. Pg. 4.

21. Brush, Mary Isabel. *Special to The New York Times*. "Vanderbilts Abroad Again After Making Summer Plans." April 6, 1913. Pg. H2.
22. Ibid.
23. Ibid.
24. Ibid.
25. *The Chicago Daily Tribune*. "Chicagoans Flock to Paris from All Over the Globe." May 11, 1913. Pg. H2.
26. Ibid.
27. *The Chicago Daily Tribune*. "Vanderbilt Women Chummy." May 11, 1913. Pg. H2.
28. *The New York Times*. "Best Year for Coaching." Jul 13, 1913. Pg. C3.
29. *The Atlanta Constitution*. "Cathleen Vanderbilt as Fairy Godmother." June 21, 1914. Pg. A2.
30. *The Chicago Daily Tribune*. "Mrs. John Astor Most Popular Woman at Newport." Aug. 10, 1913. Pg. E5.
31. *The New York Times*. "Vanderbilt Coach Wins." Jun 22, 1913. Pg. 6.
32. *The Kansas City Star*. "All Newport Snubs Them." August 22, 1913.
33. Ibid.
34. Ibid.
35. Ibid.
36. *The Kansas City Star*. "All Newport Snubs Them." August 22, 1913.
37. *The Atlanta Constitution*. "Two Mrs. Vanderbilts at War." Aug. 31, 1913. Pg. 7.
38. *The Kansas City Star*. "All Newport Snubs Them." August 22, 1913.
39. *The Christian Science Monitor*. "A.G. Vanderbilt Family Leaves." Sept. 5, 1913. Pg. 8.
40. *The Chicago Daily Tribune*. "Newporters Planning Hotel for "Right Sort of People." Sept. 7, 1913. Pg. E2.
41. *The Chicago Daily Tribune*. "Social News From Paris." Mar. 10, 1914. Pg. D9.
42. *The New York Times*. "C. Vanderbilt Gets Mansion and Art." Mar. 10, 1914. Pg. 5.
43. *The Chicago Daily Tribune*. "Can You Tell Me Why A.G. Vanderbilt Does This?" Jul 5, 1914. Pg. F4.
44. Ibid.
45. Ibid.
46. Ibid.
47. *The Atlanta Constitution*. "The Path to Paris." Apr. 7, 1912. Pg. E10.
48. Phrase is in reference to Jack London's popular novel by the same name *Call of the Wild* published in 1903.
49. Internet Broadway Data Base, IBDB.com
50. *The Atlanta Constitution*. "The Path to Paris." Apr. 7, 1912. Pg. E10.
51. Dickinson, Emily. *Emily Dickinson: The Complete Poems*. "Surrender." New York: Bartleby. 2000.
52. Ibid.

53. *The Syracuse Herald*. "Attempt of Florence Schenck To Take Her Life Said To Be Due To The Suicide Of Mrs. Ruiz." February 13, 1910. Pg. 2A.
54. *The Atlanta Constitution*. "The Path to Paris." Apr. 7, 1912. Pg. E10.
55. Ibid.
56. Ibid.
57. Ibid.
58. Ibid.
59. *Boston Daily Globe*. "New Vanderbilt and Astor Brides will Grace Newport's Summer Season." Jan. 28, 1912. Pg. 47.
60. Ibid.
61. *The Washington Post*. "Heart-Suit Beauty Dying." Dec. 8, 1913. Pg. 5.
62. Ibid.
63. *Boston Daily Globe*. "Florence Schenck Dies." Nov. 20, 1913. Pg. 13.
64. *The New York Times*. "Dr. Schenck Waits a Day." Dec. 12, 1913. Pg. 3.
65. *The Washington Post*. "Miss Schenck Fears to Die." Dec. 14, 1913. Pg. 11.
66. Ibid.
67. Ibid.
68. *The Washington Post*. "My Path Leads to the Morgue – then to Potter's Field." Feb. 1, 1914. Pg. SM1.
69. Ibid.
70. *The Washington Post*. "Florence Schenck Gone." Jan. 4, 1914. Pg. 1.
71. *The Washington Post*. "Schenck Case May Go On." Jan. 6, 1914. Pg. 8.
72. Ibid.
73. Ibid.
74. Ibid.

Chapter Sixteen

1914

The year 1914 was a momentous year. Change was brewing overseas and had made its way to American shores. While Alfred busied himself with preparations for horse shows at home, Europe had become embroiled in a war of global proportions.

On June 28, 1914, Archduke Franz Ferdinand, the heir to the Austro-Hungarian Empire, was assassinated by Gavrilo Princip, a Bosnian Serb citizen. Austro-Hungarian forces unleashed brutal retaliations against the Kingdom of Serbia, leading to the outbreak of conflict all over Europe. Over the past decade, England, France, and Russia had, through a series of treaties, coalesced to create a coalition titled the Entente Powers. Kaiser Wilhelm II of Germany united with the Austro-Hungarian Empire to form the Central Powers to take action against Serbia. On August 3rd, 1914, France declared war against Germany; England followed soon after the next day. In the bloodbath that would ensue, the full imperialistic ambitions of both Germany and England pitted them in direct opposition to one another.

In the last week of August 1914, Alfred Gwynne was in Dijon, France to acquire his passport when officials demanded full payment of ninety dollars for paperwork, which three American teachers traveling from Cleveland were not able to pay.[1] Protesting on their behalf, A.G. chivalrously came to their aid, working the crowd for sympathy and procuring enough funds to pay for all three teachers as well as others who were unprepared for the expensive tariff.

Newport society was buzzing again with a different kind of story. In September of 1914, Charlie Wilson was at the Westchester Horse Show, exhibiting *Grace* and *Queen* in the ring to fine applause, garnering second place ribbons. With a fine flourish, he brought the team back into the stable. Immediately a young man by the name of Frederick Schultz accosted him, screaming and shooting, and fired a revolver directly at Wilson. Jumping off his horse, a terrified Wilson backed up against a stable wall, trying to hide from Schultz who was yelling passionately, "You ruined that girl! Now I'm going to kill you."[2] Wilson cowered behind one of Alfred's prize-winning stallions and Schultz, not wanting to hurt the animal, hesitated before shooting the only part of Wilson that was exposed: his foot.[3] Just as Schultz fired and shot Charlie in the foot, stablemen surrounded him, forcing him to drop the gun, while other workers rushed to attend to Wilson who had collapsed on the floor, breathing hard.

The loud gunshot was heard in the boxes and show ring yet all the spectators assumed it was the backfiring of an automobile. Reginald, who had been told by his employees what had occurred, jumped away from his post and ran immediately over to the wounded Wilson. Reggie made arrangements for Charlie to be taken right away to the nearby White Plains Hospital. The police had already been called; within a few minutes, Sheriff Boyle arrived and handcuffed Schultz who did not resist the men holding him back. Instead, he engaged with a growing crowd of curious spectators, telling them in a feisty manner that he had come to avenge the death of Florence Schenck, whose life had been ruined by Charlie Wilson. His declaration spurred murmurs of disapproval among the crowd but before he could say more, Schultz was whisked away by the police and taken immediately to a prison cell.

Again lurid details of the events aboard the *Wayfarer* and in Alfred Gwynne's stables resurfaced in the news as Schultz's arraignment was brought to the court in White Plains two days later. While Wilson denied any previous contact with Schultz to Justice Moorehouse, Schultz had an entirely different story. Schultz's real name was Frederick Fickinger and he claimed that not only did Charlie know him, but had actually employed him in connection with Florence Schenck. The testimony of Walter Kelly, a stable manager for the Felix Warburg stable, confirmed that Frederick Fickinger had shot Wilson.[4] Frederick was adamant that Wilson had previously threatened him with trouble and that he had attacked Charlie out of retaliation for deserting Florence and destroying her life.[5] He claimed to be Florence's only friend in her last year.

Defiantly, Schultz proclaimed that he would not conceal any of the facts at the upcoming trial in January:

> When my trial comes, I will tell everything. This man Wilson can't scare me. I was threatened before and after Miss Schenck's death.[6]

That very day, Alfred and a heavily pregnant Maggie quietly left for the Adirondacks.[7] As the trial would only commence in January, Newport society turned its gaze away from the Wilson affair, following the social pursuits again of the young generation of wealthy millionaires, listing a summary of the richest individuals with incomes of more than a million dollars a year. Old favorites like Uncle Willie and Alfred G. Vanderbilt came as no surprise, but the appearance of Neily as a new member to the list was a surprising revelation of how his fortunes had changed.[8]

When Harry Payne Whitney put the massive steam yacht *Warrior* up for sale, Alfred G. acquired the boat. Renaming it the *Wayfarer*; A.G. prepared the vessel for a winter cruise in warmer waters. In October, a young healthy baby boy George Washington Vanderbilt III, named after Alfred's uncle, was born.[9] Alfred Junior now had a baby brother to play with and Maggie's hands were full.

Two days before Christmas, Maggie took little Alfred and her infant newborn George with her to *Sagamore Lodge* in the Adirondacks. Alfred rushed across the country to Pasadena, California to be by the bedside of his ailing friend from Yale, Frederick Martin Davies. He planned on spending the Christmas holidays with his sick former schoolmate. Greeted by reporters immediately upon his arrival in Los Angeles, Vanderbilt revealed a carefree and sunny spirit. After explaining his desire to be with Davies, who was now showing remarkable improvement, he also expressed his intent to enjoy Southern California on his way back.[10] Immediately a reporter suggested that his winsome smile "belongs in Southern California"[11] to which Alfred responded with another smile.

Three weeks later on January 18th, Frederick Schultz stood trial at the New York Supreme Court. The two sides faced off against each other as the assistant district attorney William J. Fallon presented the assault case against Schultz. Schultz's defense lawyer was a passionate and eloquent young man, Lee Parsons Davis, who had formerly served as district attorney in New York.

When Wilson took the witness stand, he denied any previous knowledge of Schultz. Lee Parsons Davis disagreed, offering to bring in the famous architect Stanford White who had, in fact, introduced Schultz to Wilson. Immediately, Charlie Wilson screamed, "He is a liar!"[12] But Davis persevered, calling Wilson "a real criminal because of his relationship with Schenck."[13]

Charlie described how Schultz had fired four or five times at him before shooting him in the foot. Parsons Davis interrogated Wilson about his relationship with Schenck:

> Mr. Wilson did you know Florence Schenck, and did you take advantage of her before she was eighteen years of age?[14]

Wilson hesitated before replying, "I have never said anything in public against that lady and I don't think I should now."[15]

Tensions rose instantly as the prosecutor Fallon objected and while Davis countered that he was trying to establish that Wilson had committed a felony, Judge Morschauser responded, "That didn't give the defendant a right to shoot the witness."[16]

For the first time, on the witness stand, Charlie Wilson would publicly admit his relationship with Florence Schenck. Denying that he had eloped with her, he said she had voluntarily come to live with him in New York and that they did not live together as man and wife there. He denied any knowledge of committing a crime and said that he had married Schenck believing that his wife in Newport had already divorced him. He vehemently denied any knowledge of bigamy and of deserting Schenck later in London when he found out that his marriage to her was illegal and considered void. As Davis pushed his questions, trying to get an emotional confession from Wilson, he met with repeated threats of contempt of court from Judge Morschauser. Tempers flared and many heated words were exchanged but, despite the judge's frequent interlocutions, Davis did not give up.

Hanging on the edge of their seats, the jury and spectators sat in pin drop silence, waiting for each blow to fall as Davis continued to draw more juicy details from Wilson. The focus shifted towards a condemnation of Wilson's behavior more than a conviction of Schultz.

As Davis questioned Wilson, details about how he had met Florence Schenck were revealed. Listening to the comments of other men from the horse show in Norfolk, Virginia standing outside a hotel nearby, Charlie Wilson paid note to a pretty girl walking by. Making eye contact with the young beauty, he approached her and talked to her. He said, "like other men, I fell for her."[17] Wilson said Florence had told him she wanted to go to New York and that he offered to take her there.

His own counsel Mr. Fallon asked Wilson why he left Schenck, which rendered Charlie deeply uncomfortable and squirming. Refusing to answer, Wilson also denied that he had left her "because of the influence of any prominent men."[18]

Next up on the witness stand was the stable manager for Felix Warburg who testified that he saw Schultz fire at Wilson, yelling, "I meant to kill you but I am glad I didn't, as shooting is too good for you."[19]

Despite this declaration, Davis was able to calm the court down when Schultz came to the stand. Right away, the young man claimed that he had acted out of self-defense[20] and that he had seen Wilson place his hand on his hip pocket, and fearing that Charlie would pull out a pistol, he had fired first. While the prosecutor Fallon was able to establish that Schultz was not acting out of self-defense, he also accepted that Wilson and Schultz had a prior relationship. He went even further, suggesting that Schultz had blackmailed

Wilson and that when the stable manager failed to pay up at the Westchester horse show, Schultz had fired four successive shots and then one shot aimed at Wilson's foot.

When Davis called Schultz to the witness stand, the young man revealed how he met Florence Schenck. On January 2, 1913, he had met Schenck in the backroom of a saloon at Eighth Avenue and Forty-Third Street. Breaking down into tears, the defendant recalled how pitiful her condition was and how she was "down and out."[21] Frederick gave her money to return home to her father but Dr. Schenck would not accept her and she returned to New York. Schultz would take care of the young woman until her death.

Frederick Schultz was first a stenographer and a secretary, before becoming a detective and later investigator. He had been living under the alias of Schultz to pursue his leads while his real name was Frederick Fricklinger. On the witness stand, Schultz said that Stanford White introduced him to Charlie Wilson in 1905, subsequently seeing him again in various places.

After Schultz took Florence under his wing, they lived together in about seventeen different areas, initially first received graciously at boarding houses. Schultz said he was always complimented on Florence's beauty but

Florence Schenck. Library of Congress. Bain Collection.

after a few days, the landlady would always want them to leave, saying, "I don't want the refuse of the Vanderbilt stable in my house, take her away."[22] Frustrated beyond belief, Schultz at last approached a legal firm and sued Wilson on behalf of Schenck for $50,000 in punitive damages. The young woman died before legal proceedings were completed in court.

After taking care of Florence, Schultz was completely broke. He said, "The reason I went to see Wilson at White Plains was to try and get money to leave the country. I didn't go there to shoot him."[23] He had demanded money from Wilson for taking care of his wife and "lifting her out of the gutter."[24] Wilson was furious, yelling that Schultz deserved to be buried in a box stall and threatened, "If you don't get out, I'll kill you,"[25] and as he moved towards his hip pocket, Schultz panicked and fired at him point-blank.

The courtroom was definitely moved by Schultz's tale and the judge was uneasy. The prosecutor Fallon established that Schultz had lived with Florence for eleven months. After Schultz denied blackmailing Wilson, Fallon rephrased his question.

> Fallon: In other words, you are an ordinary cheap blackmailer?
> Schultz: Morally Wilson owed me money, but not legally.[26]

Soon after this remark, the judge sent the jury off to chambers. Lee Parsons Davis, the defense counsel, was furious, jumping up from his seat and declaring the charges to be biased, favoring the prosecution and completely "unfair to the defendant."[27] Judge Morschauser was livid, angry about his authority being challenged and demanded that the young man return quietly to his seat. As the two further exchanged vitriolic looks, the jury returned with their verdict. The court waited in suspenseful silence.

The verdict was "not guilty." While Schultz visibly relaxed, the judge was completely surprised and disappointed, vocalizing his disagreement with the verdict, but accepting the jury's decision. He called it a "clean case of blackmail."[28] He chastised the jury:

> You can't give license to any one to do promiscuous shooting…I am going to discharge you, but when you get home search your conscience and think it over and see if you do not find that there has been a miscarriage of justice. I do not approve of the verdict.[29]

Schultz however would not escape scot-free. Prosecutor Fallon pushed for trial against the defendant for carrying an automatic revolver. Despite protests by Davis, a date was set and Schultz returned to jail, held on a different count.[30]

Four months later, Schultz reappeared in front of Judge Morschauser on the charge of carrying a revolver. However, the defendant had been in prison since the last arraignment and had been suffering another kind of punishment: he had contracted tuberculosis. Lee Davis, pleading on his behalf, passionately cried for compassion from the court since the prisoner would die if incarcerated further. While the judge said that Schultz did not have the right to possess a revolver, he was going to "give him the benefit of the doubt,"[31] suspending the sentence for a year because of the "serious condition of his health."[32] Schultz could finally go home.

At last, someone had stood up to defend Florence Schenck. Even with all the evidence and an eyewitness, the jury failed to condemn Schultz to a lifetime behind bars for shooting Wilson; they were able to see beyond his murderous intent to a greater condemnation of Wilson's behavior that had entirely ruined the life of a young woman. There could be no greater repudiation of the lifestyle of the stable manager and by association, Alfred and his equine culture. While A.G. did not respond to the court action, he was not immune to its ramifications. He was fully aware of the implications of his close association with Wilson, a tie that had mired his reputation in a sordid mess that he could not easily extricate himself. It was a web of entanglements that stretched farther than anyone could have imagined.

Perhaps, in reaction to Wilson-Schultz trial, Alfred saw that his equine days were over. The Great War was being fought in Europe and the British required assistance. In one swift action, the British government requisitioned all horses from stables in support of the war effort. As all horses were being seized from private stables, the equine culture in England that had been flourishing from international competition, unceremoniously suffered an ignoble rapid decline as all attention was diverted to supporting the war. All thoroughbreds from American exhibitors positioned in England and France, estimated at two million dollars in value, were requisitioned.[33]

Prior to formal requests, Alfred donated his prize-winning champions, which included more than one hundred horses, many of which were from Vermont and had been procured at great expense, as well as his seasoned team of grays that he had driven across the Brighton road. A.G. also said goodbye, at least temporarily, to his coaching lifestyle in England. He offered his coach *Venture* and horses to the British military in support of the war mobilization efforts.[34]

Next to go were French chefs from Newport who quickly volunteered to be in the war. As Alfred Gwynne contributed $5,000 in support of the British forces, his cousin Consuelo, the Duchess of Marlborough, spearheaded relief work for families in England.[35] Change was coming and it was happening fast. With England and France engaged in heavy warfare, news about social functions receded into the background and stories about fighting in the trenches filled the front pages of newspapers.

A lamp presented in 1914 to Alfred Vanderbilt, then president of the National Horse Show (NHS). The bottom of the lamp reads, "We extend a sincere, warm appreciation for the design and consultation effort contributed by E.G. Hubbard NHS 1914." Apparently Hubbard, who would soon die on the Lusitania, *and founder of the Roycroft Society of artists, had some consultative role in crafting the piece.*

It was the end of an era. The age of aristocrats with gilded balls, horse carriages, and festive entourages was fading rapidly from the limelight as the country united to face the onslaught of battle. While it would take several more years before America too would engage fully in the war effort, she was already committed in many ways through the ammunition, money, supplies, and Red Cross workers that she was sending.

Initially, Newport society maintained its social decorum. A.G. and Maggie entertained more at Oakland Farms, hosting intimate dinner parties with guests such as Mr. and Mrs. Barwell of London. Dinner was followed by an impromptu horse show outside in the ring as music wafted from a phonograph on the balcony.[36] Soon after, Alfred announced his plans to travel abroad again; but this time, his gaze turned south and westward.

Alfred Gwynne turned his eye towards travel in the Americas now that Europe was embroiled in heavy conflict. His yacht *Wayfarer* was outfitted comfortably to accommodate a nursery and playroom for the children.[37] William Henry III was now two years old and an active toddler. Maggie was very occupied with taking care of their infant son, George Washington Vanderbilt III. The *Wayfarer* would travel through the newly built and celebrated Panama Canal up to San Francisco.

Despite the best of intentions, Maggie had to withdraw from her social efforts when her firstborn Alfred Jr. fell sick with inflamed tonsils. After the doctor removed his tonsils, the boy appeared to be recovering well and both his parents lavished attention on him, carefully watching him with great tenderness.

While Maggie nursed Alfred Junior back to health, A.G. prepared to return to England to meet with the organizers of the International Horse Show. War raged across Europe, littering the continent with dead bodies daily. Travel now posed some serious safety issues. For the first time in years, Maggie would be staying at home with the two young children while Alfred would travel alone across the Atlantic. His valet Ronald Denyer would be accompanying him.

On April 30, 1915, the day prior to his departure aboard the *Lusitania*, Alfred attended a meeting of the National Horse Show Association, making plans for their upcoming fall show. After dining with their children, who remained behind in their suite at the Vanderbilt Hotel, A.G. and Maggie enjoyed a couple's night out. Along with their friends Mr. and Mrs. H. Vander Horst Kochs, the pair attended a theater performance of *A Celebrated Case* produced by David Belasco and the celebrated theater manager Charles Frohman, whose eye for talent and reputation for delivering masterpieces drew large appreciative crowds.

NOTES

1. *The New York Times*. "No Wagner Cycle Here Next Winter." Aug. 22, 1914. Pg. 3.
2. *The Washington Post*. "Noted Whip is Shot." Sept. 18, 1914. Pg. 3.
3. Ibid.
4. *The New York Times*. "Held for Wilson Shooting." Sept. 20, 1914. Pg. 10.
5. Ibid.
6. Ibid.
7. *The Chicago Daily Tribune*. "New York Society." Sept. 20, 1914. Pg. F5.
8. *The Kansas City Star*. "All Newport Snubs Them." August 22, 1913 "Million a Year List Still Grows." Oct. 25, 1914. Pg. 14.
9. *The New York Times*. "A. Vanderbilt Under Knife." April 14, 1915. Pg. 9.
10. *The Los Angeles Times*. "Millions Not a Burden." Dec. 22, 1914. Pg. II6.
11. Ibid.
12. *The New York Times*. "Florence Schenck a Victim of Wilson." Jan. 9, 1914. Pg. 7.
13. Ibid.
14. Ibid.
15. Ibid.
16. Ibid.
17. Ibid.
18. Ibid.
19. Ibid.
20. Ibid.
21. Ibid.
22. Ibid.
23. Ibid.
24. Ibid.
25. Ibid.
26. Ibid.
27. *The New York Times*. "Jury Acquits Schultz." Jan. 20, 1915. Pg. 7.
28. Ibid.
29. Ibid.
30. Ibid.
31. Ibid.
32. Ibid.
33. *The New York Times*. "Will Seize Blooded Horses for Mounts." Aug. 7, 1914. Pg. 7.
34. Brown, Norman. *Alfred Gwynne Vanderbilt: London to Brighton Coach*. Private Collection. London: 1930.
35. *The Washington Post*. "War Relief Work In Great Britain Led by the Duchess of Marlborough." Aug. 19, 1914. Pg. 3.
36. *The New York Times*. "Vanderbilts Entertain." Jan. 18, 1915. Pg. 9.
37. *The New York Times*. "A.G. Vanderbilt to Cruise." Jan. 30, 1915. Pg. 9.

Chapter Seventeen

Leaving Pier 54

A light spring drizzle greeted passengers who arrived at the Cunard pier ready to board the mammoth liner *Lusitania*, scheduled to depart promptly at ten o'clock in the morning from New York on Saturday, May 1, 1915. It was a cold and damp day.[1] Snow had blanketed the city in an unexpected late winter storm. Cold northern winds[2] blowing at seventy-five miles per hour zipped through city streets and as the snow accumulated, visibility decreased significantly. If weather would not cause delays, surely the April 22nd notice issued by the German Embassy from Washington D.C. with a thick black border[3] and printed by all the major newspapers throughout the city would. It read:

> Travellers (sic) intending to embark on the Atlantic voyage are reminded that a state of war exists between Germany and her allies and Great Britain and her allies; that the zone of war includes the waters adjacent to the British Isles: that, in accordance with formal notice given by the Imperial German Government, vessels flying the flag of Great Britain, or of any of her allies, are liable to destruction in those waters and that travellers (sic) sailing in the war zone on ships of Great Britain or her allies do so at their own risk.[4]

The warning ran right next to Cunard advertisements boldly promoting the *Lusitania* as the "Fastest and Largest Steamer now in Atlantic Service"[5] with "Round the World Tours"[6] offered in addition. It would be the 101st crossing for the *Lusitania* across the Atlantic waters.[7]

The warning issued by the German embassy was undoubtedly a disconcerting message. While reporters and photographers rushed in a frenzy to document what was called the "Last Voyage of the Lusitania,"[8] many arriving passengers grew increasingly uncomfortable. Alfred G. Vanderbilt however was unflappable. He remained unconcerned, dismissing warnings about

Lusitania *at the Chelsea pier in 1914. The piers were constructed between 1902 and 1907 and served Cunard, French, Red Star, White, and Atlantic Star lines. In 1914 they handled over two million passengers.*

Captain William Turner on the Deck of the Lusitania. *1915. International News Service.*

Charles Frohman, the Broadway producer.

impending attack and placing his faith in the capability of the *Lusitania*. He along with the captain and many of the passengers had an unwavering confidence in the boat's ability to surpass the German naval force.

Measuring seven hundred and eighty-five feet in length and eighty-seven feet in width, the RMS *Lusitania* was formidable in the water, weighing almost thirty-two thousand tons and built of steel. Powered by twenty-five Scotch boilers, with four Parson steam turbines[9] at seventy-six thousand horsepower, the *Lusitania* could travel at twenty-five knots,[10] the fastest boat of its kind in the water. The powerful ship was equipped to carry more than two thousand passengers as well as eight hundred and fifty crew members and was divided into first, second, and third class compartments.

Regal and powerful, the *Lusitania* exuded a domination and prowess that became a symbol of national pride for the English. Her distinctive profile with its high graceful bow, three long decks, and four heavily raked funnels, painted in the rich orange and black custom colors of the Cunard line, was unmistakable on the seas. She presented an image of "power, speed, and seaworthiness never since equaled."[11]

Alfred A. Booth, the chairman of the Cunard Line, had great confidence in the *Lusitania*.[12] Since the beginning of initial skirmishes and full-fledged naval conflict up to April 1915, no ship traveling over a speed of fourteen knots had been successfully attacked by a German U-boat. Sinking the *Lusitania* seemed highly improbable because of her reputation as a "speed queen of the seas"[13] and the accepted gentlemanly code of conduct where ocean vessels carrying a large number of civilians would not come under attack. This chivalrous code known as the Cruiser Rules that came into effect in 1512 under King Henry VIII,[14] was openly being challenged by the German naval fleet.

Under Cunard's directive, the *Lusitania* would not be traveling at twenty-five knots. Instead, in order to economize its operation and cut down on coal consumption, the ship would sail at a lowered speed of twenty-one knots. The cost of fuel had skyrocketed as war raged in Europe and the *Lusitania* was losing two thousand pounds per journey. Hence, Booth ordered that the Boiler Room 4 be closed down, saving an estimated sixteen hundred tons of coal per voyage.[15] One turbine considered faulty, was turned off for repair. The mighty liner could easily consume a thousand tons of coal per day. This slowing down in speed however was not considered a danger to the ship's safety since the *Lusitania* still operated at seven knots faster than ships that German U-boats had been able to sink successfully.[16]

Yet concerns about safety were valid considering the ambiguous nature of German naval warfare, where some U-boat skippers had been known to attack passenger lines. Many ships such as the *Cameronia* had already been requisitioned by the Admiralty to become armed merchant cruisers or loaded heavily with ammunition.[17] The British had mined German ports. Declaring the marine region around the British Isles a war zone on February 4, 1915, the Germans retaliated by threatening to attack all enemy vessels with or without warning. Six days later, American President Woodrow Wilson issued a diplomatic warning to Germany threatening that "if an American vessel or the lives of American citizens"[18] was lost due to the war zone declaration, that the United States would hold Germany to a "strict accountability."[19]

Competition between England and Germany on the seas was fierce. The first sea Lord of the Admiralty was held a decidedly opinionated and passionate young man by the name of Winston Churchill.

Churchill had swept through the Navy, making changes and incurring the ire of many old traditionalists. Among them were seventy-three year old Admiral Fisher and Captain Reginald Hall who supported a plan to divert Germany's attention by sending misleading messages of increased British shipping off the southern coast of Ireland. This was a ruse to occupy German naval forces while the British launched a naval expedition in the eastern Mediterranean. The British sought to take over the heavily guarded region of the Dardanelles, which linked the Aegean and Black Seas in the Baltic, a pivotal area of power. By gaining control of the region, the British hoped to allow the flow of supplies to Russia while isolating Turkey and quelling her support for the Austro-Hungarian regime.[20]

Churchill vehemently opposed the plan, proposing instead an amphibious landing at Gallipoli.[21] The Germans, under the directive of Hermann Bauer, the commander of the Third U-boat Half-Flotilla,[22] fooled by false reports sent by Captain Hall that announced large sailings of British forces along England's southern and western ports, unleashed U-boats into the waters surrounding the British Isles to hunt down such transports. While their opponent was thus occupied, the British sent their forces secretly to the Dardanelles.[23]

Captain Dow who had guided the *Lusitania* along her transatlantic journey in 1914 and the early part of 1915, had taken extreme precautions, painting her signature black and orange funnels a dark somber gray[24] and turning out all the lights at night-time, so that the massive ocean liner sailed invisibly at sea. He had also attached an American ensign flag[25] to her stern, signaling peaceful passage of a passenger line, a move greatly appreciated by the travelers on board. After several successful trips, society's elite also resumed travel aboard the *Lusitania* by November of 1914. For a brief period of time, *Lusitania* also resumed its traditional Cunard funnel livery, repainted in their smokestack orange-red color and black bands[26] but as her May voyage approached, a fresh coat of paint again was applied to camouflage the liner, with the funnels painted gray once again while her superstructure remained white.[27]

On May 1, 1915, six months later, travelers arrived in large numbers to board the gangway, despite the increase in hostilities abroad. Passengers and the crew alike were ignorant of how severely the war had digressed. Poison gases floated in deadly clouds above trenches on the Western Front.

Tension was high, however, among the boarding passengers who grew anxious as photographers snapped their photographs and reporters scurried around, questioning them about their fears.

Worried about the possibility of sabotage, Cunard officials had tightened security and were performing searches of boarding passengers and their luggage. In single file, every passenger had to wait while his or her cases, packages, trunks, and valises were opened separately. Stationed at the pier at the bottom and top of gangways, Cunard clerks and detectives checked the tickets of all boarding passengers.[28] Three nervous tugs steamed in wait as passengers made their way up the gangplank. Yet no signal was given for departure.

More discomfort arose when passengers from the Cunard ship *Cameronia* transferred to the *Lusitania*. The British had requisitioned the *Cameronia* for war purposes. The transfer of new passengers added another two and a half hours to the departure time.[29] These forty-odd passengers were glad to switch vessels since the *Lusitania* was far more luxurious and swifter than their previous ship.

As passengers anxiously continued to board the gangway, Charles P. Sumner, the general agent for the Cunard Company in New York, downplayed rumors. He acted as though the Embassy warning was not a matter of huge concern and insisting that no one had cancelled their tickets, he said to reporters, "You can see how it has affected the public."[30]

While Sumner tried to allay fears about possible German attacks, the general manager of the Dewar's distillery nearby echoed his support, confidently adding, "The *Lusitania* can run away from any submarine the Germans have got and British Admiralty will see the she (sic) is looked after when she arrives in striking distance of the Irish coast."[31]

After a roundtrip journey aboard the *Lusitania*, Captain Dow returned to Liverpool in March of 1915. Worried about her safety in the submarine-infested waters of the North Atlantic, he expressed his disapproval directly to the Cunard chairman Alfred Booth about the *Lusitania* carrying both passengers and munitions. Booth immediately relieved Dow of his charge and replaced him with William Thomas Turner as the new captain.

Fifty-eight year old Turner was not new to the *Lusitania*. He had commandeered the ship on her maiden voyage across the Atlantic. Turner had steered other powerful Cunard ships including the swift *Mauretania* and *Aquitania*. Well-seasoned on the seas, Captain Turner was eager to resume his former post. Casting a distinctive profile with his stocky, muscular frame and commanding visage, and attired in a classic navy uniform with four stripes and a gold braided visor on his hat, Captain Turner was every bit the senior captain.

Turner was known for his high efficiency and meticulous nature.[32] Boarding the ship soon after Dow's departure, Captain Turner was dismayed by the lack of sufficient lifeboats and most importantly, the low morale[33] and competence of the crew. He immediately set out to acquire the best men that he could in the month prior to departure. Through his authoritative stance and jovial nature, Turner appeared entirely confident.

Turner's first voyage at the helm of the *Lusitania* was deemed successful and largely uneventful. Following the Admiralty's advice, he had the ship turn off all of its lights as it steamed ahead at night while they were in the war zone area.[34] After he brought the steamer safely into New York's harbor on April 24, 1915, the *Lusitania* waited for one week, undergoing cleaning and repairs before her next scheduled departure on May 1st.[35]

The night before the *Lusitania* planned to sail, Turner was out on the town just as Alfred and other passengers were in New York. He took in a show and ate dinner at his favorite restaurant *Luchow*.[36] A typical "self-assured skipper"[37] with certain gruffness, Turner was married but estranged from his wife and had few friends. Taciturn at times, the skipper often grew annoyed by idle chitchat of passengers, preferring instead to leave that to his more outgoing staff captain, John Anderson. Instead, Turner confided sometimes to his housekeeper and to his niece Mercedes, whom he called upon that night before his departure.

Most passengers however put the published warnings behind them, including Alfred. As Alfred G. Vanderbilt arrived and checked in to his cabin, a reporter Jack Lawrence rapped on the door. Since his valet Ronald Denyer was busy unpacking, A.G. quickly answered the door, letting the gentleman in. Lawrence held in his hand a telegram that read: "THE LUSITANIA IS DOOMED. DO NOT SAIL ON HER."[38] It was signed dramatically, "MORTE." Despite his surprise, Alfred Gwynne quickly regained his composure, ignoring the warning, saying, "Somebody is trying to have a little fun at my expense."[39]

Despite steaming impatiently at ten o'clock, the *Lusitania* did not depart on time. Immediately, reporters capitalizing on the delay cornered the ship's captain William Thomas Turner, Alfred Vanderbilt and the producer Charles Frohman, who stood on the upper deck in discussion.

Charles Frohman was an American producer who had made a fortune on Broadway. Frog-like in appearance, with a short, stout body, Frohman was decidedly unappealing in appearance yet nonetheless attracted an admiring crowd anxious to fall into his graces. Ten years prior, Charles had produced a little play by Sir James M. Barrie called *Peter Pan*.[40] The play became an instant success overnight and a classic theater performance that was a favorite of both the stage and the screen. Frohman also launched the career of a young actress Maude Adams who he cast as *Peter Pan*. Nearly crippled when he accidentally tripped on his porch in White Plains, New York, the theater manager also suffered from articular rheumatism. This had left him with an ungainly gait. Leaning heavily upon his walking stick, which he called "his wife," Frohman hesitated when he walked, revealing his physical frailty despite his intellectual and social prowess.[41]

Producer of more than five hundred plays, Charles possessed the intuitive and shrewd ability to recognize talent and to suitably match actors with roles. Shying away from theater traditional favorites such as the plays of Ibsen, which he detested, Frohman always sought to entertain audiences. Frohman easily grasped what popular audiences wanted to see and he brought it to them. Money flowed into all of his efforts and he became a veritable legend in the theater, with actors and actresses clamoring for his attention.[42]

As reporters asked A.G. whether he was afraid of being attacked by a submarine, Alfred Gwynne appeared confident and even amused, querying,

The Verandah Café where much of the socializing occurs on the Lusitania. Ca. 1907 period post card. Davidson Bros.

Lusitania *May 1, 1915, as she leaves New York on her fatal voyage. Wide World Photo.*

"Why should we be afraid of German submarines? We can outdistance any submarine afloat."[43] Another reporter referencing how Vanderbilt had fortuitously canceled his berth aboard the Titanic at seemingly the last minute, asked, "Do you think your good luck will hold up?"[44] Alfred merely smiled.

Confidently, and with the appearance of close friends, Turner easily placed his hand upon A.G.'s shoulder, wisecracking:

> Do you think all these people would be booking passage on board the *Lusitania* if they thought she could be caught by a German Submarine? Why, it's the best joke I've heard in many days, this talk of torpedoing![45]

His smile was broad as he continued:

> I wonder what the Germans will do next. Well, it doesn't seem as if they had scared many people from going on the ship by the look of the pier and the passenger list.[46]

Both Turner and Vanderbilt enjoyed a good laugh after that pronouncement. Germany did not have submarines fast enough to pursue the *Lusitania*.[47] Boasting of how they would elude the Germans if necessary, Turner said, "We can do that, and we are willing to show them when the opportunity arrives."[48] Despite his bravado, the reporters did not relent in their questioning, asking him whether he would observe the same precautions taken by his predecessor Dow, such as traveling with the neutral flag of America. Turner refused to comment and ended the interview session.

Later, as he conversed in his comfortable *Lusitania* cabin with a New York companion, George Kessler, a multimillionaire and financier, the unflappable Vanderbilt reaffirmed his dim views of German behavior. "They have disgraced themselves," he spat, "and never in our time will they be looked upon by any human being valuing his honor, save with feelings of contempt. How can Germany, after what she has done, ever think of being classed as a country of sportsmen and of honor on a par with America, England, and France?"[49] Questions of honor and proper conduct appeared forefront in Alfred's mind.

As for Frohman, reporters pestered him about Ellen Terry, an actress whom he was quite familiar with, who had chosen to travel aboard the liner *New York* to England. Protected by a flag of neutrality, the *New York* was slower than the *Lusitania* but deemed safer because of the armistice of protection that it sailed under. Terry had switched from the *Lusitania* to the *New York* at the last minute along with the entire troupe of dancers from the *Isadora Duncan* ensemble. In fact, many of Frohman's friends had begged him to reconsider but he had laughed it off, and then seriously refused to do so. He said, "When you consider all the stars I've managed, mere submarines make me smile."[50] In response to the reporter's leading question, the producer did not answer directly but said instead that the popular actress Rita Jolivet, whom he had mentored on Broadway, and the lead in *What it Means to be a Woman,* was still aboard the *Lusitania*.[51]

The ship was a little over half full and there was plenty of space aboard the luxurious liner. The first class passenger list contained many notables, the most famous of whom undoubtedly was Alfred Gwynne Vanderbilt and included theater favorites such as the playwrights Justus Miles Forman and Charles Klein, and the writer and publicist Elbert Hubbard. Also on board were Guglielmo Marconi, the inventor of the wireless,[52] Charles E. Lauriet, Jr. a Boston bookseller,[53] Commander Joseph F. Stackhouse, who was raising money for a polar exploration and working for the Belgian relief effort,[54] Oliver Bernard, an English theatrical designer, Thomas Slidell, a close friend of A.G. Vanderbilt from the Knickerbocker Club in New York City, and George Kessler, another good friend of Alfred's.

Prior to Alfred Gwynne's arrival, the ship hummed with rumors about his pursuits, including coaching and women. Unlike many of the passengers who traveled for business or to reconnect with family, A.G.'s travel was considered by many to be one for frivolous reasons, an easy assumption to make of millionaires[55] and Alfred in particular, because of his previous reputation. How did A.G. feel about this? His reaction was typical; he ignored public opinion. He did what he always did; he went about doing what he wanted to do.

Vanderbilt would soon take up the company of Rita Jolivet, Charles Frohman, and his friend Thomas Slidell. Slidell hailed from a well-known family in the South with roots in both the civil war and back to the American Revolution.[56] He too, like Alfred Gwynne, had attended an Ivy League school; in his case it was Princeton. Slidell was connected to the Belmonts and a Baroness through family marriages. Slidell had taken up residence in New York and was part of the same exclusive set as A.G.[57]

The theatrical designer Oliver Bernard from England wandered around the deck after putting his bags away with noticeable irritation. The child of a successful theatrical couple, Bernard had grown up attempting to follow in the footsteps of his parents and failed.

Frustrated and with a satirical bent given to strong criticism, born largely out of his own distant relationship with his parents, Bernard worked his way up as a designer. Eventually he left England and escaped to New York to be free of the critical eye that he was so sensitive to and yet adopted naturally in his own relationships and judgments of others. In New York however, he was unhappy to discover that most people expected him to fight for his homeland. He also came to detest the American obsession with making money, which he described later as an "enterprise driven sky-high by insatiable greed."[58]

Moving to Boston, Bernard worked for William Lindsey on a "deplorable play"[59] and growing increasingly frustrated, decided to throw in the hat and return to England. Lindsey asked Bernard to keep an eye on his young daughter Leslie who was also traveling aboard the *Lusitania* with her newly wedded husband Stewart Mason. Bernard wanted to have nothing to do with the happy young couple whose gushing affectionate behavior towards each other and privileged lifestyle only stirred up deep resentment and annoyance within him.[60]

The passenger aboard the *Lusitania* that elicited the strongest disapproval from Bernard was Alfred Gwynne whom he considered among the "idle rich"[61] that lived in "fake homes like royal brothels"[62] and "steam yachts like harems."[63] Bernard dripped with sarcasm when he was in A.G.'s vicinity. He deeply resented the man who did not have to struggle to work and who had "nothing better to do than driving a four-in-hand to Brighton and coming three thousand miles to do it."[64]

Also on board was Elbert Hubbard, the theatrical writer, vaudeville actor, and producer with his wife. Known for his wry humor, Hubbard had achieved cult status through his numerous essays and self-publishing. He was a prolific writer and loquacious to boot. His appearance attracted considerable attention with his luxurious locks, large bow tie, and slouchy chapeau.[65]

While the *Lusitania* lay berthed at pier 54 in the New York harbor, a regular landmark at the Fourteenth Street waterfront in Manhattan,[66] Staff Captain Anderson, Turner's right hand man, had prepared a series of boat drills as per regulations. He also found new men to replace those who had jumped ship in fear of facing war hostilities.[67] While these men were willing and able, they were not true seamen of any skill. By the time the *Lusitania* was ready to sail, the crew would number seven hundred and two men in total.

The cruiser contained a mixed cargo that included enormous amounts of cheese, beef, bacon, Connecticut oysters, live chickens, brass, leather, machinery, automobile parts, and also four thousand and two hundred cases of small caliber rifle ammunition along with shrapnel shells and fuses, which could be labeled war contraband by the Germans. All of the cargo contents had been listed with Dudley F. Moore, the collector at the New York port and was valued at $750,000. However, rumors circulated that $6,000,000 worth of gold bullion lay below in a strong room.[68] Having changed attire from sporty white jackets to dark turtlenecks and heavy windbreakers, the crew secured the cargo hatches and busied themselves with final touches all over the ship prior to leaving port.

Turner was well aware of the British Admiralty's eight-point plan of strategy to avoid becoming a target of German submarines; tactics that included turning the ships lights off at night and zigzagging. With one less steam turbine and a boiler room shut down, Turner recognized that the *Lusitania* would outdo a fast U-boat by seven knots, a considerable amount. However, given the variations depending upon the proximity of the boat to the *Lusitania,* Turner also knew that the best way to avoid a German U-boat would be to zigzag through the North Atlantic waters. The Germans would not be able to predict the location of the boat and hence the *Lusitania* would be very difficult to torpedo.[69] Submarines lost speed when submerged and it would be nearly impossible for a U-boat to position itself for a good shot if the *Lusitania* kept changing direction above the water while traveling at a far greater speed. The submarine would lag behind. Torpedoes when launched magnified their impact upon contact and hence, a closer target was far more appealing. Sending a torpedo at an oblique angle towards a swiftly moving cruiser that kept shifting direction would most probably result in the torpedo careening off to the side.[70]

An extraordinary ship, the *Lusitania* offered every possible amenity from a nursery for babies and a hospital with doctors and nurses to special innovations that included elevators, telephones, electric lights, kennels, and architectural flourishes that included Doric columns, arched doorways, inlaid mahogany, roof gardens, and candelabras.[71] She was a wonder to behold.

The *Lusitania* could carry five hundred and fifty-two passengers in first class; four hundred and sixty in second class; and one thousand one hundred and eighty-six passengers in third-class. Apart from her crew on deck, she also had an additional team of three hundred and eighty-nine members for passenger dining services and another three hundred and sixty-nine members in the hot engine and boiler rooms.[72]

Designed by the Scottish designer James Millar, the *Lusitania* differed from other British liners, which were more subdued and mediocre in appearance. Georgian in style, the first class domed two-deck saloon featured dramatic Louis VI furnishings; luxurious and comfortable with satinwood furniture, dark mahogany paneling, and large fireplaces stoked readily with dry wood. Passengers could enjoy lounging in one of the many easy chairs and recliners in the vast room, and gaze up at the striking stained glass ceiling that depicted the twelve months of the year. The saloon also displayed fine contrasts in color with rich Italian reds in the Queen Anne smoking room and matte silk finishes in the writing room.[73]

Nearby, the Verandah café with its wicker chairs, numerous tropical plants, and direct access to the deck, conveyed the easy familiarity of a sidewalk café. Miller had given in to his artistic impulses in the wide range of two-room suites offered in first class, with styles ranging from eighteenth century Colonial to Empire designs. Every deck possessed a long sweeping hallway that ran along its breadth, along with two elevators in the center. A grand white marble staircase connected all six decks.[74]

The second-class public rooms were also luxuriously outfitted and resembled traditional first-class Cunard travel. For most passengers traveling in third-class, the rooms were far more comfortable than their accommodations back home. Between the three galleys, twenty pantries, and accompanying still rooms and refrigerators, the *Lusitania* was equipped to feed three thousand passengers if necessary.

Akin to his residences at the Vanderbilt hotel that he had just left a few hours prior, Alfred's digs were located on the promenade level of the boat. Fittingly titled Regal Suite B-65 and B-67, the two most luxurious quarters aboard the *Lusitania*, faced forward towards the bow of the boat. Styled in magnificent Louis XVI décor, each suite consisted of two bedrooms, a dining room, parlor, small bathroom, and water closet.[75] Paneled in walnut and burnished gold moldings, the dining room had matching chairs and a long oval table with a stunning white marble fireplace on one end. A sliding glass screen door led directly to the parlor. Painted floral motifs and carved gilt moldings brought color and delicate refinement to the white paneled walls. Gauzy heliotrope and cream-colored curtains accented the parlor room, softening the mahogany furniture upholstered in light green.[76]

The two bedrooms could be accessed from the parlor. One bedroom was decorated with satinwood furniture inlaid with pale green and silk panels of rose, while the other room possessed a gorgeous white and gold décor replete with Wedgwood cameos, with soft blue silk brocade curtains delicately embroidered with floral sprays.[77]

While the crew readied themselves for departure, the passengers found plenty to do. Some were busy talking to the Chief Steward about their dining arrangements; others were busy acquiring steamer chairs for one dollar apiece; and yet others were making reservations for use of the bathrooms with the Room Steward.[78] A few passengers requested changes in their accommodations and the crew assisted them as best as possible in moving those who were discontent to new quarters. The ship, although traveling with the largest number of passengers for a Cunard liner, with one thousand two hundred and fifty-seven travelers on board, was still far from capacity. Other passengers spent their time in their cabins or in the Writing Room, dashing off last minute letters and notes to loved ones.[79]

At last, the order for departure was given. It was half-past twelve. After Turner's niece Mercedes was let off the boat, the gangplanks were pulled up and hawsers were cast on to shore, while turbines slowly hummed. As the gongs sounded and the crewmembers yelled, "All Ashore!" the passengers waved goodbye to family, friends, and lovers waiting on the pier. The mood was serious as the bronze horn blared three times. Engines roared beneath the behemoth as thick black soot bellowed out from the funnels. As her propellers churned slowly, the *Lusitania* began to inch away from the pier after three powerful tugs *John Nichols*, the *E. M. Millard*, and the *Lewis K. Pulver* turned her bow south. Her massive hull pointing in the right direction, the *Lusitania* made her way out to sea a little after twelve o'clock on May 1, 1915. Turner walked down the starboard Bridge wing out to the bulwark, from where he could see the fore and aft length of the *Lusitania* as she pulled away from the dock.[80] Charles Frohman stood by the rail of the upper deck, staring out morosely to sea.[81]

A five-man orchestral band played the song *Tipperary* from the main boat deck while the Welsh group, The Royal Gwent Male Voice Singers, belted out *The Star Spangled Banner*.[82] The festivities offered a welcoming relief to the somber feeling that had marked much of the boarding process and many passengers relaxed to familiar sounds.

The *Lusitania* pushed outward and began to pick up speed in the North river as she headed out towards the open water. Within a few minutes, she had disappeared from sight, disappearing into the distant horizon, as the faint echo of her horn lingered behind.

NOTES

1. Kent, J. and Layton. *Lusitania: An Illustrated Biography of the Ship of Splendor*. North Carolina: Lulu Press, 2007. Pg. 171.
2. Ibid. Pg. 163.
3. Ibid. Pg. 171.
4. Imperial German Embassy, Washington D.C., April 22, 1915.
5. Hoehling, A. A. and Mary Hoehling. *A Thrilling Tale of Disaster At Sea: The Last Voyage of the Lusitania*. London: 1957. Pg. 22.
6. Ibid.
7. Ramsey, David. *Lusitania: Saga and Myth*. New York: W.W. Norton & Company. 2002. Pg. 19.
8. Hoehling, A. A. and Mary Hoehling. *A Thrilling Tale of Disaster At Sea: The Last Voyage of the Lusitania*. London: 1957. Pg. 34.
9. Ibid.
10. Ibid.
11. Isherwood, J. H. Excerpt from David Ramsey's *Lusitania: Saga and Myth*. New York: W.W. Norton & Company. 2002. Pg. 19.
12. Kent, J. and Layton. *Lusitania: An Illustrated Biography of the Ship of Splendor*. North Carolina: Lulu Press, 2007. Pg. 163.
13. Ibid. Pg. 161.
14. Preston, Diana. *Lusitania: An Epic Tragedy*. New York. The Berkeley Publishing Group, 2002. Pg. 70.
15. Kent, J. and Layton. *Lusitania: An Illustrated Biography of the Ship of Splendor*. North Carolina: Lulu Press, 2007. Pg. 155.
16. Ibid. Pg. 161.

17. Ibid. Pg. 173.
18. Ibid. Pg. 157.
19. Ibid.
20. Ibid.
21. Ibid. Pg. 162-3.
22. Ibid. Pg. 76.
23. Ibid.
24. Thomas, Lowell. *Raiders of the Deep*. Doubleday, Doran and Company, Inc. New York: 1928. Pg. 91.
25. Ibid. Pg. 160.
26. Ibid. Pg. 170.
27. Ibid.
28. *The New York Times*. May 2, 1915. Pg. 1.
29. Kent, J. and Layton. *Lusitania: An Illustrated Biography of the Ship of Splendor*. North Carolina: Lulu Press, 2007. Pg. 172.
30. *The New York Times*. May 2, 1915. Pg. 1.
31. Ibid.
32. Kent, J. and Layton. *Lusitania: An Illustrated Biography of the Ship of Splendor*. North Carolina: Lulu Press, 2007. Pg. 162.
33. Ibid. Pg. 163.
34. Ibid. Pg. 165.
35. Ibid.
36. Hoehling, A. A. and Mary Hoehling. *A Thrilling Tale of Disaster At Sea: The Last Voyage of the Lusitania*. London: 1957. Pg. 30.
37. Kent, J. and Layton. *Lusitania: An Illustrated Biography of the Ship of Splendor*. North Carolina: Lulu Press, 2007. Pg. 169.
38. Preston, Diana. *Lusitania: An Epic Tragedy*. New York. The Berkeley Publishing Group, 2002. Pg. 100.
39. Lawrence, J. Coronet. March 1950.
40. Kent, J. and Layton. *Lusitania: An Illustrated Biography of the Ship of Splendor*. North Carolina: Lulu Press, 2007. Pg. 155.
41. Preston, Diana. *Lusitania: An Epic Tragedy*. New York. The Berkeley Publishing Group, 2002. Pg. 96-97.
42. Ibid.
43. *The New York Times*. "Sails, Undisturbed by German Warning." May 2, 1915. Pg. 1.
44. Ibid.
45. Ibid.
46. Ibid.
47. Ibid.
48. Ibid.
49. *The New York Times*. May 16th 1915. Pg. 1.
50. Kent, J. and Layton. *Lusitania: An Illustrated Biography of the Ship of Splendor*. North Carolina: Lulu Press, 2007.

51. Preston, Diana. *Lusitania: An Epic Tragedy*. New York. The Berkeley Publishing Group, 2002. Pg. 97.
52. Kent, J. and Layton. *Lusitania: An Illustrated Biography of the Ship of Splendor*. North Carolina: Lulu Press, 2007. Pg. 165.
53. Ibid. Pg. 168.
54. Ibid. Pg. 174.
55. Ibid.
56. *The New York Times*. Magazine Supplement. Oct. 5, 1902. SM11.
57. Ibid.
58. Bernard, Oliver P. *Cocksparrow: A True Chronicle*. London: Jonathan Cape. 1936. Pg. 95.
59. Ibid. Pg. 142.
60. Ibid. Pg. 143.
61. Ibid. Pg. 153.
62. Ibid.
63. Ibid.
64. Ibid.
65. Ibid. Pg. 42.
66. Kent, J. and Layton. *Lusitania: An Illustrated Biography of the Ship of Splendor*. North Carolina: Lulu Press, 2007. Pg. 169.
67. Ibid. Pg. 168.
68. A.A. Hoehling, A. A. and Mary Hoehling. *A Thrilling Tale of Disaster At Sea: The Last Voyage of the Lusitania*. London: 1957. Pg. 27.
69. Ibid.
70. Isherwood, J. H. Excerpt from David Ramsey's *Lusitania: Saga and Myth*. New York: W.W. Norton & Company. 2002. Pg. 22-24.
71. A.A. Hoehling, A. A. and Mary Hoehling. *A Thrilling Tale of Disaster At Sea: The Last Voyage of the Lusitania*. London: 1957. Pg. 41.
72. Isherwood, J. H. Excerpt from David Ramsey's *Lusitania: Saga and Myth*. New York: W.W. Norton & Company. 2002. Pg. 26-27.
73. Ibid.
74. Ibid.
75. Peeke, Mitch, Kevin Walsh-Johnson, and Steven Jones. *The Lusitania Story*. Maryland: Naval Institute Press. 2002. Pg. 20.
76. Ibid.
77. Ibid. Pg. 19-20.
78. Kent, J. and Layton. *Lusitania: An Illustrated Biography of the Ship of Splendor*. North Carolina: Lulu Press, 2007. Pg. 172.
79. Ibid.
80. Kent, J. and Layton. *Lusitania: An Illustrated Biography of the Ship of Splendor*. North Carolina: Lulu Press, 2007. Pg. 176.
81. A.A. Hoehling, A. A. and Mary Hoehling. *A Thrilling Tale of Disaster At Sea: The Last Voyage of the Lusitania*. London: 1957. Pg. 39.
82. Kent, J. and Layton. *Lusitania: An Illustrated Biography of the Ship of Splendor*. North Carolina: Lulu Press, 2007. Pg. 176.

Chapter Eighteen

At Sea

Soon after the *Lusitania* departed from the New York pier, Alfred retired to his room for a post-lunch nap. His valet Ronald Denyer finished packing while carefully keeping aside A.G.'s travel clothes and storing the remainder. Three German stowaways found aboard the cruiser, who apparently were searching for photographic evidence that the *Lusitania* was operating as a war vessel, were immediately detained and summarily locked in the brig. Passengers settled into their cabins and the crew went about their duties. A refreshing calmness descended upon the liner.

A light fog enshrouded the ocean vessel as the *Lusitania* accelerated into the open sea and the harbor faded into the distance. While some passengers jokingly tried life jackets on their kids,[1] others changed attire and proceeded to the first-class dining saloon.[2] The day was largely uneventful and after the orchestra played an evening tune, the officers blackened the ship, drawing dark curtains over the large windows, closing portholes and hatches, and turning out the lights, as a precaution against "German surface raiders."[3]

The British Admiralty was fully aware of the threat German U-boats posed to the *Lusitania.* Captain Reginald Hall, the former director of naval intelligence, had intercepted a message from the German *U-20* as she tested her radio.[4] The *U-30* had recently sunk the *Gulfight,* a ship in the same area that the *Lusitania* was now steaming toward. In an effort to throw the Germans off track, Hall sent out fake information to convince the Germans that supplies and troops would be sent to the Dardanelles in the Mediterranean, moving from Liverpool through the Irish straights.[5] Immediately upon receiving this material in April, the German naval commander Hermann Bauer sent out three submarines to intercept these transports with the message to travel fast, hold them off as best as possible, and if necessary, not to spare any ship whether it was a warship or a merchant passenger liner.

Turner anxiously kept his post in the early hours of Sunday morning as the *Lusitania* forged ahead, ensconced in fog. Slowly the ship felt her way out into the cold Atlantic waters and the fog began to lift, as sunlight streamed aboard the decks, releasing the *Lusitania* from its dark grip. Known for his agility and endurance, Turner epitomized the classic gruff sailor and sea captain, who lived to breathe the ocean waters. The son of a sailor, Turner had run away from home at an early age, forsaking his father's ambition that Turner become a clergyman with a stable life and instead took right to the sea as a cabin boy.[6] A powerful swimmer, Turner was stubborn and refused to quit even under extreme duress. He was determined to become a captain and so he did, learning under his father and others.

Under Turner's watchful eye, the *Lusitania* was a "taut ship"[7] known for his discipline and love of the open water. When he returned back to the ship after Dow departed, Turner was overjoyed. While his crew was far from perfect, as the British government had reserved the best and fittest men for the Royal Air Force, the Army, and Navy, Turner was determined to discipline his ragtag team. His resilience was deeply respected among the British naval fleet and even the German Admiralty had a reluctant admiration and fear of the man.[8]

Later that evening, the captain would dine with first-class passengers in his cabin. Among them was the suffragette Lady Mackworth, known for her militancy including planting bombs in mailboxes and who wore her prison time like a badge of honor; the Arctic explorer J. Foster Stackhouse, and the spiritualist Ms. Theodate Pope.[9] Turner did not enjoy entertaining many of the prominent people, preferring instead the easy familiarity he had with Vanderbilt and Frohman, who were frequent travelers aboard the *Lusitania* and with whom the captain did not have to engage constantly in frivolous chatter.[10] In fact, Alfred Gwynne was probably one of Turner's favorite passengers because it was his custom to spend the majority of the trip in his cabin, which is where A.G. went soon after dinner.

While in his cabin, Alfred received a Marconi gram from Maggie that read: "FREDDIE DIED EARLY THIS MORNING LOVE MARGARET."[11] The news was not altogether shocking since his Yale friend had been sick for a while. The two had been fast friends ever since their collegiate days, traveling extensively together. Davies too had been infatuated with Alfred's sister Gertrude,[12] to whom he had professed his undying affection. Gertrude had rejected him and Davies had married another but always remained a close friend of Alfred and his family.[13]

One can only imagine how Alfred felt upon receiving the news. Boarding the ship, A.G. had revealed his strong opinions about gentlemanly conduct when he had protested the German lack of sportsmanship.[14] Frederick's death could only have exacerbated this feeling since in many ways his Yale chum epitomized in every way a gentleman. Good-natured and sincere, Davies was a wonderful friend, father, and husband.

Others aboard the Lusitania assumed that Alfred was keeping to his room because he was grieving for his lost friend. However, George Kessler, the famed city planner, later explained, "Mr. Vanderbilt kept mostly to his stateroom. There he had his meals served and there he saw his friends. He was always like that. On the voyage he always enjoyed being quiet. We had long talks together in his room chiefly on finance."[15]

A.G. and Kessler discussed a variety of topics, which included "some serious conversations" about the "Mercantile National League, of which Mr. Vanderbilt, myself, and J.P. Morgan have been the founders. This league which has been organized by P.H.W. Ross of Washington seeks to establish an American mercantile marine." Vanderbilt was eager to talk about establishing closer business ties between America and the Entente Powers; being "in favor of closer and more reciprocal relations than have hitherto prevailed."[16]

The idea of a merchant marine fleet was not an altogether new one. J. P. Morgan had pursued building an Atlantic fleet, conspiring with E. H. Harriman and William Kissam, Alfred's uncle. It was an elusive dream, powered by the desire to create an American fleet to carry American goods. To that end, Morgan and colleagues had joined with the Germans in an arrangement to ally with the *North German Lloyd*, the Kaiser's fleet. Morgan had not stopped there and had purchased the *White Star Line*, which included the *Titanic* and other significant vessels. The British, fearing that they would not have adequate troop transports in time of war, committed financial support to the construction of the *Lusitania* and her sister ships. Of all the Cunard ships, only the *Lusitania* remained in public service. In one of her luxury cabins, Alfred Vanderbilt, the scion of the Vanderbilt family, was denouncing the alliance that had served as an inspiration for his uncle and close alliances.

Why would A.G. express such disdain for the Atlantic fleet? It appeared that he was deeply rankled by German warfare. "He was very emphatic in his denunciation of German methods of barbarism."[17]

According to Thomas Slidell, Alfred Gwynne had professed a desire to support the British war effort by offering his services as a driver of an ambulance corps. In many of the areas of trench warfare, arrival by horse was useful because of the uneven terrain that cars could often not easily traverse. While everyone around him was losing horses, Alfred could put requisitioned horses to use for the war. Vanderbilt's coaching pastime had often come under heavy censure and ridicule but now, through this service, Alfred's expensive hobby acquired immediate relevance. He would be removed from criticism while indulging again in a pursuit that he so obviously excelled in. His sport would gain a nobility and glory through public service, catapulting him into the status of a hero. However, upon his departure, A.G. had promised to return within a three-week period, curtailing the ability to truly delve in deeper and be of long-term benefit.

Slidell also reported that Vanderbilt was intent on attending a meeting with members of the committee powering the Olympia horse show. This however was in sharp contrast to what A.G. apparently expressed to George Kessler: "There will be no coaching for me this year…I am sorry, but to drive a coach in these times is out of the question."[18]

To Kessler, it was obvious that Alfred Gwynne had a passion for the sport:

> I could see by his manner how devoted he was to this favorite recreation of his. He mentioned his flat in Gloucester House, Park Lane, which he had taken on an extended lease, and he was anxious to know whether I would like to take up the remainder of his lease.[19]

By the next morning, the ship's occupants had already settled into a familiar routine of eating, sleeping, lounging, reading, and playing bridge or cards. They also began to form new friendships with dining companions. Some passengers were anxious about safety measures in light of the *Titanic* disaster, questioning crewmembers about lifeboats, jackets, and rafts. A crew of eight members performed boat drills. The drills were never fully practiced since none of the actual passengers participated. Instead, after an announcement from a commanding officer, crewmembers climbed davits, boarded the boat, and acted as though they were ready for the boat to be lowered.

As Oliver Bernard wandered about the ship, he was alarmed to notice that the crew did not actually lower the boats and worried how the crew would actually perform under duress. The process was decidedly odd and the drill appeared pointless. Deployment of flotation devices and lifeboats under severe conditions required speed, agility, and practice. Bernard wondered if the crew would be able to truly handle an emergency if it arose.

"These sanguinary drills" persuaded Bernard "that the possibilities of submarine attack were to be regarded as extremely remote," but, he wondered, "What will happen if all the boats have to be lowered about fifty feet…fully loaded (with passengers)."[20] Bernard comforted himself and other onlookers by saying the *Lusitania* would require a lot of sinking.[21] Most of the passengers however remained untroubled, relaxing into a comfortable routine. Many had gotten over their mal de mar, or initial seasickness. While the sky was free of clouds, and the sun shone brightly, the ocean too was calm as the mighty ship rocked ever so slightly. The weather was perfect for a cruise.

Eating was by far the most popular pastime. The food aboard the *Lusitania* was sumptuous and the surroundings delightful and appealing. Cynical and vocal in his criticism, Oliver Bernard antagonized some passengers that were dining near him; they retreated far away to avoid the irritating man. Maneuvering his way to acquire the best table in the dining saloon like many others, he was particularly annoyed by the "abominably supercilious"[22] steward who had given away the table he desired to someone Bernard insecurely surmised was of more importance.

Bernard was acutely jealous of the upper class and in particular Vanderbilt and Frohman. He seethed internally at the presence of rich men like Alfred Gwynne whose passion for horses he could not comprehend, a pursuit he considered wasteful and frivolous. Bernard hated Frohman who, unlike him, had succeeded tremendously in the theater business. Bernard was filled with a deep-seated jealousy of the theater manager. Charles and Alfred socialized easily and naturally. Both had traveled on the *Lusitania* previously and both shared common interests. They inhabited a world that Oliver Bernard vocally detested but in many ways, secretly desired to be a part of.

Charles Frohman had a particular weakness: his fondness for sweets and all things chocolate. One of his close friends Maude Adams, a star whom he had launched, had sent him a boat-shaped basket filled to the brim with sweets, fruits, and flowers, to which he had replied, "The little ship you sent is more wonderful than the big one that takes me away from you."[23] Frohman was a complicated man; he morosely predicted the sinking of the Lusitania, drawing a picture of a passenger liner being chased by a submarine in a farewell note to a friend. He exuded a towering presence in the theater as he juggled multiple productions simultaneously. Frohman had the ability to make a star; transforming the life of some ordinary individual to that of a famous actor through his beloved plays. While he was sometimes perceived as being sullen and withdrawn, Frohman still possessed an insatiable need for their affection.[24] Two of his handpicked stars were also on board the *Lusitania*: Justus Forman and Charley Klein. While the former was deemed a dilettante and failure in the public eye, the latter had succeeded with his play *The Lion and The Mouse*.[25] At the time of sailing, Frohman had two plays in production: *The Shadow* and *The Celebrated Case*.

Despite dismissing the fears of his friends who were concerned about his safety aboard the *Lusitania*, Charles Frohman dictated the entire program for the next theatrical season before sailing, a precaution he had hitherto never followed.[26] He joked with friends, "When you consider all the stars I have managed, mere submarines make me smile."[27]

Frohman's valet William Stainton recognized that the theater manager was suffering from arthritic pain and had acquired some pills from the ship's doctor to ease Charles' suffering. Charles smiled warmly at his valet, eternally grateful for the faithful attendance the man offered him without requiring words.[28] As Frohman made his way into the dining lounge, leaning on his

German Captain Schwieger, commander of U-20 that sunk the Lusitania. *Photograph ca. 1915.*

German submarine U-20 second from left in foreground in port with her sister boats prior to sinking of the Lusitania. *Undated postcard.*

cane, he stopped by the table where Alfred Vanderbilt sat looking out the window.[29] Alfred was fashionably attired in a gray fitted suit and a matching tweed cap, striking a dashing figure and as usual, drawing a lot of attention from curious spectators. When the waiter offered A.G. a menu, he refused it, replying, "I'll have whatever your head chef recommends."[30] They engaged in a light banter before Charles ambled over to his own table in a corner.

The day before the *Lusitania* left the Cunard pier, thirty-two year old Kapitanleutnant Walther Schwieger had also taken his command, the *U-20*, out to sea. Wrapped in a heavy grey fog, the German submarine *U-20* departed from Emden harbor[31] on April 30th, like a shark, leaving the bobbing buoys of the sleepy Dutch town and into the fast and choppy waters of the North Sea.[32] Unlike the *Lusitania* whose departure attracted reporters and revelers, the German *U-20* slipped away from her wharf, jettisoning out to sea with nary an onlooker. Austere in its simplicity, the vessel lacked any luxuries. Her profile was distinctive with her single vertical conning tower. Her top speed was fifteen knots on the surface and nine knots when submerged.

Hailing from an old Berlin family, Schwieger was poised and well educated. A bachelor at thirty-two, he possessed a distinguished bearing and striking blue eyes and was a "particularly fine-looking fellow."[33] Tall, blond, and handsome, Walther Schwieger was known for his tough command and his team of thirty-eight men worked closely together like the cogs of a tightly oiled machine, in synchronicity and without words.[34] Schwieger had two loves: submarine warfare and classical music.[35] Commanding his first submarine at twenty-seven, the young man had entered the naval service at the age of eighteen. Witty, joyful, and kind, Schwieger inspired both respect and gaiety among his crew and was a general favorite in the German Navy.[36]

Sworn to uphold the honor of their Fatherland, Schwieger's crew possessed an uncannily high morale. Well trained for a singular purpose, each member brought his own particular skills. Seamlessly, they worked together in one unfailing motion, united in mind, body, and spirit. They were all well aware of the inherent dangers and discomfort associated with the mission, just as much as they keenly strived for glory and success. Not a whisper of complaint issued from these men.

After peering wearily through his periscope for hours, Schwieger was relieved when the heavy fog lifted, as the sun shined brightly, illuminating the dark waters and the skyline. Immediately, the *U-20* emerged out of the water, breaking the surface and blowing her tanks. The crew greedily drank in the fresh air that wafted into the fetid hull. As the captain took his position at the helm, the crew stood along the surface. However, they would not stay visible for long. When a watch officer alerted them with a shout, "Destroyers!" the sailors immediately scrambled back into the hull as they slammed the hatches shut and the *U-20* plummeted downwards sixty feet into the water.

Schwieger turned the periscope until he could see a band of six destroyers protecting a British fleet at Scapa Flow. Sunday evening, as passengers aboard the *Lusitania* enjoyed one of the finest meals while a dreamy waltz wafted through the ship, life aboard the *U-20* was in sharp contrast. Crew members shivered, rubbing their arms and legs as they fought to keep warm, trapped in their damp metal hull as water droplets condensed along the inside, turning their cabin into a refrigerator in the cold sea. For hours they would remain stuck in their tube below the water until the destroyers were no longer in view and then they could resurface for a short while and ride the open sea.

When Oliver Bernard fretted about the poor quality of the drills being practiced aboard the *Lusitania*, he did not know how right he was. Since war had been declared nine months prior, some sixty-six merchant vessels had been sunk by German U-boats. In fact, the German Admiralty started promoting a tonnage contest between commanders to figure out who could sink the greatest weight of vessels including neutral vessels deemed to be "in the service of the enemy."[37]

On Sunday afternoon, when Alfred received the sad news of the death of his friend Frederick Davies, the *U-20* boat crew sighted Fair Island, a lonely outpost north of Scotland, between the Orkneys and the Shetlands.[38] Celebrating, the crew rejoiced that the halfway mark was in sight and before long, they would be dropping helm as the submarine headed towards the Irish coastline. More signposts that signaled progress along their sea journey came into view such as Cape Wrath and Nun Lighthouse off the Hebrides by Scotland. Many submarines preferred to take a longer route here and avoid the Dover Straits. As the *U-20* passed Fair Island, the darker waters of the North Sea gave way to the colder, greenish tinged waters of the immense Atlantic Ocean. The *U-20* also had its own enemies to avoid, including minefields and submarine traps. Her large steel cabled masts protected her from these traps and periodically, she dipped below the surface, closing the conning tower as she submerged.

At last, the outpost of St. Kilda in the Outer Hebrides came into view. Large distinctive red cliffs made this small island easily recognizable.[39] Inhabited by a small population of human beings who lived in stone huts, St. Kilda was wild and untamed. The *U-20* steamed past the desolate island out into the open waters.

As the *U-20* passed the islands off the coast of Scotland, she swam through a floating mass of wreckage, planks, and flotsam; the shattered remains of former merchant and fishing fleets.

By Monday as the passengers aboard the *Lusitania* basked in the beautiful weather, the *U-20* navigated through the watery depths of the ocean unnoticed. Unlike her previous records of six hundred and eighty miles a day, the

Lusitania was limited to five hundred miles per day, due to shutting down one of her boiler rooms. She would arrive slightly later than anticipated in Liverpool. Everyone reveled in the fabulous weather and there was great merriment aboard the ship among the passengers.

Tuesday was another beautiful day. The British Admiralty did not send out any messages warning of submarine attack. The *U-20* was almost beyond Scotland and would soon be reachable by the wireless station. Firing twice at freighters, the submarine failed to sink any enemy targets and Schwieger and his crew grew anxious.

Accompanied by nurses, the children of first-class passengers played in a nursery on the C deck, next to their own private dining room while those of the second class were let loose in a spacious "corral-like playpen."[40] The third class children unfortunately had to remain in their cabins. Some passengers, like the bookseller Charles Lauriat, placed wagers on the *Lusitania*'s speed.

On Wednesday, May 5th the *Lusitania* officially passed the invisible halfway mark, averaging about four hundred and sixty miles a day[41] on her eastbound journey. At this rate, she would reach Liverpool by 4:30 a.m. on Saturday. The sky was mostly clear with a few patches of fog appearing that caused Turner some consternation, but he did not dare slow down for fear of submarine attack. Charting a course not too distant from Fastnet Rock by the southwest tip of Ireland, an area most likely patrolled by submarines, Turner was aware that he was bringing the *Lusitania* right into harm's way by the next day.

Underwater at periscope depth, Walther Schwieger spotted the light of two ships. Recognizing that they were armed trawlers, he veered the *U-20* carefully away. The *U-20* would remain below the surface until she was safely miles away off Fastnet rock. Without a ship in sight, Schwieger ordered the crew to get ready. While Schwieger peered through the periscope, flanked by the Chief Engineer in the control room of the conning tower, the *U-20* slowly surfaced. The coast was clear and no other vessels were in sight. The water laid vast and wide open in front of them. The solemn silence inside the boat was broken by the loud hissing sounds of roaring water as the steel bow and gun rose up into the light.

Schwieger's men worked nonstop as they lined up the tiers of the *U-20* to charge its water-cell storage batteries. The conning tower hatch opened and fresh air streamed into the compartments below. As oxygen renewed below the decks, some of the nasty smells of cooking, oil, human breath, and body odor, left the cramped quarters below.[42] The seabed lay three hundred feet below and the *U-20* bobbed along the swells. The diesel engines hummed. The deck was soaking wet and bits of yellow and green seaweed clung to the sides. Wearing a pair of binoculars around his neck, Schwieger in a leather jacket, stood out by the conning tower, looking out to sea, enjoying the fresh mild air.[43] A thick fog still lay around them and visibility, although improving gradually, was still low.

As the submarine rose out of the water to a ringing clamor of metal, her commander stared out to sea across the cold Atlantic waters off the coast of Ireland. The morning was misty and mild and the deep waters off Fastnet Rock by the southwest tip of Ireland were salty, dark, and foreboding. Immense white seagulls with black-tipped wings dipped through the thick fog to grasp for herring. Schwieger too was ready to hunt. By Fastnet Rock, the *U-20* lay patiently in wait for a passing steamer.

At noon, the fog began to clear and Schwieger, peering through his binoculars, made out the landmark of Old Head Kinsdale rising 256 feet out of the water.[44] Just three miles seaward from the mainland, the houses of Kinsdale appeared as dim shapes. The fog that shrouded the vessel had now lifted and as the sun was now bright, illuminating the Irish shore, the *U-20* was no longer invisible. It lay unmasked in the light like a giant whale, exposed and in full view from the shore.

Schwieger took off his jacket, warming up under the rays of the sun now dazzling the entire deck with bright light. Towering waves stronger in intensity hit the conning tower and sides of the boat while reflected beams of sunlight revealed a range of blue and green colors in the water. Frothing surf hit the beach in the distance. As gulls swooped closer in to the vessel, Schwieger maintained his attentive lookout.

Finally at two o'clock in the afternoon, his patience was rewarded. A little schooner, the *Earl of Latham,* carrying eggs, bacon, and butter from Ireland to Liverpool, came into view.[45] Saving a torpedo, Schwieger chose instead to surface and order the crew of the schooner to abandon ship. Glad to survive, the crew immediately complied and Schwieger's men rapidly destroyed the boat with a few hand grenades. Several hours later that evening, the *U-20* encountered a three thousand ton Norwegian steamer flying under a neutral flag but the torpedo they fired failed to launch and remained stuck in the tube.[46] Avoiding possible engagement with the steamer, the *U-20* immediately dove to seventy feet.

The sinking of the *Earl of Latham* did not go unnoticed. The British Admiralty was well aware of the dangers looming in the waters surrounding the British Isles. However, the attention of the naval secretary and first sea lord Winston Churchill was diverted to the future of the Dardanelles and securing British control of the region. If Turner hoped that a destroyer or other armed vessel would appear to escort the liner through the troubled waters, then he would be sorely disappointed.

The morning of Thursday May 6, 1915, passengers on the *Lusitania* awoke to sounds of the crew as they practiced lowering the lifeboats. Again the drill wasn't fully carried out but Turner was apparently satisfied with this half-hearted effort as an adequate compliance with the Admiralty's safety orders. There were enough lifeboats aboard to carry the entire contingency of some two thousand passengers and crew with room for an additional six hundred. This was not the *Titanic*; some lessons come hard.

Turner also positioned men on various spots all over the vessel as lookouts. Two men were stationed at the forecastle, another two on either side of the bridge, and two in the crow's nest area in addition to the regular two officers of the watch.[47] Turner was well aware of the probable dangers that lay ahead as the ship entered the war zone. The *Lusitania* had to enter the *Mersey River* at high tide on the way to Liverpool and the passage would be impossible at any other time. Waiting between tides was out of the question because then the *Lusitania* would be an easy prey for "any U-boat on the prowl."[48]

After failing to sink the Norwegian liner the previous evening, Schwieger was determined to have a victory. Surfacing quietly, the *U-20* opened fire on

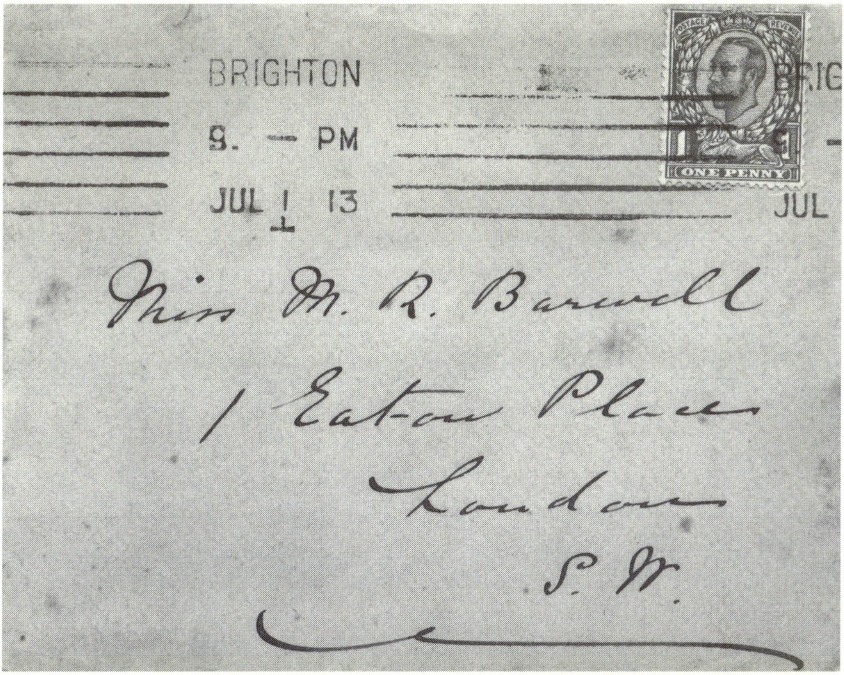

Envelope of letter sent by Charles Wilson to Miss Barwell with enclosed invitation to ride from London to Brighton seated next to Alfred Vanderbilt.

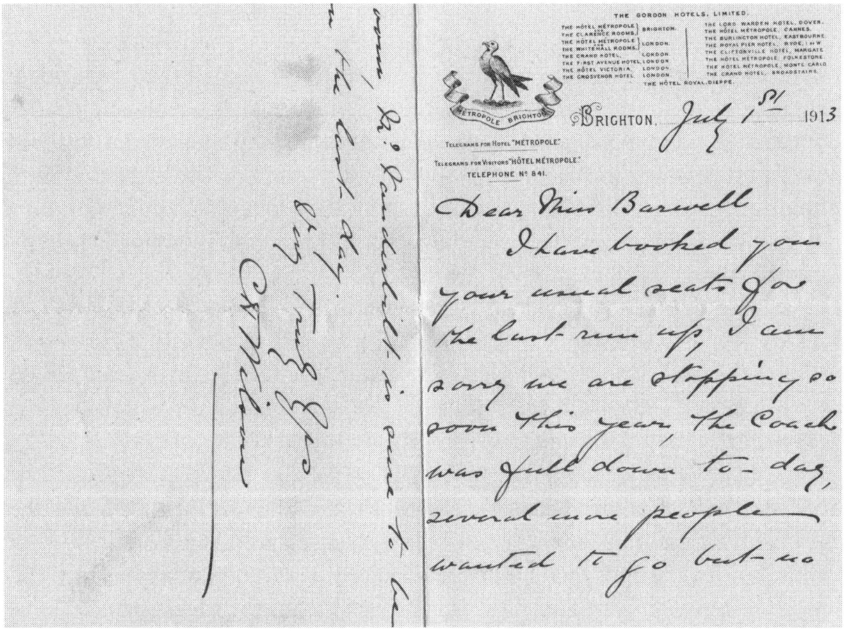

THE GORDON HOTELS, LIMITED.

BRIGHTON, July 1st 1913

Telegrams for Hotel "MÉTROPOLE"
Telegrams for Visitors "HÔTEL MÉTROPOLE"
TELEPHONE No 841.

Dear Miss Barwell
I have booked you
your usual seats for
the last run up, I am
sorry we are stopping so
soon this year, the Coach
was full down to-day,
several more people
wanted to go but no

Very truly yours

Letter to Miss Barwell indicating that she would get her usual seats. One for herself next to Alfred and the second for a chaperone.

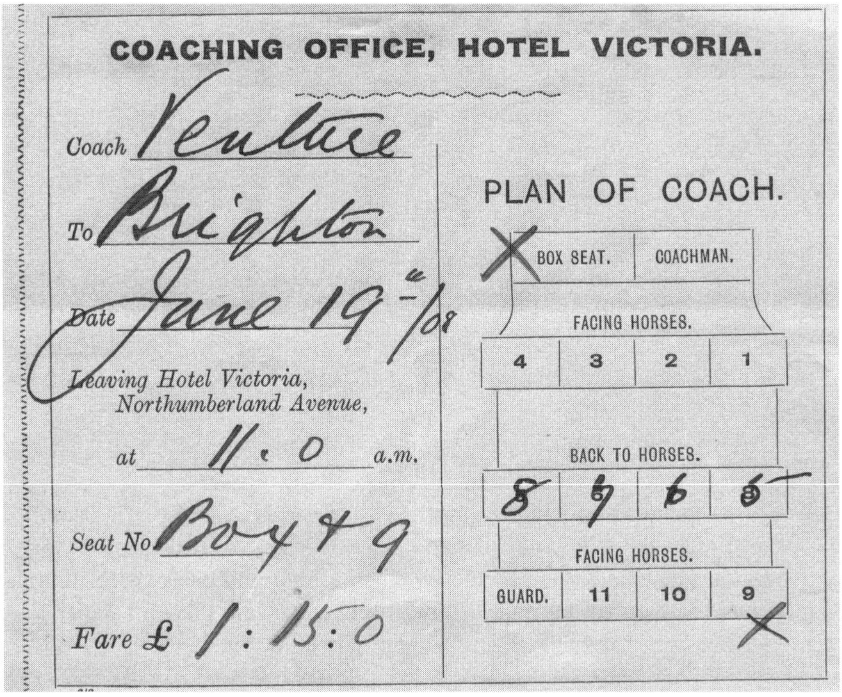

COACHING OFFICE, HOTEL VICTORIA.

Coach Venture

To Brighton

Date June 19th/08

Leaving Hotel Victoria,
Northumberland Avenue,

at 11.0 a.m.

Seat No Box & 9

Fare £ 1:15:0

PLAN OF COACH.

BOX SEAT.	COACHMAN.		
FACING HORSES.			
4	3	2	1
BACK TO HORSES.			
8	7	6	5
FACING HORSES.			
GUARD.	11	10	9

Tickets of Miss Barwell to ride the Venture from London to Brighton on June 19, 1908. Note that she had the box seat and the ninth seat reserved.

the armed Harrison steamer *SS Candidate* from Liverpool without warning. Riddled with bullets, the ship swayed precariously as crewmembers on board immediately abandoned ship, jumping aboard lifeboats that were lowered right away. Schwieger finished the assault with a torpedo that slammed right into the engine room. The ship began to sink and with a few more close-range gunshots from the deck gun, the ship finally keeled over, and sunk heavily beneath the waves, disappearing from view in a tremendous ring of concentric, frothing waves.

Soon after, a second armed trawler, the *Lawrenny Castle SA 52* appeared on the scene, and on seeing the *U-20*, she did not fire but instead turned around and fled. With a thick fog all around, Schwieger kept the submarine underwater in fear of being stalked.

Spotting a steamer by periscope and seeing the fog clearing, the *U-20* surfaced, gasping for escape from the fetid air below. She was the *Centurion*, the sister ship of the *Candidate*, another armed Harrison Line steamer. Schwieger would take no chances and immediately fired a torpedo at the vessel. The *Centurion* however remained afloat, stubborn and powerful. It would take another torpedo to finish her off, while her crew escaped.

With the taste of two victories, Schwieger could have enjoyed the moment. The hunting had been very good. Only three torpedoes waited in their tubes. Two torpedoes were required for the return journey; and now only one remained to stop supplies from reaching Liverpool.

As the evening approached, passengers yearned for a good celebration. So much of the journey had been punctuated by fear and anxiety about possible attack and as Liverpool would be reached by Saturday morning, most travelers intended on packing Friday evening. Hence, Thursday night assumed the privilege of being the night to party and forget all of one's worries.

Chief among the revelers was the theatrical manager Charles Frohman who vivaciously entertained a large number of guests in his suite. Attired in a handsome dark suit with a crisp white shirt, Frohman was debonair and playful. Like many others on board, he was relieved that the final destination would be reached in less than forty-eight hours. A.G. was among his favorite guests. Alfred had finally surfaced from his cabin to join his fellow passengers.

A few minutes before Alfred Gwynne was about to depart to join Frohman's festivities, his valet Denyer was handed a Marconi gram by a bellboy who sang out, "Cable for Mr. Vanderbilt" in a loud and clear voice. Immediately, Denyer handed the note to his employer. A thin piece of paper, the Marconi gram was handwritten and signed by the sender. It read:[49]

HOPE YOU HAVE SAFE CROSSING LOOKING FORWARD VERY MUCH TO SEEING YOU SOON MAY BARWELL

May Barwell, an attractive twenty-five year old, was the daughter of a wealthy London family who owned the sprawling estate, *Barkford House,* in Billingshurst, Sussex. The Barwells had been friends with A.G. for many years, frequenting social events in Newport.[50] The previous year she had accompanied Alfred and Margaret, along with friends Mr. and Mrs. William Whitehouse, G. Mifflin Wharton, and Worthington Whitehouse when they attended the opening of Verdi's "*Un Ballo in Maschera*" at the Metropolitan Opera.[51] They sat together in A.G.'s Box 31 and enjoyed a good time together.

Earlier in the year, in January of 1915, Mr. and Mrs. Barwell, probably Osborne and Agnes, her parents, had called upon Alfred and Margaret for a house party at Oakland Farms.[52] May arrived in New York on the *Baltic* and returned to England on the *Lusitania* in January of 1915.

May frequented Alfred's coach each year. In 1908 she purchased a ticket to sit on the box next to Alfred and for the next six years, she faithfully traveled aboard the *Venture*, accompanied frequently by another coaching companion, likely a chaperone. She always saved the personal memento books that A.G. handed out to all of his guests. On July 13th 1913, she received a note from Charles Wilson:

> I have booked you your usual seats for the last run up, I am sorry we are stopping so soon this year, the coach was full down today (sic), several more people wanted to go but no room, Mr. Vanderbilt is sure to be on the last day.
>
> Very truly yours,
> C. H. Wilson"[53]

Theater stars Rita Jolivet and Josephine Brandell bolstered Frohman, wrapping him in the adoration he enjoyed so heartily. At twenty-five, Rita Jolivet was a striking brunette with large eyes, an oval visage, and womanly figure. She was one of Charles Frohman's protégés, and enjoyed the privilege of being a sought-after actress for both Broadway and Hollywood. Rita had boarded the *Lusitania* to visit her brother in France on an impulse.[54] She was surprised to find her brother-in-law George Vernon, who was married to her sister Inez, on board the ship. Chatty and outgoing, the actress kept the company of her brother-in-law, Frohman, the other theater people on board, Alfred G. Vanderbilt, and her admirer Wallace Phillips.

Captain Anderson, of a more amicable nature than Turner's, was there to participate for a short while in pleasantries. Dinner in Frohman's suite was delightful for all the guests who reveled in the good company and food, which included trays of canapé and glasses of celebratory champagne.[55] Despite discussing the war, the overall mood was upbeat. After dinner, the guests slowly proceeded, many of them arm-in-arm, to the First Class Lounge to listen to the evening's entertainment, a concert and comedy show.

Turner, however, did not attend the concert but instead went to his office, where he was greeted by a wireless telegram with an alarming if predictable warning that read: SUBMARINES ACTIVE OFF SOUTH COAST OF IRELAND. The British Vice Admiral Sir Charles Coke, who was very concerned about Schwieger's sinking of three ships, sent a wireless message from Queenstown in Ireland that was received eight minutes before eight p.m. that evening.[56]

While Turner puffed away at a cigar and anxiously paced inside his office, another encoded wireless message arrived thirteen minutes later.

> BETWEEN SOUTH FORELAND AND FOLKESTONE KEEP WITHIN TWO MILES OF SHORE AND PASS BETWEEN THE TWO LIGHT VESSELS TAKE LIVERPOOL PILOT AT BAR AVOID HEADLANDS PASS HARBOURS AT FULL SPEED STEER MID-CHANNEL COURSE SUBMARINES OFF FASTNET

The concert would be the last large social event and the men and women attending were dressed appropriately, festive in their silk, satin, and other luxurious fabrics. Arriving with Charles Frohman, Rita Jolivet did not want to be seen consorting with amateur actors and instead took up the company of some spectators, men who gladly volunteered to be her company.

While the Gwent choir sang in the spectacular Palm Lounge with its enormous palm trees, plush carpeting, and painted ceiling,[57] a group of women approached guests one by one, petitioning them to donate money to the seamen's fund by purchasing programs for the Seaman's Charitable Concert. One among them was Phoebe Amory, an elderly Canadian woman who was traveling with two of her friends and was going to see her sons off to war. She approached Alfred G. Vanderbilt and offered him a ten-cent program.[58]

"I'm sorry, but I've already bought a programme," he said. She was about to withdraw when he offered her a $5.00 bill. "There," he told her, "that's for your lovely smile."

She blushed and said, "I shall have to look for change. Our programmes cost only ten cents."

"Certainly not," Alfred replied, smiling warmly at her.[59]

A pianist struck the major C chord with emphasis as he played the catchy tune "I Love a Piano" by Irving Berlin. The audience applauded loudly when he finished. He was followed soon after by a Scottish comedian with a quick tongue whose references could only be understood by his countrymen who laughed heartily at his one-liners while other spectators watched in silence. As the comedian ended his performance to a cheer of applause, Captain Turner took center stage.

Tremors of anxiety had vibrated throughout the entire concert performance. Fear was rampant and although temporarily subdued, it resurfaced again in a restless unease among the passengers. Captain Turner thanked his passengers for sailing on the *Lusitania* and extended his hope that the voyage had been a good one. He made mention that submarines had been active in the war zone, "But of course there is no cause for alarm. We shall be arriving at Liverpool early on Saturday morning."[60]

Many passengers staring at the stoic Turner, who smiled confidently back at them, drew comfort in his strength. While he talked to them, however, the lifeboats swung out on davits in a state of frightening readiness. A concerned passenger asked Turner if they were in any danger. The captain replied honestly, "In wartime there is always danger. But I must repeat that there is no cause for alarm. I will make one request to those gentlemen who are fond of cigars. Please do not light them on deck." He told them of the precautions that had been taken, such as blackening the portholes, locking the watertight doors, maintaining speed, quadrupling the watch, and swinging out the lifeboats in preparation.[61]

Some passengers however, could not be appeased by Turner's placating statements, and instead, chose to go in search of lifejackets and start fitting them on themselves and their children, in preparation. One group organized a campaign to instruct others on the proper method for donning a life jacket. They received consent from Turner but were instructed not to panic the passengers.

Charlotte Pye, a second-class traveler with an eighteen-month old baby in tow, was visibly upset. Her husband had encouraged her to take the swifter *Lusitania* from Edmonton to England, but now she regretted her selection. Terrified at the idea of being sunk by a submarine, she kept replaying the horror in her mind and despite being comforted by fellow passenger Reverend H.L. Gwyer, a young clergyman, she could not be consoled. Gwyer slept on the deck nearby her suite in readiness in case anything happened.

Turner was at his watch early the next morning, Friday May 7th. Worried about protecting his ship as she entered the danger zone, the captain ordered that the ship lower speed to fifteen knots because of the thick fog. As he brought the *Lusitania* to Liverpool, he knew that he was bringing the vessel into a busy port and wanted to time it right to catch the tide. However, by reducing speed, the *Lusitania* would not make the four o'clock morning high tide, forcing him to cycle the ship in the waters while in port.

If Turner knew that in the last few days since the *Lusitania* had set sail twenty-three merchant ships had been sunk,[62] he would have been even more vigilant. He was happily ignorant of this alarming news. The only communication he had with London was with the Admiralty who knew of the *Lusitania*'s position in the waters surrounding Ireland.

Through the protective blanket offered by the fog, the fog horn sounded loudly again and again. Oliver Bernard could not understand why it was necessary to sound the fog horn. He thought the sound invited attack.[63] What he failed to realize however was that Captain Turner was searching for the *Juno,* an older cruiser that could be an escort to the *Lusitania* and with whom the *Lusitania* could not risk a collision.[64] Turner wasn't aware that the *Juno* had already headed to port with no intention of escorting the *Lusitania.*[65]

The fog lifted, revealing a clear and sunny day but Turner did not increase the ship's speed, keeping a steady pace of fifteen knots. While passengers fretted that the captain did not speed back up, Turner kept fast to his plan. He had decided to arrive at the Liverpool Bar at 6:53 a.m. at high tide and steam into the protected waters of Liverpool without stopping. However, they still had to pass through the hotly contested war zone area.

Late in the morning when the *Lusitania* was off *Fastnet,* Turner received a wireless message that read:

> SUBMARINES ACTIVE IN SOUTHERN PART IRISH CHANNEL; LAST HEARD OF TWENTY MILES SOUTH OF CONINGBEG LIGHTSHIP.

As passengers whispered about submarines, the tension aboard the *Lusitania* was unmistakable. However, by noon the Irish shore grew visible. Many passengers such as second-class traveler Mrs. Alice Loynd took comfort in

Lusitania *photographed in an earlier voyage at the spot off the Old Head of Kinsdale, where she would later sink after being struck by a torpedo launched from U-20 on May 7, 1915.*

its proximity, expressing their relief and gratitude, "We can see Ireland quite well now. Thank God for a safe journey."[66]

Captain Turner sighted what he believed to be Brow Head, concluding that he was northwest of Fastnet Rock. Turning hard to port, Turner chose a course at sixty-seven degrees east.[67] An officer handed him another foreboding message at one o'clock. It read ignominiously:

> SUBMARINES FIVE MILES SOUTH OF CAPE CLEAR PROCEEDING WEST WHEN SIGHTED AT TEN A.M.[68]

Soon after, he saw another signpost, which he recognized as Galley Head, a location some forty miles from Brow Head. Despite traveling at least a hundred times on this journey from New York to Liverpool, Turner was confused. He was unsure of his location. Turner knew that he had not traversed the distance between Brow Head and Galley Head in that short amount of time. Turner realized that he had made a navigational error and wondered which signpost he had passed. He ordered that the *Lusitania* shift direction, adjusting her course.[69]

Twenty minutes after one p.m., Schwieger spotted by periscope the distinctive profile of the *Lusitania* at a course perpendicular to his own vessel. Delighted to see a large passenger liner, Schwieger realized that the ship was too far for the *U-20* to reach. He patiently waited and watched the cruiser. Immediately, the crew recognized that she was one of five British four stackers and while a crewmember hurried to find a naval journal to identify her, Schwieger got ready to fire a torpedo at their new target. The *U-20* submerged instantly to a depth of eleven meters, charging full speed ahead, in a direct collision course with the steamer. Schwieger hoped that the *Lusitania* might change its course to starboard along the Irish coast, which would set the *U-20* up for a perfect shot of its target.[70]

Finally spotting a familiar landmark, the Old Head of Kinsdale, Turner breathed a sigh of relief at 1:40 p.m. He positioned the *Lusitania* to eighty-seven degrees east, running parallel with the shoreline. Turner still could not place his exact bearing and so taking extreme precaution, he decided to make a four-point bearing on to Old Head ten minutes later. To maintain this position, the *Lusitania* would have to stay in a straight line for the next forty minutes at a steady speed.[71] Unwittingly, Turner had placed the *Lusitania* right into the range of the *U-20*.

The *Lusitania*'s steady course made her an easy target. Schwieger could not have been more pleased than the exaltation he felt as the *Lusitania* corrected course straight at the *U-20*. The last maneuver had brought the four-funneled treasure into a course that would bring her for a perfect bowshot within a short distance. Schwieger had time to position himself several times for the best shot before he fired. The entire crew aboard the *U-20* knew that the target was a massive passenger liner, most likely the *Lusitania,* and would be carrying hundreds of women and children. Sinking a cruiser with so many innocent passengers on board weighed heavily upon the mind of the *U-20*'s Quartermaster Charles Voegele.[72] Voegele knew instantly that his refusal to carry out the order would result in the loss of his position in the navy as well as a possible court indictment for treason. When Schwieger gave the order to ready the torpedo, Voegele became overcome with emotion: "I'm sorry, sir, but I cannot bring myself to destroy a ship with innocent women and children on board. Such an act is barbaric."[73]

Schwieger called another seaman immediately to carry out his order while Voegele was relieved of his duty. As the announcement "Torpedo is ready" came back, Schwieger was calm and purposeful, never losing his focus for a second.[74]

At a distance of seven hundred meters or two thousand three hundred feet, Schwieger ordered the release of a G torpedo ten feet below the surface. Blasted with air to launch the missile, the chamber housing the torpedo hissed loudly. The missile catapulted out of its hold at an angle of ninety degrees, bursting forth with foam before it sped towards the liner initially at twenty-two knots, and accelerating as it headed straight for a clean bow shot.[75]

NOTES

1. Kent, J. and Layton. *Lusitania: An Illustrated Biography of the Ship of Splendor*. North Carolina: Lulu Press, 2007. Pg. 57.
2. Ibid. Pg. 59.
3. Ibid. Pg. 60.
4. Hickey, Des and Gus Smith. *Seven Days to Disaster*. G. P. Putnam & Sons, 1981. Pg. 93.
5. Preston, Diana. *Lusitania: An Epic Tragedy*. New York. The Berkeley Publishing Group, 2002. Pg. 162.
6. Ibid. Pg. 64.
7. Ibid. Pg. 66.
8. Ibid.
9. Ibid. Pg. 68.
10. Ibid.
11. *The New York Times*. "Will Leaves a Gift to A.G. Vanderbilt." May 19, 1915. Pg. 14.
12. Hickey, Des and Gus Smith. *Seven Days to Disaster*. G. P. Putnam & Sons, 1981. Pg. 116.
13. *The New York Times*. "Will Leaves a Gift to A.G. Vanderbilt." May 19, 1915. Pg. 14.
14. *The New York Times*. May 16, 1915. Pg. 1.
15. *The New York Times*. "Vanderbilt Called Notice Ridiculous." May 16, 1915. Pg. 1.

16. *The New York Times*. "Vanderbilt Called Notice Ridiculous." May 16, 1915. Pg. 1.
17. Ibid
18. Ibid.
19. Ibid.
20. Bernard, Oliver. *Cock Sparrow: A True Chronicle*. Oxford: Alden Press. 1936. Pg Pg. 149.
21. Ibid.
22. Bernard, Oliver. *Cock Sparrow: A True Chronicle*. Oxford: Alden Press. 1936. Pg. 148.
23. Hickey, Des and Gus Smith. *Seven Days to Disaster*. G. P. Putnam & Sons, 1981. Pg. 87.
24. Ibid. Pg. 88.
25. A.A. Hoehling, A. A. and Mary Hoehling. *A Thrilling Tale of Disaster At Sea: The Last Voyage of the Lusitania*. London: 1957. Pg. 78.
26. Hoehling, A. A. and Mary Hoehling. *A Thrilling Tale of Disaster At Sea: The Last Voyage of the Lusitania*. London: Madison Books, 1957. Pg. 78.
27. Preston, Diana. *Lusitania: An Epic Tragedy*. New York: The Berkeley Publishing Group, 2002. Pg. 97.
28. Cussler, Clive and Craig Dirgo. *The Sea Hunters*. New York: Simon & Schuster Inc, 2003. Pg. 271.
29. Ibid. Pg. 272.
30. Ibid.
31. Hoehling, A. A. and Mary Hoehling. *A Thrilling Tale of Disaster At Sea: The Last Voyage of the Lusitania*. London: Madison Books, 1957. Pg. 48.
32. Ibid. Pg. 51.
33. Thomas, Lowell. "Raiders of the Deep." Doubleday, Doran and Company, Inc. New York: 1928. Pg. 91.
34. Bergen, Claus and Karl Neureuther. *U-boat Stories*. London: The Naval & Military Press Ltd. Pg. 16-17.
35. Preston, Diana. *Lusitania: An Epic Tragedy*. New York: The Berkeley Publishing Group, 2002.
36. Hoehling, A. A. and Mary Hoehling. *A Thrilling Tale of Disaster At Sea: The Last Voyage of the Lusitania.* London: Madison Books, 1957. Pg. 16.
37. *Germany's Submarine Campaign*. Living Age. October 31, 1925. Pg. 327.
38. Ibid. Pg. 52.
39. Ibid. Pg. 53.
40. Ibid.
41. Lauriat, Charles E. *The Lusitania's Last Voyage*. London: Charles E. Lauriat, 1915. Pg. 4.
42. Ibid. Pg. 15.
43. Kent, J. and Layton. *Lusitania: An Illustrated Biography of the Ship of Splendor*. North Carolina: Lulu Press, 2007. Pg. 172.
44. Hoehling, A. A. and Mary Hoehling. *A Thrilling Tale of Disaster At Sea: The Last Voyage of the Lusitania*. London: Madison Books, 1957. Pg. 15.
45. Ibid. Pg. 80.

Chapter Nineteen

Eighteen Minutes

The weather was perfect for a leisurely stroll and Oliver Bernard was one of the many passengers taking advantage of the calm and clear day. Nearing the Verandah café, Bernard was lost in his own thoughts, pondering his own meaning in life and wondering, "How the hell did one learn to love everybody: Did anybody really and truly love their enemies, he wondered, and why, and—what's that flickering, what?" when something off in the distance, a few hundred yards from the ship, caught his eye. Immediately, he turned to look and was astonished by what he saw:

> "What the hell was this? A frothy track was snaking up to them like an express; an experiment, a signal, his mind tried to register, to persuade him anything but that it was a torpedo!"[1]

He turned away as a sickening sensation convulsed through him. He saw the trail of "bluey-white" foam[2] disappear under the starboard counter. Seconds later, the torpedo slammed into the liner, striking the hull of the mighty ship and the coalbunker of Boiler Room No. 1. Three hundred pounds of swiftly moving metal crashed into the outer hull at forty-five miles an hour, shooting a plume of water and debris straight up into the air at least sixty feet while the booming explosion shook the vessel "like the banging of a door on a windy day."[3]

The blast in the boiler room sent an enormous high-pressure shock wave that reached into the main stokehold, creating a deafening sound as men working there were thrown to the floor, holding their ears in sheer agony. Within seconds, the heat of the boiler room, at one hundred and twenty degrees Fahrenheit, was replaced by cold seawater rapidly flooding the bunker and stokeholds. As the men tried to escape, they feared the possibility of a steam explosion.

Torpedo striking the Lusitania. New York Herald. *Undated ca. 1915.*

Schwieger watched in amazement at the success of his torpedo that hit the starboard side of the *Lusitania* right behind the bridge with an "unusually heavy explosion" and a large cloud that reached far beyond the front funnel. Meanwhile, passengers aboard the liner panicked as wood, cinders, and metal shards rained down on them. Friends and families rushed forward, clutching each other tightly.

Exactly two minutes later at 2:12 p.m., Captain Turner ordered the helmsman and quartermaster Hugh Johnston to steer hard to starboard. Turner knew that the damage was serious but he was not aware of its full impact. The *Lusitania* did not respond. Then he simply ordered that the ship be held on course, bringing her into Kinsdale, but there she could not be controlled. She acted like a rudderless sailboat, moving forward without stopping. While Turner yelled the order "hard-a-starboard", the *Lusitania* plunged towards the bow. She moved forward unable to be steered; the controls were gone.

Turner knew that she was making too much headway for lifeboats to be launched and sought to reduce her speed. The *Lusitania* could give her master nothing in return for his anguished requests. As the steam pressure had plunged, no power was left to reverse engines. The screws would slowly come to a halt but provide no counter force as she plummeted ahead. To make matters worse, beginning with a slow rumble that increased in volume to a terrifying roar issuing from deep within the ship, there was a second explosion that raised the ship's bows right out of the water. Glass and metal screeched in loud torment and the *Lusitania* shuddered.

Bernard "stood spellbound."[4] Feeling "a slight shock through the deck, as if a tug had run into the enormous hull of the liner,"[5] Bernard closed his eyes "for a fraction of a second"[6] just before he heard "a terrific explosion."[7] A young mother, Charlotte Pye, holding her baby, collapsed to the floor as the explosions hit the ship.

Charles Lauriat, who was leaning on the rail outside the First Class dining saloon with fellow passengers Mr. and Mrs. Hubbard, distinctively heard a second explosion from deep within the ship's innards with a terrifying sound.[8] Women, some of them clutching their babies, clamored to the door to get out of the public lounge areas where splintered glass and debris fell in a huge avalanche that rolled out to the sea.

Rita Jolivet, who was in her cabin when the first explosion occurred, was thrown around her cabin like a rag doll. Tired from the previous night's festivities, she was confused and frightened. Through her window, she could see a female passenger trying on a lifejacket so she grabbed her own lifejacket and scurried upstairs immediately to the first-class deck. Immediately, she saw her brother-in-law George Vernon, who assisted her and fastened the lifejacket securely upon her.[9]

Lady Mackworth and her father had just returned from dining and were about to enter the elevator to return to their cabins when they heard the first explosion. Instinctively, Lady Mackworth stepped back from the elevator and into the hallway. Although she wanted to get out into the open air of the boat deck, she wondered if it was safer to remain covered. As she and her father climbed up the stairs to the first class promenade deck, the suffragette remarkably kept her cool, despite fighting back fears that she would have to get in the water. Lady Mackworth knew how to swim but was terrified of water going over her head.[10]

Passengers crowded the stairs, leading to the upper decks. The crew requested that all passengers make it to the promenade deck where the boats were but their pleas fell on deaf ears. A mad rush of people frantically scrambled to put on their lifejackets. Shrieking hysterically, Lesley Mason, whose care her father had entrusted to Bernard, came running towards Bernard just as he reached the Verandah café on the port side of the ship. She did not know where her husband was. Bernard shook her violently and told her to "pull yourself together."[11] He promised to get lifejackets and asked her to wait there by the port deck. Rushing past passengers trying to climb

Alfred in white scarf, hat and overcoat. International News Service.

into boats while crewmembers held them off until the boats were lowered, Bernard almost crashed into Alfred G. Vanderbilt.

Unlike the hysteria that was sweeping all the decks, Alfred was remarkably calm and poised. He grinned at Bernard. Attired fashionably in a dark gray suit with a polka-dot tie, A.G. held a purple leather case in his hand, the kind of elegant container that a lady would use for storing jewelry; he was possibly safeguarding them for Lady Mackworth.[12] "Absolutely unperturbed,"[13] Alfred Gwynne was the "figure of a gentleman"[14] as he waited patiently and with "sportsmanlike coolness."[15]

With a wide grin, Alfred said dryly, "They got us this time alright."[16]

Bernard stumbled down the stairs leading to his cabin just as the power failed. Plunged into darkness, Bernard tripped and fell, crashing at the bottom of the stairs. Quickly getting back up, he made his way to his cabin where he found his life jacket. Terrified that he might get stuck below, Bernard ran back up the stairs to the deck. Making his way to the port side, Bernard returned to find Lesley gone.

Another woman screaming, "Where did you get that?" pointed at Bernard's lifejacket. Before he could reply, she snatched it out of his hands and ran with all her might down the deck.[17]

Loud shrieks erupted from the lower decks and elevators as passengers unfortunately remained stuck behind the iron bars. Among them were many able-bodied seamen, whose assistance would have been of great help to the crewmembers on the main deck of the forecastle, struggling with screaming mobs of anxious passengers.[18]

In the *U-20*, some seven hundred yards away, while one of the three dachshunds on board barked, Schwieger closely watched the torpedo slam between the first and second funnels. The submarine rattled heavily with the impact from the two detonations. The second explosion shook the *U-20* so powerfully that light bulbs burst while the submarine was tossed around on the high ocean waves. Schwieger could not have hoped for a better outcome. The massive ocean liner was hit and rapidly sinking after the second explosion. He watched as the "superstructure right above the point of impact and the bridge" were ripped asunder, as a fire broke out, and a thick haze of smoke began to envelop the high bridge. Rapidly, Schwieger deduced that the first explosion had hit a boiler room, resulting in a greater second explosion with coal or gunpowder. The mighty ship heeled over to starboard soon after, as the bow dipped precariously into the water, becoming completely immersed. To all appearances, it looked as though the *Lusitania* would capsize within moments.[19]

Pandemonium had broken loose. Passengers ran screaming, crying, and yelling up and down decks, searching for loved ones and grabbing life jackets. While Turner desperately tried to regain control of his ship, the *Lusitania* failed to respond at the helm. When the power went out, the passengers who were feverishly gathering their possessions and running out of their rooms and the second-class dining saloon were plunged into darkness. Panic ensued and many fell to the floor below with loud thuds, as they slipped on steps, screaming desperately, just as torrents of water poured into the engine room, quickly enveloping the lower decks.[20]

The chief officer of the Marconi wireless, Robert Leith, ran up to the Sun Deck as fast as he could, making his way to the Marconi room. A junior officer was already at the key typing. Leith immediately took over and began to tap out a message rapidly and methodically; the second time carefully adding in the ship's location that an officer quickly informed him of:

> S.O.S. COME AT ONCE. BIG LIST. TEN MILES SOUTH OLD HEAD KINSDALE. MFA.[21]

Within seconds of the torpedo striking, Martin Mannion from St. Louis noticed that all of his poker companions had deserted him. Tables and chairs were overturned and the bar itself was tilted at a crazy angle, sending glasses and bottles smashing against the floor and counter. He sat alone in the second-class smoking saloon. Jauntily making his way uphill to the bar, he approached the bartender who was quickly untying his apron and said, "'Let's die game anyway.'" Angrily, the bartender retorted, "'You go to hell!'" and jumping over the counter, bolted out the back door. Sighing, Mannion pulled out a bottle of ale from among the splintered glass on the table and settled back down on to a stool for a drink.

As panic swept the second and third class compartments, first class passengers tried to maintain some form of composure.[22] Most notable among these passengers for his sense of calm was Charles Frohman. Frohman had just finished a late lunch with his entourage of playful companions and was strolling along the upper promenade deck when the torpedo struck. Alfred Gwynne was with the group initially at lunch but had slipped away soon after. George Vernon, Rita Jolivet's brother-in-law, was engaged in a conversation with Frohman who smoked a cigar. Just as the English officer Alick Scott approached him, the reverberations of the torpedo sent a shock wave through the ship. Frohman, cigar in hand, kept his composure, saying unperturbedly, "This is going to be a close call."[23]

Joining Frohman, Rita Jolivet noticed how calm the theater manager was in stark contrast to the chaos that was overtaking the ship as people ran helter skelter, screaming with looks of complete desperation as the ship moaned. Charles Frohman began to make small talk as everyone around him lost their initial composure and panicked. Alick Scott slipped away, reappearing with life jackets. He fastened one on Frohman. When Frohman noticed that Scott did not have a life jacket himself, he protested, insisting that Scott have one, to which the officer replied, "If I'm going to die, it's only for once."[24]

Frohman comforted Rita Jolivet by telling her to stay close and hold tight to the railing, saving her strength. While he continued to puff on his cigar, Frohman looked out towards the sea and commented, shaking his head, "I didn't think they would do it."[25]

Thomas Slidell was in the smoking room with another passenger, Herbert Stone, when the torpedo struck. Immediately, they both leapt to their feet, uttering "Torpedo!" and fleeing the room, Slidell running downstairs while Stone made for the upper deck.[26]

Schwieger noticed that the mighty ship did not have a flag astern and saw the bright golden lettering of the name *Lusitania* on the bow as the ship continued to blow off steam. He reckoned that the liner would not stay afloat much longer. Schwieger gave the order to dive to a depth of twenty-four meters and run out to sea. A second torpedo did not seem necessary as the ship was falling asunder so quickly on its own from the impact of the explosion in the boiler room. He considered it "impossible for me, anyhow, to fire a second torpedo into this crowd of people struggling to save their lives."[27]

Propaganda Postcard issued by the French showing civilian victims of the sinking.

The elevator, once a sign of luxury, now became a terrifying steel cage. The dining hall was awash with floating timber, debris, and wreckage as water flowed in, ruining the fine furniture as chandeliers came crashing down. On the port side, passengers struggled, pushing against each other to reach the boats. While the crew tried to get the lifeboats out the edge of the deck so that they could be lowered, many passengers climbed aboard the boats and refused to get out, despite pleas from the ship's men. The starboard side faced opposing problems where the boats had swung out so far that the distance between the deck and gunwale was at least six feet. The *Lusitania* was making so much headway that when the lifeboats hit the surface of the water, many of them flipped, spilling out passengers into the frigid waters.

As they were lowered, many of the lifeboats were ripped right out of their davits, colliding with each other, crushing passengers on board and even killing some passengers who unfortunately stood too close. Others were torn to pieces. There was little hope the boats could be dragged along the hull safely. Nonetheless, people clamored to get into the boats, screaming in terror and had, in at least one case, to be held at bay by a sailor who wielded a powerful axe in front of them.

In mute horror, C.W. Bowring, a shipper, watched a boat proceed downwards about half the way, before dumping her passengers into the sea. Within seconds, another boat became tangled in the lines of the first, collapsing on top of the survivors of the first boat and smashing them. Fleeing down a companionway to grab his life jacket, he passed Alfred Gwynne who sat calmly on a sofa, striking a remarkable figure because of his calmness. A.G. was stoic and resolute, "just sitting, thinking, not a bit excited."[28]

Some passengers, such as the wealthy wine merchant from New York, George Kessler, refused to accept that the *Lusitania* was sinking, all the while assisting women on board the lifeboats. It would take Herculean effort by a team of adrenaline-driven men to launch boats along the port sides.

James Brooke, a first-class passenger, swiftly came to their rescue of women such as Lady Mackworth and Theodate Pope. "Tall and husky," Brooke immediately inspired confidence among the women, as he offered them one hand, while he held boat davits with his other hand.

James Brooke was getting ready to play a game of shuffleboard with his friends when the torpedo struck. Rushing from the Marconi deck to reach other friends, he became enveloped in a cloud of steam and escaped, coughing, wet, and delirious to the forward starboard deck. There he watched Captain Turner wearing a life preserver, wave orders to crewmen below as he clung desperately to chairs. Initially rebuked by Isaac Lehmann, a stockbroker who threatened to shoot any passengers boarding the lifeboats before they were ready, who put a pistol to his head, Brooke retorted, "Who in hell is trying to?"

He watched in horror as a boat swinging from a davit, came crashing down on to the deck as Lehmann blocked off other passengers, wounding Lehmann in the right leg severely. Dazed and confused, the man lay senseless on the deck and before Brooke or any other passenger could reach him, a gigantic ocean wave swept over him, pulling him off the deck and into the surging waters below.

Within the last ten minutes, the *Lusitania* had tilted some twenty degrees starboard, jettisoning wailing passengers into the sea. The North Atlantic water was very cold, about fifty degrees Fahrenheit. A terrible moaning and groaning ensued from the vessel as her bow dipped further underwater. The *Lusitania* was sinking fast, now picking up water from the portholes that had once allowed refreshing air into the dining halls. The crew, cursed by inexperience, could do little. The flotsam formed a wake of blood and dead bodies, as *Lusitania* kept moving forward.

All the while, Robert Leith continued tapping out an SOS message in the Marconi room, resolute and unwavering in his determination. He had switched to emergency batteries when the main generators failed.[29] His efforts were not in vain. The cry for help was immediately picked up by three Anglo-American ships, the *Narragansett, Etonian,* and *City of Exeter*, whose captains pushed their vessels to maximum speed.[30] The Germans and English admiralties heard it too. The English Admiralty sent out four boats,[31] the *Julia, Stormcock, Flying Fish,* and *Warrior*, while alerting all ocean vessels to the terrible predicament. More and more ships, fishing vessels, and trawlers all changed course, traveling at top speed to reach the sinking *Lusitania.* From the Irish shore, local fishermen and the coastguard watched[32] the massive distinctive ship plunge forward, her funnels tilting sharply, as her lower decks became submerged.

Many of the women who stood watching the lifeboats being loaded became appalled that the boats filling rapidly with people had hardly any children.[33] There was an unusual amount of children aboard the *Lusitania*, and no one seemed to be stopping to help them. Several gentlemen aboard took notice of the predicament, and among them was Alfred Gwynne Vanderbilt.

While the water threatened to sweep people off decks, A.G. dashed to and fro, along with his valet Ronald Denyer, rescuing little children and babies. Lott Gadd, the ship's barber who had met A.G. the previous night at Frohman's party, witnessed Alfred putting lifejackets on both women and children as the "ship was going down fast. When the sea reached them, they were washed away. I never saw Vanderbilt after that. All I saw in the water was children---children everywhere."[34] Without ceasing for a moment, Alfred and his valet worked together quietly and efficiently as a team despite the rising waters that now surged up to their knees. Calm and collected, A.G. ordered his valet to "Find all the kiddies you can, boy."[35] Denyer collected the children and brought them to Alfred who, "dashed to the boats with two little ones in his arms at a time."[36] Some said he looked as composed as if he was waiting for a train.[37]

Pushing forward with a relentless determination, Vanderbilt rushed into the nursery where terrified children cried helplessly in fear, alone and bewildered. A baby in each arm, he waded through the surging waves that foamed and threatened to submerge the lower decks. The water continued to rise, reaching past his knees and up to his chest, but A.G. pressed on: a quietly determined and remarkably calm figure amidst the ensuing mayhem. Six days prior, Alfred had indicated that being considered a sportsman and a gentleman, in essence, a man of caliber, were very important to him. Here, in this time of travail, those thoughts would translate with lightning speed to immediate action.

Many women clasping babies in their arms, tried to make their way out of the second-class dining room and on to the deck near the lifeboats. Desperately trying to hold on to their babies, many of the women slipped repeatedly, falling down on the deck of the swaying *Lusitania.* Hysterical, these women tried to climb aboard the lifeboats, donning lifejackets whenever possible. Screaming babies, their faces red and swollen, slipped out from the hands of mothers, disappearing immediately below the surface. Crewmembers tried to get as many women and children into the lifeboats but many of the boats with passengers capsized, and those fortunate to be wearing lifejackets, bobbed back to the surface, grabbing on to pieces of driftwood and floating wreckage. A.G. lent a hand wherever he could: attempting to calm down women that were hysterical[38] and shepherding young children safely to boats. Second Steward Robert Chisholm shouted at Vanderbilt in vain, "Hurry, Mr. Vanderbilt, or it will be too late!" as he passed him on the B deck.[39]

As the list grew more severe, Oliver Bernard fell down repeatedly. Abandoning his own efforts to assist the newlywed couple left in his charge, Oliver Bernard focused on purely his own survival. In the open sea, he saw a naked man swimming in hope of being found by an approaching ship.[40] Watching him, Bernard decided to get rid of his extra clothes and removed his coat, vest, tie, and collar. He was overcome with his own thoughts about how insignificant so much that had previously consumed him now appeared. Instead, he felt like he was sinking deep into a "sea of agonizing futility"[41] and wondered what the point of his whole life had been. Frustrated beyond belief, Bernard threw himself into a lifeboat still on a davit and freed the boat from the ropes holding it hostage. He helped another passenger on to the lifeboat and was relieved to find himself alive and safe.[42]

Lady Mackworth who had fallen out of a lifeboat, clung to one end of a floating piece of wood while another passenger clung to the other side.[43] Slipping in and out of consciousness as the frigid waters ensconced her, she held on with all of her might, noting that the other passenger had lost his grip and drifted mercilessly away into the ocean's embrace. Four members of the Royal Welsh Choir all clamored aboard the same lifeboat, singing a Scottish hymn in supplication.

Electrician George Hutchinson helped Alfred Gwynne Vanderbilt get lifebelts on the remaining passengers on board the deck. Some of the men and women refused, but the two men kept working until water forced them apart.[44]

The torment of children and women trying to find safety in lifeboats convinced Rita Jolivet to consider suicide; she decided she preferred a bullet from her own small pearl-handled pistol to the horrifying death of drowning in the freezing water. Jolivet stood on the deck next to Charles Frohman, tightly clasping his hand. Despite the limitations of his crippled, weak body, Charles exhibited an uncanny fortitude of spirit. While the bow of the ship sunk rapidly into the clutches of the dark ocean waters below, Frohman remained remarkably calm, saying aloud, "To die will be an awfully big adventure,"[45] a line from his famous Peter Pan play.[46]

Just then a magnificent cliff of cold green water assaulted them, flinging them apart. Ripped right out of her shoes by the sheer force of the water,

Rita Jolivet sunk deep under the water in a torrent of bubbles. She resurfaced briefly before being drawn back down again by powerful undercurrents, disappearing from view and reappearing some hundred yards away by a lifeboat, clinging desperately to a wandering piece of driftwood.

Like a man possessed, Alfred Gwynne continued to rescue little babies although his efforts seemed futile in the wake of disappearing lifeboats and the carnage of death surrounding him. The water up to his chest, the millionaire frantically strapped babies into Moses Baskets, lifejackets secured to their wrappings, releasing a flotilla of young ones into the crashing green waters as he vainly attempted to beat the relentless forward march of the inevitable sinking. A massive wave had knocked his valet Denyer off the deck into the Atlantic. Alfred could have jumped into the water or escaped on to a lifeboat in those last few minutes. Instead, the millionaire made no effort to save his own life. While everyone around him including the ship's hands had abandoned the liner, Alfred did not cease his work for a minute, desperately trying to empty the nursery of the children. His thick overcoat did not protect him as his clothes were soaked and stuck to him.[47] Hatless and dripping from head to toe, A.G. was scarcely recognizable as the millionaire that the world knew. Drenched to the bone, his handsome face soaked with water dripping from his hair down his nose, he pushed against the overwhelming force of water with the mammoth strength of an avenger. A bear inside the man had been released; an unquenchable spirit that could not rest.

Swimming with all of her might, fifteen-year old Virginia Bruce Loney, who had fallen out of an overturned lifeboat, saw Alfred Gwynne still on board. She took one last look at the man who had attempted to save her life by placing her and her parents on a lifeboat.[48]

Another woman, Alice Middleton, a Seattle nurse[49] and second-class passenger, struggled to keep her bearing on the ship. Alfred Gwynne approached her and, taking off his own lifebelt, gave it to her immediately.[50] Thomas Slidell, Alfred's friend, witnessed the deed as A.G. moved away "without a word."[51]

As he gave Alice his lifebelt, Alfred gave up any possibility of his own survival. He could not swim and the freezing waters of the Atlantic rose higher, threatening to envelop him in its squid-like embrace.

A solitary figure staring at the deck of his ship looming above him and that now threatened to topple him over as the *Lusitania* plunged down into the ocean depths, Turner stood on the bridge of the mighty ship as she took her final breath. Just a few moments earlier, he had told his dutiful Quartermaster Johnson to abandon ship and save himself as the *Lusitania* reported a twenty-five degree angle.[52] The *Lusitania*, which had moved forward undeterred by any of the crew's efforts to stop her course, now came to an abrupt end when she scraped the ocean bed, plowing downward. Groaning and twisting, the liner fell below the surface with colossal waves, spinning people and furniture in a vortex around her. Grabbing a hold of a floating wooden chair, Turner held on tightly to a wooden arm until a fishing trawler found him.

He watched helplessly as the forward funnel slid below the surface, followed by all the grandiose public rooms, and the Verandah Café. Rolling back to starboard, the *Lusitania* pinned down four passengers including detective William Pierpoint, who were sucked into the vortex. Within seconds, they were shot back into the air, covered in soot, as a powerful blast of air issued from deep within the ship's innards. Turner noticed Pierpoint swim quickly away with a terrified expression on his face.[53]

In just eighteen minutes, at 2:28 p.m. on May 7, 1915, the mighty *Lusitania* sank. The ship, which had moved forward undeterred by any of the crew's efforts to stop her course, came to an abrupt end when she plowed into the ocean bed. The world's greatest liner disappeared under the frothing, raging ocean waters.

In the *Lusitania*'s last moments, with the imminent threat of death looming in front of him, A.G. demonstrated a willpower and vitality that surpassed all expectations of him. In the ultimate test of chivalry, A. G. "measured up."[54] Alfred transcended his image of a millionaire playboy by his final acts, with a courage that defied comprehension, as he willingly gave up his own life to save another's, fighting till the very last moment to somehow save the children on board until the water finally swallowed him. While many passengers around him had fled, thinking only of their own preservation, and yet others had turned into brute savages, ripping off the lifebelts of others and pushing their way first into the lifeboats, Alfred Gwynne Vanderbilt became a hero.

NOTES

1. Bernard, Oliver. *Cock Sparrow: A True Chronicle*. Oxford: Alden Press. 1936. Pg. 154.
2. Ibid.
3. Preston, Diana. *Lusitania: An Epic Tragedy*. New York: The Berkeley Publishing Group, 2002. Pg. 192-4.
4. Bernard, Oliver. *Cock Sparrow: A True Chronicle*. Oxford: Alden Press. 1936. Pg. 154.
5. Ibid.
6. Ibid.
7. Ibid.
8. Hickey, Des and Gus Smith. *Seven Days to Disaster*. G. P. Putnam & Sons, 1981. Pg. 186.

9. Preston, Diana. *Lusitania: An Epic Tragedy*. New York. The Berkeley Publishing Group, 2002. Pg. 200.

10. Ibid. Pg. 207.

11. Hoehling, A. A. and Mary Hoehling. *A Thrilling Tale of Disaster At Sea: The Last Voyage of the Lusitania*. London: Madison Books, 1957. Pg. 139.

12. *The New York Times*. "Vanderbilt Saved Woman." May 10, 1915. Pg. 1.

13. Ibid.

14. Ibid.

15. Ibid.

16. *The Los Angeles Times*. "They've Got Us, Says Vanderbilt." May 11, 1915. Pg. I1.

17. Bernard, Oliver. *Cock Sparrow: A True Chronicle*. Oxford: Alden Press. 1936.

18. Kent, J. and Layton. *Lusitania: An Illustrated Biography of the Ship of Splendor*. North Carolina: Lulu Press, 2007. Pg. 192.

19. Ibid.

20. Hickey, Des and Gus Smith. *Seven Days to Disaster*. G. P. Putnam & Sons, 1981. Pg. 189.

21. Kent, J. and Layton. *Lusitania: An Illustrated Biography of the Ship of Splendor*. North Carolina: Lulu Press, 2007. Pg. 196.

22. Hickey, Des and Gus Smith. *Seven Days to Disaster*. G. P. Putnam & Sons, 1981. Pg. 196.

23. Hoehling, A. A. and Mary Hoehling. *A Thrilling Tale of Disaster At Sea: The Last Voyage of the Lusitania*. London: Madison Books, 1957. Pg. 150.

24. Ibid. Pg. 198.

25. Ibid. Pg. 200.

26. *Boston Daily Globe*. "Vanderbilt Placed Own Life Belt About Woman Before the End." May 10, 1915. Pg. 3.

27. Bailey, Thomas and Paul Ryan. *The Lusitania Disaster*. Free Press, Division of McMillan Publishers: London. 1975. Pg. 55-56.

28. Thomas, Lowell. *Raiders of the Deep*. Doubleday, Doran and Company, Inc. New York: 1928. Pg. 103.

29. Hoehling, A. A. and Mary Hoehling. *A Thrilling Tale of Disaster At Sea: The Last Voyage of the Lusitania*. London: Madison Books, 1957. Pg. 118.

30. Ibid. Pg. 119.

31. Ibid. Pg. 121.

32. Ibid. Pg. 122-3.

33. Ibid. Pg. 181.

34. Preston, Diana. *Lusitania: An Epic Tragedy*. New York: The Berkeley Publishing Group, 2002. Pg. 233.

35. *Boston Daily Globe*. "Come, Let Us Save the Kiddies." May 13, 1915. Pg. 1.

36. Ibid. Pg. 233.

37. *The New York Times*. "Vanderbilt Saved Woman." May 10, 1915. Pg. 1.

38. Chidsey, Ronald Barr. *The Day They Sank the Lusitania*. New York: Award Books, 1967. Pg. 96-97.

39. Hoehling, A. A. and Mary Hoehling. *A Thrilling Tale of Disaster At Sea: The Last Voyage of the Lusitania.* London: Madison Books, 1957. Pg. 149.

40. Bernard, Oliver. *Cock Sparrow: A True Chronicle.* Oxford: Alden Press. 1936. Pg. 157-9.

41. Ibid. Pg. 159.

42. Hickey, Des and Gus Smith. *Seven Days to Disaster.* London: G. P. Putnam & Sons, 1981. Pg. 225.

43. Butler, Daniel Allen. *The Lusitania: The Life, Loss, and Legacy of an Ocean Legend.* Mechanicsburg: Stackpole Books, 2000. Pg. 139.

44. The Mersey Report: *Report of a Formal Investigation into the Circumstances Attending the Foundering on the 7th of May, 1915, of the British steamship "Lusitania" of Liverpool, After Being Torpedoed off the Old Head of Kinsdale, Ireland.* Pg. 10.

45. The exact words that Frohman used are debatable. James Barrie didn't formally publish the script for Peter Pan until 1928, after revising it many times, and the newspaper articles that reported Frohman's last words used different versions of the quote. The line quoted here is from James Barrie's novel version of the play Peter Pan, entitled *Peter and Wendy*, published in 1911.

46. Barrie, J.M. *Peter Pan.* New York: Penguin Books, 2004. Pg 84.

47. *The Los Angeles Times.* "They've Got Us, Says Vanderbilt." May 11, 1915. Pg. I1.

48. Hoehling, A. A. and Mary Hoehling. *A Thrilling Tale of Disaster At Sea: The Last Voyage of the Lusitania.* London: Madison Books, 1957. Pg. 153.

49. Chidsey, Ronald Barr. *The Day They Sank the Lusitania.* New York: Award Books, 1967. Pg. 96-97.

50. *The Atlanta Constitution.* "Vanderbilt Gave Belt to Woman and Went Down with Lusitania." May 10, 1915. pg. 1.

51. Hickey, Des and Gus Smith. *Seven Days to Disaster.* London: G. P. Putnam & Sons, 1981. Pg. 223.

52. Kent, J. and Layton. *Lusitania: An Illustrated Biography of the Ship of Splendor.* North Carolina: Lulu Press, 2007. Pg. 202.

53. Ibid.

54. *The Washington Post.* "Alfred Vanderbilt." May 11, 1915. Pg. 6.

Chapter Twenty

Aftermath

As the liner disappeared beneath the waves, few survivors remained. Local residents near the landmark red and white lighthouse by Old Head of Kinsdale watched as Captain Turner, dazed and bewildered, drifted to shore a few hours later, tightly grasping the leg of a wooden chair. Survivors arrived one by one or clutching each other; some in lifeboats, others holding on to pieces of driftwood. Many who had jumped aboard lifeboats had fallen into the sea and perished. In less than eighteen minutes, the *Lusitania* had sunk, taking one thousand one hundred and ninety-eight people down with her, of which seven hundred and eighty-five were passengers.

Her SOS was too late. By the time her rescuers arrived, ranging from fishing boats to trawlers, the *Lusitania* had slipped beneath the ocean surface. As news of the ship's demise spread, the count for the living began.

Some reports were harsh, such as *The New York Times'* "Disaster Bears Out Embassy's Warning," condemning the Cunard company for its failure to take the published warnings more seriously.[1]

Having just completed a luncheon party at the Ritz-Carlton, Margaret was "almost prostrated when she heard the news"[2] of the sinking of the *Lusitania*. Rushing back to the *Vanderbilt* hotel, accompanied by two friends Eleanor Sears and Ethel McCormick, she frantically "kept the cables busy"[3] in a desperate effort to acquire information about her husband. Anxiously, she awaited news of his fate but none arrived. Her secretary stayed with her all night, hoping to receive word.[4]

She did not give up hope. Refusing to accept that her husband was dead, Margaret said firmly, "I will not believe Mr. Vanderbilt has gone down with the vessel. None of the reports I have received thus far is (sic) conclusive, and until absolutely reliable information coming from sources which I cannot doubt proves the contrary I shall believe my husband is safe."[5]

Family of survivors in Queenstown. May 1915. American Press Association.

While survivors reunited with their families and friends,[6] Mrs. A. G. Vanderbilt feverishly waited, her hope mixing with dread as no news surfaced. To all accounts, Alfred had gone down with the ship. The papers now were filled with matter-of-fact reports about his life – where he was born, his fortune, marriages, and lifestyle.[7] His mysterious disappearance was immediately ascertained as a likely death by drowning.[8]

Waiting with her father Colonel Isaac Emerson, Maggie did not abandon her hopes, but the chances of A.G. returning grew increasingly slim. Cablegrams were sent via the New York Central Railroad to charter tugs and to search the area once the local authorities gave them access.[9] Those who came to visit, Mrs. Harry Payne Whitney and Mrs. Reginald Vanderbilt, said she was holding on to hope, but as the hours passed it became evident that any chance of Alfred's survival was slipping away.[10] At last, word came from Walter Webb-Ward, the family representative, at four o'clock on May 9th.[11] The message was definitely not encouraging. Of the six hundred passengers who had been rescued, no trace of A.G. Vanderbilt could be found. Heart-broken, Colonel Emerson conceded that the lack of news could only be interpreted to mean that Alfred was lost. He was certain that "a man of Mr. Vanderbilt's prominence would be recognized, if he was saved, even though seriously injured."[12]

More and more bodies were found and among the dead, lay the body of Charles Frohman. Oliver Bernard, who had tenaciously survived, identified Frohman's body among countless others in the three makeshift morgues housing more than one hundred bodies along the Irish coast.[13] He noted that Charles' body was intact and not disfigured and that his face was remarkably calm and peaceful, having "died without protest, before the sea could do its worst."[14] The only body that Bernard could recognize was that of Charles Frohman and in respectful words, his former rage transformed into admiration: "perhaps it will interest his many friends in London and New York to know that the famous manager's face in death gives uncommonly convincing evidence that he died without a struggle. It wears a serenely peaceful look."[15] Bernard looked among all the dead but could not find his employer William Lindsey's "little girl"[16] or her husband Mason.

While the consul distributed clothes and money to numerous destitute Americans, supported by military staff from London, most passengers who had survived the ordeal remained in shock, dripping in seawater with faces ravaged from their experiences.[17] Captain Turner was found wandering the town of Queenstown with a bewildered expression, a shrunken version of his former self.[18] Slowly, survivors began to share their own reports and Alfred's heroism made its way back home to American shores. W. B. Phillips shared:

> "I saw Alfred Vanderbilt standing on the starboard deck five minutes before the ship sunk. He was with Mr. Frohman and Miss Rita Jolivet. The latter was saved. Mr. Vanderbilt's calmness was heroic. It struck me even in that moment of crushing disaster. Mr. Frohman was nearby and also quite collected. That was the last I saw of either of them."[19]

Some interpreted Vanderbilt's death as the result of fate, since he had purportedly "escaped death on the *Titanic* only to be drowned three years later."[20] A.G. had initially planned to travel on the White Star Liner in 1912 but had changed his mind at the last minute.

Alfred's death came upon the eve of his mother's most elaborate evening of entertainment; Alice was about to entertain royal guests, the Maharajah of Kapurthala, his wife Princess Prem Kaur, and his son, Prince Karlmjit Singh.[21] Her New York residence was being decorated lavishly. The Maharajah had courteously entertained American guests at his home in India and was now returning a visit. When Mrs. Vanderbilt received the news of her son's drowning, she immediately withdrew from the public.

Maggie arrived with the children to her mother-in-law's residence in New York on Fifth Avenue where they remained sequestered for the next three days, anxiously awaiting news. Maggie and Alice held on tightly to each other, refusing to accept his death. However, Maggie's hopes were dashed when Uncle Willie K. arrived calmly on Monday morning and turning "her dry-eyed gaze upon him,"[22] she "broke down"[23] into tears, sobbing, "I know now that he is dead!"

Immediately, she asked to see little Alfred. The young child appeared soon after, a chubby "little scion of a great house as was ever summoned to bear the burden of a vast fortune."[24] Considered the "living image of his father," little Alfred resembled his father much more than his younger brother George. He cried with his mother, not knowing what had transgressed; unaware that he had both simultaneously lost his father and acquired an enormous fortune with one fell stroke.[25]

Many social engagements were still on the horizon. The Whitneys had offered their Long Island residence for the Meadowbrook Steeplechase Association's annual meet and as generous hosts, did not want to halt the event. Invitations had already been sent and acknowledged, but they would not attend themselves, withdrawing with heavy hearts, as Mrs. Whitney, Alfred's sister, mourned the death of her brother, with whom she had enjoyed so many romps as a child.[26]

Considered a "spectacular figure,"[27] A.G. was the celebrated lover of horses and also the center of ugly rumors and speculations following his divorce and affairs with Agnes Ruiz. For years, his name had occupied the front page of many newspapers, caught up in the lurid details of the scandals Alfred had become embroiled in. Now, a new story began to emerge.

Thomas Slidell, who had survived the sinking, spoke to the press passionately on behalf of his friend:

> "Just as the *Lusitania* was heeling over its final plunge an old woman, apparently without friends, came along. Seeing that she was without a life belt, Mr. Vanderbilt without hesitation took off his own and fastened it around her. Then the boat went down. What happened to the old woman I don't know, but I do

know that Mr. Vanderbilt is dead. He could not swim and must have known that by surrendering his life belt he was sacrificing his own life."[28]

Slidell had last seen Vanderbilt standing on the B deck wearing his lifebelt along with two or three other people, including a young fifteen-year old girl by the name of Miss Virginia Loney.[29] Alfred had placed Virginia and her parents in a life boat. Miss Loney survived to tell Slidell the tale of Alfred's sacrifice.

Slidell also shed light on A.G.'s intentions for traveling to England. He said that he had spoken with Alfred on the night prior to the sinking. In confidence, A.G. had shared with Thomas that despite giving large amounts of money to the Red Cross, "he felt every day that he had not done enough."[30] He was compelled to go to England "to do more."[31] Slidell revealed that Vanderbilt was planning on fitting up two more ambulances and to accompany them to France to assist in the war effort, directly helping "the British and American Red Cross people personally in one capacity or another."[32]

The final tally came in: six hundred and forty-five passengers had survived the terrifying experience.[33] Quartered in hospitals and makeshift residences, many of the survivors had to remain in Queenstown because of the severity of their wounds while the first trickle of passengers who could leave finally boarded trains to Dublin to their families. "Heartrending stories"[34] poured in of the perils faced as the steamer was torpedoed, and the sea became a watery grave, littered with the dead bodies of men, women, and children floating among the froth of debris, split wood, oars, chairs, and flotsam.

Alfred's gallantry surfaced. A.G. had placed his lifebelt around the waist of a woman, saving her life at the cost of his own while everyone agreed that Alfred had sacrificed his life by giving his life jacket to another, but somewhere in the panic of the tragic event, the exact identity of who the fortunate woman was got lost. Some said she was old, while others described her as a young woman. Some thought her to be Charlotte Pye, a young mother aboard the ship with her eighteen-month old baby. Others claim they saw Alfred give his life jacket to the nurse Alice Middleton. The truth may never be known, but the fact remained that Alfred was universally proclaimed to be a hero.

Slidell's story was verified by another passenger, Norman Ratcliffe of Gillingham, Kent[35] who shared how he had heard the story from a steward with whom he had clung on a wooden box floating in the middle of the ocean for three hours. Ratcliffe said:

"This steward told me he had seen Mr. Vanderbilt on the *Lusitania's* deck, shortly after the ship was struck, with a life belt about his body. When the ship gave every indication that it would sink within a few minutes, the steward said, Mr. Vanderbilt took off his life belt and gave it to a woman who passed him

Funeral of Lusitania *victims at the Queenstown grave yard. Service at the graves. May 1915. International News Service.*

Flag draped victim in Queenstown. May 1915. Library of Congress.

The S.S. New York *loads the casket of an American Victim. Pierre Lorillard would be a passenger on this voyage. He carried "papers for Vanderbilt's widow." International News Service.*

on the deck, trembling with fear of the fate she expected to meet. The steward said Mr. Vanderbilt turned back, as though to look for another belt and he saw him no more."[36]

The tale of Alfred's heroics now began to take shape. Dr. Owen Kenan of Wilmington, North Carolina, a passenger, added that as the ship was going down he spied Vanderbilt coolly leaning against a door and that the millionaire called out to him: "They have got us now."[37]

Oliver Bernard filled in details:

> "I last saw Alfred G. Vanderbilt standing at the port entrance to the grand saloon. He stood there the personification of sportsmanlike coolness. In his right hand was grasped what looked to me like a large purple leather jewel case. It may have belonged to Lady Mackworth, as Mr. Vanderbilt had been much in company of the Thomas party during the trip, and evidently had volunteered to do Lady Mackworth the service of saving her gems for her. Mr. Vanderbilt was absolutely unperturbed. In my eyes, he was the figure of a gentleman waiting unconcernedly for a train. He had on a dark striped suit, and was without cap or other head covering."

A Canadian woman Mrs. Lines shared her own glowing testimony to Alfred's valor and that of his valet Ronald Denyer in saving the lives of many children. Warmly, she shared:

> People…will not talk of Mr. Vanderbilt in the future as a millionaire sportsman and a man of pleasure. He will be remembered as the children's hero and men and women will salute his name. When death was nearing him he showed gallantry, which no words of mine can adequately describe. He stood outside the palm saloon on the starboard side of the *Lusitania* with Ronald Denyer by his side. He looked around on the scene of horror and despair with pitying eyes.
>
> 'Find all the kiddies you can, boy,' he said to his valet. The man rushed off collecting children and as he brought them to Mr. Vanderbilt the millionaire dashed to the boats with two little ones in his arms at a time. When he could find no more children he went to the assistance of the women and placed as many as he could safely in the boats. In all his work he was gallantly assisted by Denyer, and the two continued their efforts until the very end.[38]

Passionately she added:

> "I hope the young men of Britain will act with the same cool bravery for their country that Mr. Vanderbilt showed for somebody's little ones."[39]

Like wildfire, her story spread, stirring up palpable emotions and eloquent words as newspapers described Alfred, a man whose character had hitherto been largely misunderstood. Another bit of information was revealed: Alfred Gwynne could not swim.

The *Washington Post* eloquently explained:

> "The unselfish heroism of Alfred Gwynne Vanderbilt in the face of death, and at the expense of his own life, was an act that reflects honor upon American manhood. This was at a moment when death was imminent, when the instinct of self-preservation in selfish mortals is likely to transform them into savages.

Young Vanderbilt was unable to swim; he had no knowledge that he could procure another lifebelt, and probably he failed to find one. But, with innate chivalry and heroism, he performed the duty which is clear to such men."[40]

Boldly, the *Washington Post* proclaimed: "Americans of all kinds and degrees, when they read of Alfred Vanderbilt's death, are proud that he was one of them."[41] Vanderbilt had proved his mettle under duress when "suddenly confronted with an elemental situation in which manhood, and not social position, was the test of their worth; and nobly they measured up to the test."[42]

More philosophical questions were raised from the pulpits of Sunday sermons. Reverend Dr. William Harman van Allen at the Church of the Advent, offered:

"Did not this man, in the act of trying to save the lives of children, enter into a more blessed and speedy purgatory than he had ever dreamed of-than he would have done had he been spared and his life permitted to pursue its natural course to an end?"[43]

Another preacher, the Bishop of London was more generous:

"There is one incident the world will remember in connection with the sinking of the *Lusitania*, when Alfred G. Vanderbilt was face to face with death he said to his valet: 'Come and let us save the kiddies.' Those words will run 'round the world in a way no millionaire's millions could ever do."[44]

As his actions grew legendary, Alfred's name inspired those performing civic service to care for war babies[45] and as a rallying cry in the Liverpool riots after the sinking.[46] While Yale University flew its flag at half-mast to commemorate the lives of Yale graduates who perished aboard the *Lusitania,* and their President Hadley offered his condolences for the men who "met death like Christian gentlemen," not everyone was so warm in their praise.

Critics at the *Chicago Daily Tribune* described A.G.'s death as the closure to "one of the most conspicuous international New York and Newport Society."[47] The newspaper counted six divorces, including Alfred's own separation from Elsie and the suicide of Agnes Ruiz, which "fell along the merry road of life on which 'the millionaire coachman' cracked the whip."[48]

Immediately, the *Los Angeles Times,* in sharp contrast, offered a full-page glowing tribute to Vanderbilt as a woman, Doris Collins, wrote a charming full-page description of a ride she took on A.G.'s coach *The Venture* from London to Brighton and back:

"The center of interest, was of course, the tall and rather young looking man in the formal coaching costume of checked trousers, long blue coat and gray hat,

> who came out adjusting his red and white boutonnière…and prepared to mount to the box."[49]

Collins described a delightful trip, one that she enjoyed every step of the way. She lamented the loss of this "quiet gentleman and lover of horses, who did so much to keep alive the interest in coaching"[50] and who "was never too occupied to wave"[51] to spectators or to "acknowledge their friendly greetings."[52] She extolled his kindness to a dumb, crippled man and how A.G. "understood so well all that the brown eyes tried to express, but which could not be spoken."[53]

Yet despite all the lavish press reports, Alfred's obituary was starkly simple. It read:

> "On Friday, May 7, 1915, at sea, Alfred Gwynne Vanderbilt, son of Alice Gwynne and the late Cornelius Vanderbilt, in the thirty-eighth year of his age. Notice of service hereafter."[54]

There was no mention of his heroic deeds or even of his death aboard the *Lusitania.* Why were these details omitted? A mysterious shroud enveloped Alfred's death and perhaps the answer lies in the envelope that Pierre Lorillard brought to the widow, Margaret Emerson.[55] Lorillard was obviously distressed but he would not reveal the contents of the secret envelope.

What information did these papers contain? Many rumors circulated about possible statements of Alfred's heroism sent to console the widow. No such statements ever surfaced. An alternative was that the contents of Mr. Lorillard's envelope would provide help in settling the estate.

Perhaps Pierre Lorillard carried the letters left by his wife when she committed suicide; one in her hand and the second in the hand of another. If the letter written in the hand of another had been penned by Elsie, then it conveyed a message to Margaret from the grave that she could not ignore. If Pierre's wife's suicide was linked to Alfred, and the letter he delivered to Margaret revealed the connection between the two, it would have been quite difficult for Lorillard to remain silent when the villain of his life was being championed a hero. Lorillard would have been in a very uncomfortable position; if he revealed the contents of the letter, he would forever stain the reputation of his wife and his own family name. Yet at the same time, he could not remain silent when the world was now heralding Alfred as a hero. Perhaps, then, a bargain was struck between Pierre Lorillard and Margaret Emerson, where neither tale of Alfred's affair nor his heroism would be brought to light. Thus Lorillard took the next ship from London to New York and the obituary remained mute.

The offer of $1000 for Alfred's body failed to produce results.[56] A memorial service was held at his mother's home, 1 West Fifty-Seventh Street, and anyone who chose to join in mourning was welcomed with open arms. More than two hundred guests arrived to mourn Alfred's death. There was no mention of the *Lusitania* sinking except for the recital of the Episcopal prayer "for the burial of the dead at sea."[57] His epitaph was as brief and solemn. Despite his purported friendship, Pierre Lorillard failed to attend.

NOTES

1. *The New York Times*. "Disaster Bears Out Embassy Warning." May 8, 1915. Pg. 3.
2. *The Washington Post*. "Mrs. Vanderbilt Refuses to Believe Her Husband Has Not Been Saved." May 9, 1915. Pg. R17.
3. *The Boston Daily Globe*. "Some Well-Known Men Who Sailed on the Lusitania." May 8, 1915. Pg. 9.
4. Ibid.
5. *The Washington Post*. "Mrs. Vanderbilt Refuses to Believe Her Husband Has Not Been Saved." May 9, 1915. Pg. R17.
6. *The Atlanta Constitution*. "Alfred Vanderbilt Among the Missing." May 9, 1915. Pg. B2.
7. *The Washington Post*. "Mrs. Vanderbilt Refuses to Believe Her Husband Has Not Been Saved." May 9, 1915. Pg. R17.
8. *The Atlanta Constitution*. "Alfred Vanderbilt Among the Missing." May 9, 1915. Pg. B2.
9. *The New York Times*. "Vanderbilt Family All but Hopeless." May 9, 1915. Pg. 3.
10. Ibid.
11. Ibid.
12. Ibid.
13. *The Washington Post*. "Calmly Waited to Die." May 9, 1915. Pg. 3.
14. Bernard, Oliver. *Cock Sparrow: A True Chronicle*. Oxford: Alden Press. 1936. Pg. 166.
15. *The New York Times*. "Vanderbilt Saved Woman." May 10, 1915. Pg. 1.
16. Ibid.
17. *The Washington Post*. "Calmly Waited to Die." May 9, 1915. Pg. 3.
18. Hickey, Des and Gus Smith. *Seven Days to Disaster*. London: G. P. Putnam & Sons, 1981. Pg. 260.
19. Ibid.
20. *The Los Angeles Times*. "Death of Vanderbilt Recalls Titanic Escape." May 9, 1915. Pg. 14.
21. *The Chicago Daily Tribune*. "New York Society." May 16, 1915. Pg. D8.
22. Ibid.
23. Ibid.
24. Ibid.
25. Ibid.

26. Ibid.
27. Ibid.
28. *The Chicago Daily Tribune*. "A. G. Vanderbilt Hero in Death." May 10, 1915. Pg. 2.
29. Ibid.
30. *The New York Times*. "Vanderbilt Saved Woman." May 10, 1915. Pg. 1.
31. *The Chicago Daily Tribune*. "A. G. Vanderbilt Hero in Death." May 10, 1915. Pg. 2.
32. Ibid.
33. *The Atlantic*. "Smear of Flotsam Marks Ocean Grave of Slain Innocents and the Lusitania." May 10, 1915. Pg. 1.
34. Ibid.
35. *The New York Times*. "Vanderbilt Saved Woman." May 10, 1915. Pg. 1.
36. Ibid.
37. *The Los Angeles Times*. "They've Got Us, Says Vanderbilt." May 11, 1915. Pg. 11.
38. *The New York Times*. "Many Children Owe Lives to Vanderbilt." May 11, 1915. Pg. 2.
39. Ibid.
40. *The Washington Post*. "Alfred Vanderbilt." May 11, 1915. Pg. 6.
41. Ibid.
42. Ibid.
43. *The Boston Daily Globe*. "Assassin of Civilization." May 17, 1915. Pg. 3.
44. Ibid.
45. *The Washington Post*. "Urges Civic Work by Women." May 16, 1915. Pg. 4.
46. *The Washington Post*. "Caring for 'War Babies.'" May 17, 1915. Pg. 6.
47. *The Chicago Daily Tribune*. Alfred Gwynne Vanderbilt. May 9, 1915. Pg. 5.
48. Ibid.
49. *The Los Angeles Times*. "Her Ride with Vanderbilt." May 30, 1915. Pg. III4.
50. Ibid.
51. Ibid.
52. Ibid.
53. Ibid.
54. *The New York Times*. "Obituary 2---No Title." May 23, 1915. Pg. 16.
55. *The New York Times*. "Survivor Here Saw Trap for Lusitania." May 25, 1915. Pg. 4.
56. *The Washington Post*. "Hunt for Vanderbilt." May 11, 1915. Pg. 2.
57. *The New York Times*. "Vanderbilt Prayer is Burial At Sea." May 28, 1915. Pg. 13.

Afterword

As Alfred Gwynne's last will was read, his estate was divided among his heirs.[1] The estate was valued at $26,375,000,[2] severely diminished from the $42,875,000 he inherited, and included his heaviest holdings in the New York Central securities.[3] Alfred Gwynne Vanderbilt bequeathed the majority of his income to his first son, William Henry.[4] In his divorce settlement with Elsie French, A.G. had already set aside ten million dollars for William Henry. Thirteen years old, William H. received the honorary congressional medal, the symbolic heirloom of Vanderbilt family leadership. William Henry also received Alfred's cherished Oakland Farms and an annual income for its maintenance. The remaining fortune was divided among Alfred's other two sons, Alfred Jr., born September 22, 1912, his younger son George, born September 23, 1914,[5] and his widow Margaret Emerson, who received $8,000,000 and all of A.G.'s properties, including Sagamore Lodge and the Vanderbilt Hotel.

Alfred's story would remain untold for almost one hundred years. Enclosed in the murky waters of the Atlantic, Alfred's body disappeared, never to be found again. His name, similarly, was erased from history. Remembered from time to time as the Vanderbilt who coached on the Brighton path or as the Vanderbilt who died on the *Lusitania*, his legacy has been all but forgotten.

NOTES

1. The New York Times. "Vanderbilt Will Gives $26,375,000. May 30, 1915. Pg. 5.
2. The New York Times. "Vanderbilt Will Gives $26,375,000. May 30, 1915. Pg. 5.

3. The Hartford Courant. "The Vanderbilt Wealth: Three Boys to Share It." May 10, 1915. Pg. 3.
4. The New York Times. "Death of Vanderbilt Recalls Titanic Escape." May 9, 1915. Pg. 14.
5. Ibid.

Bibliography

"$10,000,000 for Wife." *The Washington Post,* April 4, 1908.
"$15,000 Flats too Rich for the Blood of Englishmen."*The Atlanta Constitution,* May 7, 1911.
"$350,000 for Ruiz Gems." *The New York Times,* Dec. 18, 1909.
"$50,000,000 Hotel Merger: A.G. Vanderbilt as Backer?" *The Chicago Daily Tribune,* March 31, 1910.
"19-Story Hotel Planned." *The New York Times,* Jan. 1, 1909.
"30,000,000 to Vanderbilt." *The New York Times,* Oct. 20, 1912.
"A Baltimore Beauty." *The Evening Post,* July 2, 1911.
"A. G. Vanderbilt Coming." *The New York Times,* Oct. 26, 1912.
"A. G. Vanderbilt Hero in Death." *The Chicago Daily Tribune,* May 10, 1915.
"A. G. Vanderbilt in Newport: The Visit Causes Revival of Report of His Coming Marriage." *The New York Times*, Jan. 27, 1900.
"A. G. Vanderbilts Here." *The New York Times,* Nov. 3, 1912.
"A.G. Vanderbilt At Home." *The New York Times,* Oct. 15, 1899.
"A.G. Vanderbilt Back In London."*The New York Times,* Apr. 13, 1904.
"A.G. Vanderbilt Coming Here." *The New York Times*, Oct. 16, 1899.
"A.G. Vanderbilt Defends Trophy." *The Christian Science Monitor,* Jun. 11, 1910.
"A.G. Vanderbilt Family Leaves." *The Christian Science Monitor,* Sept. 5, 1913.
"A.G. Vanderbilt in the City." *The New York Times,* Oct. 17, 1899.
"A.G. Vanderbilt Leaves." *The New York Time,* Apr. 24, 1911.
"A.G. Vanderbilt Narrow Escape." *The Wall Street Journal,* Oct. 14, 1905.
"A.G. Vanderbilt Returns in Summer." *The New York Times,* April 12, 1908.
"A.G. Vanderbilt Returns: Enthusiastic Over London Horse Show, Which He Planned." *The Washington Post,* Feb. 27, 1907.
"A.G. Vanderbilt Sues Owner of Automobile." *The New York Times,* April 25, 1903.
"A.G. Vanderbilt to Cruise." *The New York Times,* Jan. 30, 1915.
"A.G. Vanderbilt to Wed?" *The Washington Post,* June 5, 1908.
"A.G. Vanderbilt was not Shot." *The Boston Daily Globe,* Aug. 26, 1909.

"A.G. Vanderbilt Weds Mrs. McKim." *The Chicago Daily Tribune*, Dec. 18, 1911.
"A.G. Vanderbilt Wins in Durland Horse Show." *The New York Times,* April 18, 1906.
"A.G. Vanderbilt's Coach Run: To Drive from Newport to Boston Today in Record-Breaking Time." *The New York Times,* August 25, 1900.
"A.G. Vanderbilt's New Team." *The New York Times,* Dec. 21, 1904.
"Advance Guard." *Boston Daily Globe*, Jul. 19, 1904.
"Alfred G. Vanderbilt Arrested for Speeding." *The New York Times,* April 1, 1905.
"Alfred G. Vanderbilt Head of New York Horse Show." *The Chicago Daily Tribune,* Aug. 14, 1910.
"Alfred G. Vanderbilt Marries Miss French." *The New York Times,* Jan 15, 1901.
"Alfred G. Vanderbilt Silent." *The New York Times,* Jul. 17, 1903.
"Alfred G. Vanderbilt Tries New Investment." *Chicago Daily Tribune*, Nov. 27, 1901.
"Alfred Gwynne Vanderbilt, His Horses, and His Coach." *The New York Times,* April 19, 1908.
"Alfred Gwynne Vanderbilt." *The Atlanta Constitution,* April 16, 1912.
"Alfred Gwynne Vanderbilt." *The Chicago Daily Tribune*, May 9, 1915.
"Alfred Vanderbilt a Father." *The New York Times,* Nov. 25, 1901.
"Alfred Vanderbilt Among the Missing." *The Atlanta Constitution,* May 9, 1915.
"Alfred Vanderbilt Cut by Smart Set of London." *The Atlanta Constitution,* Aug. 9, 1908.
"Alfred Vanderbilt is Inclined to Economy." *The Washington Post,* Jul. 23, 1905.
"Alfred Vanderbilt Loses $15,000." *The New York Times,* July 2, 1908.
"Alfred Vanderbilt Silent." *The New York Times,* Feb. 26, 1911.
"Alfred Vanderbilt Thrown." *The Atlanta Constitution,* Oct. 14, 1905.
"Alfred Vanderbilt to Wed 'Dollar Princess." *The Atlanta Constitution,* Jun. 12, 1910.
"Alfred Vanderbilt Will Drive Coach." *The New York Times,* March 29, 1908.
"Alfred Vanderbilt Will Drive Coach." *The New York Times,* March 29, 1908.
"Alfred Vanderbilt." *The Washington Post,* May 11, 1915.
"Alfred Vanderbilt." *The Washington Post,* May 11, 1915.
"Alfred Vanderbilt's Influence." *The Washington Post,* March 20, 1910.
"All Newport Snubs Them." *The Kansas City Star,* August 22, 1913.
"America's Best Horses to be Shown in London." *The New York Times,* Jul. 29, 1906.
"American Features to Lead."*The New York Times,* Apr. 21, 1907.
"American Industry Abroad." *The New York Times*, May 6, 1908.
"American Horses as Olympia Show." *The New York Times,* June 8, 1907.
"Americans in London." *The Washington Post,* April 12, 1908.
"Americans in London." *The Washington Post,* June 14, 1908.
"Americans Pay High for London Houses." *The New York Times,* March 20, 1910.
"Another Woman In Ruiz Scandal." *Oakland Tribune,* June 16, 1909.
"Arena at Olympia A Mass of Flowers." June 5, 1910. Pg. C3.
"Assassin of Civilization." *The Boston Daily Globe,* May 17, 1915.
"At Home and Abroad." *The New York Times,* March 15, 1908.
"Atlantic City Horse Show." *The New York Times,* Jul. 18, 1906.
"Attack by Knowles on Tarbell's Methods." *The New York Times,* May 2, 1905.

"Attempt of Florence Schenck To Take Her Life Said To Be Due To The Suicide Of Mrs. Ruiz." *The Syracuse Herald,* February 13, 1910.
"At Vanderbilt's Bier: Prominent Clergy and Laity To Gather Around Tomb." *The Washington Post,* Sept. 14, 1899.
"Author Deserted: Blames Wife's Chum." *The Hartford Courant,* Jun. 15, 1907.
"A. Vanderbilt Experiment." *The Wall Street Journal,* Sept. 15, 1910.
"A. Vanderbilt Meets Mrs. M'Kim." *Oakland Tribune,* April 23, 1911.
"A. Vanderbilt Under Knife." *The New York Times,* April 14, 1915.
"A. Vanderbilt's Coaching Trip: Heat Balks His Effort to Establish a Record from Newport to Boston." *The New York Times,* August 25, 1900.
"A Wonderful Auto." *The Washington Post,* Jan. 13, 1906.
"Beauty's Tragedy." *The Los Angeles Times,* June 11, 1909.
"Berlin Filled with Visitors: Americans are in the Lead." *The Chicago Daily Tribune,* Sept. 6, 1908.
"Best Show Horses for Long Branch." *The New York Times,* July 26, 1908.
"Best Year for Coaching." *The New York Times,* Jul. 13, 1913.
"Breakers Ahead for Vanderbilt." *The Chicago Daily Tribune,* April 6, 1908.
"Bride Cables Her Parents." *The New York Times,* Dec. 18, 1911.
"Bride to Be May Settle Vanderbilt Feud." *The Chicago Daily Tribune,* Oct. 4, 1903.
"C. Vanderbilt Gets Mansion and Art." *The New York Times,* Mar. 10, 1914.
"Calmly Waited to Die." *The Washington Post,* May 9, 1915.
"Can You Tell Me Why A.G. Vanderbilt Does This?" *The Chicago Daily Tribune,* Jul. 5, 1914.
"Caring for 'War Babies." *The Washington Post,* May 17, 1915.
"Cast off by Vanderbilt; Dies." *The Chicago Daily Tribune,* June 11, 1909.
"Cathleen Vanderbilt as Fairy Godmother." *The Atlanta Constitution,* June 21, 1914.
"Celebrating 111 Years of the Terminal Railroad." Vol. 14. Winter/Spring 2000. Pg. 5-6.
"Chat of Well Known People." *The Washington Post,* June 6, 1908.
"Chat of Well Known People." *The Washington Post,* Sept. 5, 1908.
"Chat of Well-Known People." *The Washington Post,* May 1, 1908.
"Chat of Well-Known People." *The Washington Post,* April 28, 1908.
"Chauffeur Sent to Jail." *The New York Times,* Sept. 2, 1908.
"Chicagoans Flock to Paris from All Over the Globe." *The Chicago Daily Tribune,* May 11, 1913.
"Citizen of Rhode Island." *Boston Daily Globe*, Aug. 23, 1903.
"Clerk of Commons Bars Ruiz Inquiry." *The New York Times,* June 17, 1909.
"Clubs and Clubmen." *The New York Times,* April 26, 1903.
"Coachers Were His Samaritans." *Los Angeles Times*, May 20, 1903.
"Coachman A.G. Vanderbilt." *The Hartford Courant*, June 29, 1908. Pg. 8.
"Come, Let Us Save the Kiddies." *Boston Daily Globe*, May 13, 1915.
"Coming Vanderbilt Wedding " *The New York Times,* Dec 22, 1900.
"Confirms Story." *Boston Daily Globe*, Jul. 17, 1903.
"Convert to Socialism Quits Dunne's Cabinet."*The New York Times,* Mar. 3, 1906.
"Covers Mile in 59 1-5 seconds." *The Chicago Daily Tribune,* Jun. 12, 1904.

"Dame Gossip's Tongue Wags." *The Los Angeles Times*, April 4, 1908.
"Dancer Ducked! Weird Doings at Vanderbilt Ball." *The Los Angeles Times*, September 12, 1908.
"Death of Vanderbilt Recalls Titanic Escape." *The Los Angeles Times,* May 9, 1915.
"Death of Vanderbilt: Head of the Family Stricken Down at New York." *The Washington Post,* Sept. 13, 1899.
"Denies Promise to Wed Her." *The Washington Post,* April 8. 1908.
"Deserted, She Tries Suicide." *The Boston Daily Globe,* Feb. 7, 1910.
"Deserts Newport." *The Washington Post,* July 23, 1908.
"Disaster Bears Out Embassy Warning." *The New York Times,* May 8, 1915.
"Divorce Makes Her So Happy." *The Los Angeles Times,* Aug. 14, 1910.
"Divorce the Vanderbilt Curse." *The Chicago Daily Tribune,* Oct. 24, 1909.
"Dog Fight Witnessed by Horse Show Crowd." *The New York Times,* Aug. 5, 1906.
"Domino Ball at Newport." *The Washington Post,* Sept. 3, 1908.
"Dr. Schenck Waits a Day." *The New York Times,* Dec. 12, 1913.
"Dr. Smith H. McKim and Wife Separate." *The New York Times,* May 22, 1909.
"East Boston Girl Bride of Vanderbilt's Whip." *Boston Daily Globe*, Jan. 20, 1911.
"Editorial Pen Points." *The Los Angeles Times,* June 12, 1909.
"Editorial Points." *The Boston Daily Globe,* July 7, 1908.
"English Horses Lead." *The Washington Post,* June 16, 1907.
"English Snub Vanderbilt." *The Chicago Daily Tribune,* June 28, 1908.
"Equitable Life." *The Wall Street Journal,* Feb. 17, 1905.
"Everything in Good Taste." *The New York Times,* Jan. 15, 1901.
"Exile Through Ruiz Case." *The Chicago Daily Tribune,* June 14, 1909.
"Fads and Fancies: A Rich Man's Book."*The New York Times,* Dec. 10, 1905.
"Fashion's Fads and Fancies." *The Washington Post,* Nov. 6, 1910.
"Fashion's New Fad." *The Boston Daily Globe*, Oct. 9, 1900.
"Fast Auto Drivers to Meet at Ormond."*The New York Times,* Dec. 25, 1904.
"Favors Divorce of Vanderbilts." *The Los Angeles Times,* May 22, 1908.
"Few American Entries."*The New York Times,* June 15, 1908.
"Few Americans at Henley." *The Chicago Daily Tribune,* July 5, 1908.
"Finest Flats in London." *The Atlanta Constitution,* June 21, 1908.
"First Coaching Party." *The Los Angeles Times,* Apr. 25, 1905.
"Flashes From the Wires." *The Los Angeles Times,* Nov. 25, 1901.
"Florence Schenck a Victim of Wilson." *The New York Times,* Jan. 9, 1914.
"Florence Schenck Dies." *Boston Daily Globe*, Nov. 20, 1913.
"Florence Schenck Gone." *The Washington Post,* Jan. 4, 1914.
"Fox Hunters at Newport: Mrs. Ladenburg in at the Death After a Hard Ride." *The New York Times,* Sept. 18, 1900.
"From Touring to Racing." *The New York Sun,* Aug. 1904.
"Gas Fumes Kill Mrs. Pierre Lorillard. Jr." *The New York Tribune,* Mar. 26, 1909.
"Gave Up Run To Lenox." *Boston Daily Globe*, Jul 6, 1902.
"Gay Charity Fete at Oakland Farm." *The New York Times,* July 9, 1908.
"General News." *The Chicago Tribune,* July 22, 1900.
"Get A Vanderbilt Mascot: Alfred G. Gives Fireman a Dog in Place of One Which Was Killed."*The New York Times,* March 13, 1907.

"Gives Dinners in Paris."*The New York Times,* Feb. 25, 1912.
"Golden Match." *The Boston Daily Globe,* April 29, 1901.
"Good Short Stories." *The Los Angeles Times,* Sept. 6, 1908.
"Gossip about Mrs. McKim Occupies New York Society." *The Atlanta Constitution,* May 15, 1910.
"Gossip of Society." *The Washington Post,* Sept. 22, 1908. Pg 7.
"Gossip of Society." *The Washington Post,* Dec. 20, 1908. Pg 7.
"Gossip of Society." *The Washington Post,* Oct. 20, 1908. Pg 7.
"Gossip of Society."*The Washington Post,* June 23, 1908. Pg 7.
"Great World's Show of Horses in London." *The New York Times,* Nov. 24, 1906.
"Grief Makes Her Ill." *The Washington Post,* Jul. 11, 1907.
"Guests of Mrs. Vanderbilt."*The Washington Post,* Apr. 7, 1907.
"Half A Million for Hope Diamond." *Los Angeles Times,* Nov. 28, 1901.
"Hanged Herself with a Trunk Strap."*The Atlanta Constitution,* Mar. 17, 1912.
"Heart-Suit Beauty Dying." *The Washington Post,* Dec. 8, 1913.
"Heir is born to Head of the Vanderbilt Family." *Chicago Daily Tribune*, Nov. 25, 1901.
"Held for Wilson Shooting." *The New York Times,* Sept. 20, 1914.
"Her Ride with Vanderbilt." *The Los Angeles, May 30, 1915.*
"Her Romance Over." *The Washington Post,* July 9, 1907.
"His Love Lost to Her." *The Washington Post,* June 13, 1909.
"Horrible Loss of Life," Says White Star Officials." *The Atlanta Constitution,* April 16, 1912.
"Horse Show Best Ever Held, Says Americans in London." *The Chicago Daily Tribune,* June 19, 1910.
"Horse Show in London Centers World Interest." *The Atlanta Constitution,* Jul. 2, 1911.
"Horse Show is opened in New York." *The Christian Science Monitor,* Nov. 16, 1912.
"Horse Show Stirring Blood of Britons; Yankees Sure." *The Chicago Daily Tribune,* Feb. 24. 1907.
"Horses Traveling In Padded Stalls." *The New York Times,* Feb. 24, 1907.
"Horses Well Cared For." *The Hartford Courant,* Feb 25, 1907.
"How a Pompeian "Alfred Vanderbilt" Wrote Love Letters to His Chloe 1900 Years Ago." *The Atlanta Constitution,* March 31, 1912.
"How One Charming Romance after Another Has Followed in the Wake of His Jolly . . ." *The Washington Post,* Oct. 24, 1908.
"How to have a Pair of Pretty Shoulders." *The Chicago Daily Tribune,* Aug. 12, 1906.
"Hunt for Vanderbilt." *The Washington Post,* May 11, 1915.
"Hurt by Heat." *The New York Times,* August 27, 1900.
"Hyde Must Quit or be Exposed." *The Chicago Daily Tribune,* Apr. 1, 1905.
"Hyde's Complaint Against Alexander: Full Text of Petition." *The New York Times,* May 14, 1905.
"In Fashion's Realm." *The Washington Post,* June 13, 1908.
"In Luxurious Flat." *The Boston Daily Globe,* Dec. 19, 1911.
"In the Public Eye." *The Atlanta Constitution*, Sept. 20, 1899.
"It Happened in New York." *The Washington Post,* Jan. 18, 1906.
"It is no gift." *Boston*, Oct. 28, 1899.
"Judges Make Final Awards." *The New York Times*, Aug. 2, 1908.

"Judges' Award Hissed at Bay Shore Show." *The New York Times,* Aug. 6, 1905.
"Jury Acquits Schultz." *The New York Times,* Jan. 20, 1915.
"King Edward Visits the Show." *The New York Times,* Jun. 12, 1907.
"Learning to Sail Yacht." *The Boston Daily Globe,* Sept. 22, 1905.
"Life Palls on Beauty." *The Washington Post,* Feb. 11, 1910.
"Lively Polo at Newport." *The New York Times,* Aug. 2, 1903.
"London Greets Many American Visitors." *The New York Times,* May 10, 1908.
"London Horse Show Plans: A.G. Vanderbilt Says Exhibition Will Be Biggest Ever Held." *The New York Time,* Feb. 27, 1907.
"London Horse Show Ends." *The Washington Post,* June 14, 1907.
"London is Jammed for the Coronation." *The Boston Daily Globe,* Jun. 22, 1911.
"London Opera Prospers." *The New York Times,* April 3, 1910.
"London Society Women Dancing like Maud Allen." *The Atlanta Constitution,* Aug. 8, 1908.
"London to Have An Early Season." *The New York Times,* April 14, 1907.
"Madame Ruiz Found Close to Gotham." *The Chicago Daily Tribune,* June 14, 1906.
"Madame Ruiz Suicide Stirs All London." *The Chicago Daily Tribune,* June 13, 1909.
"Madame Ruiz with Him." *The Washington Post,* Sept. 19, 1908.
"Many American Horses For the English Show." *The New York Times,* Feb. 3, 1907.
"Many Children Owe Lives to Vanderbilt." *The New York Times,* May 11, 1915.
"Marquis de Fontenay." *The Chicago Daily Tribune*, June 19, 1907.
"Marriage Fails to Halt a Suit." *The Chicago Daily Tribune,* Oct. 18, 1908.
"Marry In London Under a License." *The Boston Daily Globe*, Dec. 18, 1911.
"May Lose His Sweetheart: Uncle of Elsie French Opposed to Alfred Gwynne Vanderbilt as Suitor for Her Hand." *The Chicago Daily Tribune,* March 12, 1900.
"McKim Agrees Not to Sue Vanderbilt." *The New York Times,* Feb. 22, 1911.
"McKim to get $7,500 a year." *The Washington Post,* Feb. 23, 1911.
"McKims Agree to Part." *The Washington Post,* May 22, 1909.
"Men's Fashions at the Horse Show." *The New York Times,* Nov. 25, 1906.
"Methodist Picnic at Oakland Farm."*The New York Times,* Jul. 2, 1907.
"Million a Year List Still Grows." *The Kansas City Star,* Oct. 25, 1914.
"Millions Not a Burden." *The Los Angeles Times,* Dec. 22, 1914.
"Miss French Arrives." *Boston Daily Globe*, July 26, 1900.
"Miss Neilson His Choice." *The Washington Post,* August 4, 1902.
"Miss Roosevelt at Newport." *Chicago Daily Tribune*, Aug. 3, 1902.
"Miss Schenck Delays Suit." *The Washington Post,* Oct. 18, 1908.
"Miss Schenck Fears to Die." *The Washington Post,* Dec. 14, 1913.
"Mme. Ruiz Second to Die for Alfred." *The Los Angeles Times,* June 16, 1909.
"Money Delays." *Boston Daily Globe,* May 19, 1908.
"Money Halts Divorce." *The Washington Post,* April 11, 1908.
"Money Halts Divorce." *The Washington Post,* April 11, 1908.
"Moore Beats Vanderbilt." *The New York Times,* Jun. 14, 1910.
"Moore's Radiant Loses at Newport." *The New York Times,* Sept. 8, 1908.
"More Mystery in Ruiz Suicide." *The Chicago Daily Tribune,* June 12, 1909.
"Motor Wouldn't Go Slow." *The New York Times*, Jan. 2, 1905.

"Mr. and Mrs. A.G. Vanderbilt Plan Novel Function." *The Washington Post,* Jun. 17, 1906.

"Mr. Cornelius Vanderbilt Dead." *The New York Times,* Sept. 13, 1899.

"Mr. Hyde's Coaching Trip." *The New York Times,* Oct. 13, 1901.

"Mr. Reid Presides at Dante Meeting." *The New York Times,* Apr. 28, 1907.

"Mr. Vanderbilt at Newport: Spends the Day with Miss French Completing Wedding Arrangements." *The New York Times,* Jan. 2, 1901.

"Mr. Vanderbilt's Bride." *The Atlanta Constitution*, Jan. 6, 1901.

"Mr. Vanderbilt's Memory: Honored by the Foremost Railroad Men and Financiers." *The New York Times,* Sept. 15, 1899.

"Mrs. A. G. Vanderbilt Gives Birth to Son." *The New York Times,* Sept. 23, 1912.

"Mrs. A. G. Vanderbilt Sues for Divorce." *The New York Times,* April 2, 1908.

"Mrs. A. G. Vanderbilt Here." *The New York Times,* May 20, 1908.

"Mrs. A. G. Vanderbilt is Going Abroad." *The New York Times,* April 19, 1908.

"Mrs. Alfred Gwynne Vanderbilt Sues for an Absolute Divorce." *Oakland Tribune*, April 2, 1908.

"Mrs. Alfred Vanderbilt Returning." *The New York Times,* Jul. 7, 1907.

"Mrs. Antonio Ruiz A Suicide in London." *The Los Angeles Times,* June 11, 1909.

"Mrs. Antonio Ruiz A Suicide In London; Was Mentioned in Connection with the Divorce Case of Alfred G. Vanderbilt."*The New York Times,* June 11, 1908.

"Mrs. Gerken Withdraws from Bay Shore Show." *The New York Times,* Aug. 4, 1905.

"Mrs. Howard Says Husband Is Wrong." *The New York Times,* Jun. 19, 1907.

"Mrs. John Astor Most Popular Woman at Newport." *The Chicago Daily Tribune,* Aug. 10, 1913.

"Mrs. Lorillard Jr. Commits Suicide." *The Chicago Daily Tribune,* Mar. 26, 1909.

"Mrs. Lorillard Jr. Commits Suicide." *The Chicago Daily Tribune*, March 26, 1909.

"Mrs. M. E. McKim in Reno." *The Washington Post,* Nov. 2, 1909.

"Mrs. M'Kim Gets Divorce." *The Washington Post,* Aug. 4, 1910.

"Mrs. M'Kim Off to Japan." *The Washington Post,* Aug. 18, 1910.

"Mrs. McKim's Plaint." *The Washington Post,* June 1, 1910.

"Mrs. M'Kim Silent on Plans." *The Washington Post,* Oct. 24, 1910.

"Mrs. McKim Off to Japan." *The Washington Post,* Aug. 18, 1910.

"Mrs. McKim Wins Point." *The Chicago Daily Tribune,* Aug. 5, 1910.

"Mrs. Ruiz A Suicide." *The Washington Post,* June 11, 1909.

"Mrs. Ruiz Twice Tried Suicide." *The Los Angeles Times,* June 15, 1909.

"Mrs. Smith Hollins McKim May Marry Vanderbilt." *The Atlanta Constitution*, Aug. 22, 1909.

"Mrs. Vanderbilt Denies." *The Boston Daily Globe*, Sept. 20, 1908.

"Mrs. Vanderbilt Free." *The Washington Post,* May 26, 1908.

"Mrs. Vanderbilt Gives Testimony." *The Chicago Daily Tribune,* April 4, 1908.

"Mrs. Vanderbilt in Hurry to Secure Her Divorce." *The Atlanta Constitution*, April 3, 1908.

"Mrs. Vanderbilt May Marry." *The Washington Post,* Dec. 19, 1909.

"Mrs. Vanderbilt Refuses to Believe Her Husband Has Not Been Saved." *The Washington Post,* May 9, 1915.

"Mrs. Vanderbilt's Sloop Run Down." *The New York Times,* Jun. 1, 1907.
"Mrs. Vanderbilt Sues for Divorce." *The Chicago Daily Tribune,* April 2, 1908.
"Mrs. Vanderbilt to Get Divorce." *Boston Daily Globe*, April 10, 1908.
"Mrs. Vanderbilt to Wed Alfred's Chum?" *The Los Angeles Times,* Sept. 19, 1908.
"Mrs. Vanderbilt's Plans." *The New York Times,* May 29, 1908.
"Mrs. Vanderbilt's Rival." *The Washington Post,* April 26, 1908.
"My Path Leads to the Morgue – then to Potter's Field." *The Washington Post,* Feb. 1, 1914.
"Mystery Shrouds Report Mary Ruiz Is Dead Abroad." *The Chicago Daily Tribune,* May 30, 1909.
"Narrow Escape in Newport Accidents." *The New York Times,* Jul. 10, 1904.
"New Apartments for the Rich." *The Chicago Daily Tribune,* June 3, 1906.
"New Coaching Record Is Made." *Chicago Daily,* Oct. 10, 1901.
"New Vanderbilt and Astor Brides will Grace Newport's Summer Season." *Boston Daily Globe,* Jan. 28, 1912.
"New York Society." *The Chicago Daily Tribune,* May 16, 1915.
"New York Society." *The Chicago Daily Tribune,* Sept. 20, 1914.
"New York Society: The Vanderbilt-French Wedding, the Astor Ball, and Other Social Functions at the Great Metropolis." *Los Angeles Times,* Jan. 27, 1901.
"Newport Patients Do Well." *The New York Times,* Sept. 5, 1910.
"Newport Plans." *Boston Daily Globe*, Feb. 25, 1906.
"Newport Society Flocks to Horses." *The New York Times,* Sept. 9, 1908.
"Newport Society Surprised by Collier-Van Alen Wedding." *The New York Times,* Jul. 27, 1902.
"Newport to Entertain Prince Albert." *The Washington Post,* Mar. 11, 1906.
"Newport, R.I. Sick Improve." *Boston Daily Globe*, Sept. 5, 1910.
"Newport's Chrysanthemums." *The New York Times,* Nov. 12, 1893.
"Newport's Last Hunt." *The New York Times,* September 30, 1900.
"Newporters Planning Hotel for "Right Sort of People." *The Chicago Daily Tribune,* Sept. 7, 1913.
"News of Newport." *The New York Times,* Jul. 8, 1906.
"No Surprise for Newport." *The New York Times,* Dec. 19, 1911.
"No Wagner Cycle Here Next Winter." *The New York Times,* Aug. 22, 1914.
"Not to Wed Count." *The Boston Daily Globe,* Mar. 22, 1909.
"Noted Whip is Shot." *The Washington Post,* Sept. 18, 1914.
"Notes Put in Coffin with Mrs. Lorillard." *The New York Times,* Mar. 27, 1909.
"Obituary 2—No Title." *The New York Times,* May 23, 1915.
"Off on its First Trial." *The Boston Daily Globe,* Jan. 22, 1906.
"Olympia, London, to be Transformed Into an Elizabethan Village for the Coronation Year Horse Show." *The New York Times,* May 7, 1911.
"Opening the Dramatic Season." *The Chicago Daily Tribune,* October 3, 1900.
"Paid High for their Kisses." *The Washington Post,* Nov. 27, 1910.
"Peking in Port." *Los Angeles Times,* Oct. 10, 1899.
"Pioneer Horses Sold." *The New York Times,* Jun. 13, 1906.
"Plans for Vanderbilt-French Wedding." *Boston Daily Globe,* Dec. 27 1881.

"Plans of Travel for Young Vanderbilt." *The Chicago Daily Tribune,* January 31, 1900.
"Preferred Girl Chum." *The Washington Post,* June 16, 1907.
"Quits Newport for Berlin." *The New York Times,* Nov. 22, 1909.
"R. C. Vanderbilt Gives Costume Dance." *The New York Times,* Aug. 28, 1909.
"Ready for Guests." *Boston Daily Globe*, April 13, 1903.
"Referee Shields Mrs. Vanderbilt." *The Chicago Daily Tribune,* April 5, 1908.
"Reginald C. Vanderbilt Announces Ushers for his Wedding." *Boston Daily Globe,* April 3, 1903.
"Reginald Wins Over Alfred G." *Boston Daily Glob*e, May 29, 1906.
"Returns to Newport." *Boston Daily Globe*, April 14, 1908.
"Rich Men Not Bad: Vanderbilt " *The Chicago Daily Tribune,* October 21, 1906.
"Rich Men's Sons are Hard Workers." *The Chicago Daily Tribune*, Aug. 2, 1903.
"Richest Young Man Going To Work: Alfred G. Vanderbilt Surprises His Friends by Announcing that He will Try to Learn the Railroad Business." *Boston Daily Globe,* October 1, 1900.
Report of a Formal Investigation into the Circumstances Attending the Foundering on the 7th of May, 1915, of the British steamship "Lusitania" of Liverpool, After Being Torpedoed off the Old Head of Kinsdale, Ireland. Pg. 10.
"Rogue, the Brightest Coach Dog." *The Washington Post,* June 17, 1906.
"Ruiz Case Brought Before Parliament." *The New York Times,* June 15, 1909.
"Ruiz Case To Parliament." *The Washington Post,* June 14, 1909.
"Ruiz Death is a London Scandal." *Chillicothe Constitution,* June 14, 1909: 3.
"Ruiz Sues for Divorce." *The New York Times,* Aug. 2, 1908.
"Rumor Links Count Name with Mrs. A. G. Vanderbilt." *The Chicago Daily Tribune,* Mar. 21, 1909.
"Rushes from Ocean to Ocean." *The Atlanta Constitution,* Oct. 10, 1899.
"Sails, Undisturbed by German Warning." *The New York Times,* May 2, 1915.
"Says She'll Shoot." *The Washington Post,* Jul. 10. 1907.
"Schenck Case May Go On." *The Washington Post,* Jan. 6, 1914.
"Sea Romance Hits Shoals." *The Chicago Daily Tribune,* May 22, 1909.
"Secret Burial of Mrs. Ruiz." *The Los Angeles Times,* June 12, 1909.
"Secret in Shroud." *The Los Angeles Times,* Mar. 27, 1909.
"See Vanderbilt Ambulance." *The New York Times,* March 12, 1911.
"Seek Hand of Miss Gould." *The Washington Post,* Dec. 12, 1909.
"Separation Climax of McKim Romance." *The Los Angeles Times,* May 22, 1909.
"Settles for $5,000,000." *Boston Daily Globe*, May 23, 1908.
"Shall Rich Wife Pay Alimony?" *The Chicago Daily Tribune,* Mar. 26, 1911.
"Shuns English Society." *Boston Daily Globe*, June 28, 1908.
"Sidelights of the Smart Set." *The Washington Post,* Jun. 7, 1910.
"Simple Life at Newport." *The New York Times,* Sept, 27, 1908.
"Smear of Flotsam Marks Ocean Grave of Slain Innocents and the Lusitania." *The Atlantic.* May 10, 1915.
"Snapshots at Social Leaders." *The Washington Post,* Nov. 18, 1910.
"Social and Personal." *The Washington Post,* Feb. 25, 1901.

"Social Gossip." *The Washington Post,* Feb. 25, 1907.
"Social Gossip." *The Washington Post,* Feb. 12, 1907.
"Social Gossip." *The Washington Post,* June 9, 1908.
"Social Gossip." *The Washington Post,* May 12, 1908.
"Social Gossip." *The Washington Post,* May 13, 1907.
"Social Gossip." *The Washington Post,* May 2, 1908.
"Social Gossip." *The Washington Post,* May 6, 1908.
"Social Gossip." *The Washington Post,* Sept. 19. 1908.
"Social News From Paris." *The Chicago Daily Tribune,* Mar. 10, 1914.
"Social Notes." *The New York Times,* April 16, 1912.
"Social Notes." *The New York Times,* March 6, 1907.
"Social Set of Other Cities." *The Washington Post,* Feb. 5, 1909.
"Social Set of Other Cities." *The Washington Post,* Sept. 23, 1910.
"Social Sets of Other Cities." *The Washington Post,* May 25, 1909.
"Social War at Newport." *The New York Times,* Jul. 25, 1908.
"Society at Newport." *The New York Times,* May 30, 1909.
"Society at the Show." *The Washington Post,* Nov. 19, 1910.
"Society in New York." *The Washington Post,* Feb. 2, 1907.
"Society Marks The Decline of Summer." *The New York Times,* Aug. 25, 1901.
"Society Outside the Capital." *The Washington Post,* Feb. 9, 1910.
"Society Turns Out for Coach Parade." *The New York Times,* May 12, 1907.
"Society's Paper Chase." *Boston Daily Globe*, Jul. 25, 1899.
"Son Is Cut Off By Vanderbilt." *The Chicago Tribune,* Oct. 27, 1899.
"Son Will Not Listen to Her." *The Los Angeles Times,* May 11, 1908.
"Some Well-Known Men Who Sailed on the Lusitania." *The Boston Daily Globe,* May 8, 1915.
"Son with A.G. Vanderbilt." *The New York Times,* Oct. 14, 1908.
"Splendor at a Wedding." *The Chicago Daily Tribune,* Jan. 15, 1901.
"Sponsors Plan to Save Horse Show." *The New York Times,* Feb. 10, 1908.
"St. Louis Remembers Woman." *The Chicago Daily Tribune,* June 13, 1909.
"Stork Coming." *Boston Daily Globe*, Sept. 16, 1903.
"Sudden Death of Vanderbilt." *The Chicago Daily Tribune,* Sept. 13, 1899.
"Suggests Simple Life: W.K. Vanderbilt Says It's Way to be Married Happily." *The Washington Post,* April 23, 1908.
"Survivor Here Saw Trap for Lusitania." *The New York Times,* May 25, 1915.
"Swiftest Autos in the World to Compete in Daytona Beach." *The Atlanta Constitution*, Dec. 11, 1904.
"The Imp, the Merry Widow, and the Millionaires." Terminal Railroad Association of St. Louis Historical and Technical Society, Inc. Issue 53-54.
"The News of Newport." *The New York Times,* April 22, 1900.
"The News of Newport." *The New York Times,* Nov. 13, 1900.
"The News of Newport." *The New York Times,* Aug. 6, 1906.
"The News of Newport." *The New York Times,* August 13, 1900.
"The News of Newport." *The New York Times,* Dec. 27, 1903.
"The News of Newport." *The New York Times,* Jul. 30. 1906.

"The News of Newport." *The New York Times,* Feb. 8, 1901.
"The News of Newport." *The New York Times,* Jul. 14, 1899.
"The Path to Paris." *The Atlanta Constitution*, Apr. 7, 1912.
"The Referee." *The Chicago Daily Tribune,* Jan. 21, 1906.
"The Vanderbilt Will." *The Washington Post,* Oct. 27, 1899.
"The Vanderbilts Entertain." *The New York Times,* January 18, 1915.
"They've Got Us, Says Vanderbilt." The Los Angeles Times, May 11, 1915.
"This Year' Derby King Versus Belmont." *The Los Angeles Times,* Jun. 2, 1902.
"Thousands Cheer Alfred Vanderbilt." *The New York Times,* April 23, 1908.
"Throng Welcomes Opening of Opera." *The New York Times,* November 17, 1914.
"Titanic in Peril, On Leaving Port." *The New York Times,* April 11, 1912.
"To Have and To Hold." *The New York Times,* Feb. 19, 1901.
"To Newport in His Coach." *Boston Daily Globe*, August 28, 1900.
"To Smash Record." *Boston Daily Globe,* Jul. 5, 1902.
"Told In Her Boudoir." *The New York Times,* May 3, 1903.
"Tour of World." *Boston Daily Globe*, Jul. 27. 1899.
"Two Call Him Spouse." *The Washington Post,* Jun. 21, 1907.
"Two Mrs. Vanderbilts at War." *The Atlanta Constitution,* Aug. 31, 1913.
"Two Nations Enmeshed In A Woman's Suicide." *Oakland Tribune,* June 13, 1909.
"Urges Civic Work by Women." *The Washington Post,* May 16, 1915.
"Vanderbilt A Bus Driver." *The Washington Post,* Jul. 19, 1906.
"Vanderbilt Called Notice Ridiculous." *The New York Times,* May 16, 1915.
"Vanderbilt Coach on Time." *The New York Times,* May 5, 1908.
"Vanderbilt Coach Welcome in England." *The Washington Post,* May 22, 1906.
"Vanderbilt Coach Wins." *The New York Times,* Jun. 22, 1913.
"Vanderbilt Coaching Trip: Party Returns After Boston to Newport After Successful Run." *The New York Times,* August 28, 1900.
"Vanderbilt Divorce Suit." *The Atlanta Constitution*, Sept. 19, 1908.
"Vanderbilt Divorce Sure?" *The New York Times,* May 19, 1908.
"Vanderbilt Engagement: Miss Elsie French to become Alfred Gwynne Vanderbilt's Wife." *The New York Times,* April 29, 1900.
"Vanderbilt Escaped." *The Washington Post,* June 16, 1909.
"Vanderbilt Family All but Hopeless." *The New York Times,* May 9, 1915.
"Vanderbilt Four First in London." *The New York Times,* June 9, 1907.
"Vanderbilt-French Wedding." *The New York Times,* August 1, 1900.
"Vanderbilt-French: Preparations for Today's Wedding at Newport." *The Hartford Courant,* Jan. 14, 1901.
"Vanderbilt Gave Belt to Woman and Went Down with Lusitania." *The Atlanta Constitution*, May 10, 1915.
"Vanderbilt Gives Ball." *The Washington Post,* Sept. 6, 1908.
"Vanderbilt Gives Late Party." *The Chicago Daily Tribune,* July 3, 1910.
"Vanderbilt Gives to Yale." *The Atlanta Constitution*, Feb. 11, 1910.
"Vanderbilt Gives $3,700,000 to Fiancée." *The Chicago Daily Tribune,* Jan. 12, 1901.
"Vanderbilt Horses Arrive." *The Washington Post,* Feb. 21, 1909.
"Vanderbilt Horses First." *The New York Times,* Jul. 19, 1905.

"Vanderbilt In Flat." *Chicago Daily Tribune*, Nov. 16, 1903.
"Vanderbilt in Spill." *The Washington Post,* Oct. 14, 1901.
"Vanderbilt Is Sued." *The Washington Post,* April 2, 1908.
"Vanderbilt Leads." *The Washington Post,* Nov. 25, 1906.
"Vanderbilt Likes London." *The New York Times,* Nov. 23, 1912.
"Vanderbilt Loses $15,000 on Horses." *The New York Times,* July 21, 1908.
"Vanderbilt Man Arrested in Garden." *The New York Times,* Nov. 12, 1909.
"Vanderbilt Mascot Quits: Couldn't Stand Third Avenue When Presented to a Firehouse." *The New York Times,* March 24, 1907.
"Vanderbilt Papers Sealed." *The Washington Post,* May 22, 1908.
"Vanderbilt Party in N. Y. Central Wreck." *The New York Times,* Feb. 9. 1907.
"Vanderbilt Party Off: Young Millionaires Started Last Night from This City on Their Trip Around the World." *The New York Times,* July 27, 1899.
"Vanderbilt Picnic for Children." *Boston Daily Globe,* Jul. 13, 1096.
"Vanderbilt Placed Own Life Belt About Woman Before the End." *Boston Daily Globe,* May 10, 1915.
"Vanderbilt Prayer is Burial At Sea." *The New York Times,* May 28, 1915.
"Vanderbilt Saved Woman." *The New York Times,* May 10, 1915.
"Vanderbilt Saves Horse Show, Wins Plaudits." *The Los Angeles Times,* March 7, 1909.
"Vanderbilt Seeks Blue Ribbons." *The New York Times,* May 22, 1907.
"Vanderbilt Sees Horses." *The New York Times,* Feb. 10, 1909.
"Vanderbilt Shuns Society." *The Los Angeles Times,* June 28, 1908.
"Vanderbilt Stand Scares Society." *The Chicago Daily Tribune,* April 3, 1908.
"Vanderbilt Surprised." *The Boston Daily Globe*, April 2, 1904.
"Vanderbilt to Defend Suit." *The New York Times,* April 3, 1908.
"Vanderbilt to Give Wife Five Millions." *The Los Angeles Times,* April 3, 1908.
"Vanderbilt to Run Two." *The Boston Daily Globe,* Feb. 4, 1909.
"Vanderbilt to tool Trotters to His Coach on Famed Brighton Road." *The Washington Post,* March 15, 1908.
"Vanderbilt to Wed Millions." *The Washington Post,* April 29, 1900.
"Vanderbilt Troubles Old." *The Chicago Daily Tribune,* April 11, 1908.
"Vanderbilt Wealth Spent on Stage Beauty." *The Los Angeles Times,* Jun. 6, 1910.
"Vanderbilt Wedding." *Los Angeles Times,* Jan. 14, 1901.
"Vanderbilt Will Changed By Heir." *The New York Times,* Oct. 27, 1899.
"Vanderbilt Will Conference." *The New York Times,* Oct. 17, 1899.
"Vanderbilt Will Not Filed For Probate." *Chicago Daily,* Oct. 17, 1899.
"Vanderbilt Will Read." *The Chicago Daily Tribune,* Sept. 16, 1899.
"Vanderbilt Will: Only $1,500,000 Left to the son Cornelius." *The Chicago Tribune,* Oct. 27, 1899.
"Vanderbilt Women Chummy." *The Chicago Daily Tribune,* May 11, 1913.
"Vanderbilt Yarn Agitates the Town." *The New York Times,* Aug. 26, 1909.
"Vanderbilt-French Wedding: Date is Now Definitely Settled for Jan.18 Next." *The New York Times,* Nov. 6, 1900.
"Vanderbilt-McKim Wedding Expected." *The New York Times,* Apr. 23, 1911.

"Vanderbilt's Auto Exploit." *The Washington Post,* Jul. 20, 1903.
"Vanderbilt's Auto Wrecked in a Race." *The New York Times,* Jul. 19. 1904.
"Vanderbilt's Coach First at Hollywood." *The New York Times,* Jul. 29, 1905.
"Vanderbilt's Will." *Los Angeles Times*, Oct. 27, 1899.
"Vanderbilts Entertain." *The New York Times,* Jan. 18, 1915.
"Vanderbilts Here." *Boston,* Jan. 15, 1901.
"Vanderbilts Part When Cash Fails." *The Chicago Daily Tribune,* April 7, 1908.
"Vanderbilts Part; Wife Brings Suit." *The Hartford Courant,* April 2, 1908.
"Vanderbilts Santa Claus to Hundreds." *The New York Times,* Dec. 26, 1907.
"Vanderbilts' Yachts." *The New York Sun,* Aug. 1904.
"Venture Coaching Season." *The New York Times,* May 19, 1912.
"Vow Said At Newport." *The Washington Post,* Jan. 15, 1901.
"W.K. Vanderbilt. Jr., Clerk." *The New York Times,* Dec. 4, 1903.
"War Relief Work In Great Britain Led by the Duchess of Marlborough." *The Washington Post,* Aug. 19, 1914.
"Wealth in Hands of Fifty." *The Chicago Daily Tribune,* Jul. 26, 1903.
"What is Doing in Society." *The New York Times,* June 13, 1901.
"What is Doing in Society." *The New York Times,* April 28, 1903.
"What is Doing in Society." *The New York Times,* May 2, 1900.
"What is Doing in Society." *The New York Times,* Oct 16, 1900.
"While Piccadilly Halts." *Boston Daily Globe,* April 22, 1908.
"Why It's Lucky for a Millionaire's Son to be Disinherited." *The Washington Post,* June 10, 1910.
"Will Exhibit Noted Stud." *The Washington Post,* Apr. 21, 1907.
"Will Fight for Child." *The Washington Post,* May 20, 1908.
"Will Go a Mile in: 23 2-3." *The Chicago Daily Tribune,* May 7, 1908.
"Will Have Supper on Lawn." *The Washington Post,* Sept 4, 1908.
"Will Leaves a Gift to A.G. Vanderbilt." *The New York Times,* May 19, 1915.
"Will of Mr. Vanderbilt." *The New York Times,* Sept. 28, 1899.
"Will Seize Blooded Horses for Mounts." *The New York Times,* Aug. 7, 1914.
"Will Try for Record Today." *The New York Times,* August 27, 1900.
"Wilson Denies All." *Boston Daily Globe,* April 8, 1908.
"Winans Will Be Real American." *The Chicago Daily Tribune,* May 26, 1907.
"With His Wealth Vanderbilt Endows Miss Elsie French." *The Atlanta Constitution,* Jan. 15, 1901.
"With the Four Hundred: Vanderbilts May Make Up." *The Los Angeles Times,* April 22, 1908.
"Woes of Mrs. Howard." *The Washington Post,* Jun. 18, 1907.
"World's First Horse Show to be held in London." *The New York Times,* May 27, 1906.
"Yankee Girl May Get a Rothschild." *The Chicago Daily Tribune,* May 24, 1908.
"Yankee Horses Inferior." *The Chicago Daily Tribune*, June 16, 1907.
"Young Hyde's Unique Method of Expenditure." *The Washington Post,* Jul. 23, 1905.
"You're All Right." *Los Angeles Times,* Nov. 4, 1899.
"Young and Beautiful" *Boston,* Oct. 28, 1899.

BOOKS AND MANUSCRIPTS

Bailey, Thomas and Paul Ryan. *The Lusitania Disaster*, Free Press, Division of McMillan Publishers: London. 1975.

Barrie, J.M. *Peter Pan.* New York: Penguin Books, 2004.

Beard, Patricia. *After the Ball*, New York: Harper Collins, 2003.

Bergen, Claus and Karl Neureuther. *U-boat Stories*. London: The Naval & Military Press Ltd.

Bernard, Oliver. *Cock Sparrow: A True Chronicle*. Oxford: Alden Press. 1936.

Brush, Mary Isabel. *Special to The New York Times*. "Vanderbilts Abroad Again After Making Summer Plans." April 6, 1913. Pg. H2.

Butler, Daniel Allen. *The Lusitania The Life, Loss, and Legacy of an Ocean Legend.* Stackpole Books. Mechanicsburg, PA. 2000.

Carder, Tim *The Encyclopedia of Brighton.* Lewes: East Sussex County Council.1991.

Chidsey, Ronald Barr. *The Day They Sank the Lusitania*. New York: Award Books, 1967.

Cussler, Clive and Craig Dirgo. *The Sea Hunters*. New York: Simon & Schuster Inc, 2003.

Dickinson, Emily. Emily Dickinson: The Complete Poems. "Surrender." New York: Bartleby. 2000.

Ellen F. Vanderbilt Vs. Alfred G. Vanderbilt. No. 1908-2273. Supreme Court of the State of New York, New York County. 2 April 1908: 3.

Ernest Iselin, son of Mr. and Mrs. Adrian Iselin.

Garman, James. E. *A History of the Gentleman's Farm of Portsmouth*. City: 2003. Pg. 66.

Germany's Submarine Campaign. *Living Age*. October 31, 1925.

Harper, Charles G. *The Brighton Road: The Classic Highway to the South.* London: C. Tinley & Co. Ltd. Third Edition. 1922. Pg. 1.

Hickey, Des and Gus Smith. *Seven Days to Disaster.* G. P. Putnam & Sons, 1981.

Hoehling, A. A. and Mary Hoehling. *A Thrilling Tale of Disaster At Sea: The Last Voyage of the Lusitania.* London: Madison Books, 1957.

Hoehling, A.A. and Mary Hoehling. *Popular Library Edition.* New York, N.Y. 1956.

Hutto, Richard. *Their Gilded Cage: The Jekyll Island Club Members.* Macon: Indigo Custom Publishing. 2005.

Internet Broadway Data Base, IBDB.com

Isherwood, J. H. Excerpt from David Ramsey's *Lusitania: Saga and Myth.* New York: W.W. Norton & Company. 2002.

Kent, J. and Layton. *Lusitania: An Illustrated Biography of the Ship of Splendor.* North Carolina: Lulu Press, 2007.

Lauriat, Charles E. *The Lusitania's Last Voyage*. London: Charles E. Lauriat, 1915.

Oliver, Bernard P. 1936. *Cock Sparrow: A True Chronicle*. Jonathan Cape Ltd. London.

Peeke, Mitch, Kevin Walsh-Johnson, and Steven Jones. *The Lusitania Story.* Maryland: Naval Institute Press. 2002.

Perschler, Martin. *"Historic Landscapes Project: The Breakers."* Newport, RI: The Preservation Society of Newport County, 1993.

Preston, Diana. *Lusitania: An Epic Tragedy.* New York. The Berkeley Publishing Group, 2002.

Ramsey, David. *Lusitania: Saga and Myth.* New York: W.W. Norton & Company. 2002.

Ruskin, John. *Praeterita.* 1923

Ryder, Tom. *The History of the Coaching Club: 1871-2000.* London: J.A. Allen, 1999.

Thomas, Lowell. *Raiders of the Deep.* Doubleday, Doran and Company, Inc. New York: 1928.

Tschirch, John. *The Breakers.* NPS Report. The Preservation Society of Newport County. Feb. 22, 1994.

Vanderbilt II, Arthur T. *Fortune's Children: The Fall of the House of Vanderbilt.* New York, NY: William Morrow and Company. 1989.

Vanderbilt Jr., Cornelius V. *Queen of the Golden Age: The Fabulous Story of Grace Wilson Vanderbilt.* New York, NY: McGraw-Hill Book Company. 1956.

Wickham, Glenn. *A History of Theatre.* London: Phaedon Press, 1994.

Wilson, Charles. Letter to May Barwell. July 13, 1913.

Index